P9-ECV-453

DATE DUE

Looking for Heroes in Postwar France

Looking for Heroes
in Postwar France

Albert Camus, Max Jacob, Simone Weil

Neal Oxenhandler

DARTMOUTH COLLEGE

Published by University Press of New England

Hanover and London

Dartmouth College

Published by University Press of New England

Hanover, NH 03755

© 1996 by the Trustees of Dartmouth College

Printed in the United States of America

5 4 3 2 1

CIP data appear at the end of the book

Frontispiece:
left: Albert Camus, 1947 (Studio Izis, Paris);
center: Max Jacob in 1943 (collection of Neal Oxenhandler);
right: Simone Weil in 1936 (courtesy Sylvie Weil).

FOR JUDY

To read well is to take great risks.
It is to make vulnerable our identity,
our self-possession.

George Steiner

: :

Contents

Abbreviations

Chapters on Albert Camus:

TRN   Albert Camus, *Theatre, recits, nouvelles* (Pléiade I)
E   Albert Camus, *Essais* (Pléiade II)
ACB   Herbert R. Lottman, *Albert Camus: A Biography*
T   Shoshana Felman and Dori Laub, *Testimony: Crises of Witnessing in Literature, Psychoanalysis and History*

Chapters on Max Jacob:

VMJ   Pierre Andreu, *Vie de Max Jacob*
DP   Max Jacob, *Derniers Poemes et vers et en prose*
MR   Max Jacob, *Méditations religieuses*
PT   Sydney Lévy, *The Play of the Text*

Chapters on Simone Weil:

VSW   Simone Pétrement, *Vie de Simone Weil* (vols. 1 & 2)
SW   Thomas R. Nevin, *Simone Weil: Portrait of a Self-Exiled Jew*
SE   Richard Rees, *Selected Essays 1934–1943 by Simone Weil*
CS   Simone Weil, *Connaissance surnaturelle*

Translations throughout are mine unless otherwise indicated.

Looking for Heroes in Postwar France

The Pull of France

And yet I write about myself with the same pencil and
in the same exercise book as about him.

Samuel Beckett, *Malone Dies*

THIS book is about three major French literary figures
whose paths I had the good fortune to cross during a fifty-
year love affair with France. This "crossing," which involved an element of opportunity and luck, was driven from the
start by a young man's desire to possess the thought and culture
of France. From the time of my first three-day pass to Paris as an
eighteen-year-old GI in World War II, I was smitten by this
culture where writers and artists, as nowhere else, impact on
society. Over the next five decades, from 1944 to 1994, I encountered a number of memorable figures. Some I saw, a few I met;
others had left their traces still intact. I could walk down their
streets, read their books, interview their friends. Through their
vision I constructed a France to my measure, a country where I
too belonged with all my quirks and contradictions. Love of
France has been a passion that not only informs my writing and
teaching but my very understanding of who I am and how I
read the meaning of life.

Albert Camus, Max Jacob, and Simone Weil were very much
part of the French scene in 1948 when I returned to France as a
student. Camus was alive, Jacob a martyr-hero, Weil a power-

ful, if controversial, presence. From the moment I first discovered each of them, my destiny was connected with theirs, linked in complex ways that this book unfolds. They taught me morality, politics, and religion; they gave me clues to secret parts of my psychic life.

As a child, I knew instinctively that great writers could tell me what it all meant. The challenge was to decipher their art, to find their secrets revealed. I started with my father's collection —Dickens, Thackeray, Conrad, Kipling, Maugham, O'Neill. On a high shelf I found *The Hindu Art of Love*, *Psychopathia Sexualis*, and Frank Harris's *My Life and Loves*. Maybe sex was the secret. More years went by and I was reading voraciously. My father brought me armsful of books, then subscribed to a lending library that delivered books to the house. I read till my eyes glazed over, read myself to sleep at night, and picked up the book from the floor and went on reading when the alarm went off in the morning. When I wasn't reading, playing football, or in school, I day-dreamed about the deeper mysteries. Two evenings in my bedroom closet with a wonderful girl named Muriel seemed to prove that sex was the answer; but Muriel disappeared and sex became part of the enigma rather than the answer. It was many years before I found answers that seemed adequate. Of course, I found them in France.

This is not another conversion story, though it recounts *en passant* how I became lodged in a specific faith narrative. Its real subject is reading and writing. Its central concern is the question of how we invent the meaning of our lives through the stories of others, profiting from what J. Hillis Miller calls their "transferability," a quality of narrative that ensures that, no matter how eccentric or strange, stories always find their readers. My own story has several beginnings. It began in earnest in France during World War II and continued with my discovery of Albert Camus, Max Jacob, and Simone Weil after the War. It's a story of false starts, mistakes, and small discoveries; of a second marriage that worked and a first that didn't; of making my way through the traps of a challenging profession; ultimately, of awakening to a personal truth sprung from the competing and interfering and intertwined stories of others that, in unexpected ways, generated my own. And always, the pull of France.

The shape of the book is as follows: Chapters 1 through 4, grouped under the title "Success Story," discuss the rise and fall of the last great hero of modern French letters. During Albert Camus' rise to fame, there was an avalanche of books and articles about history's lucky young man; then he was swept into marginality, with Sartre, his former friend, serving as executioner of his literary reputation. According to Sartre, Camus was a mandarin, an aesthete, who conferred on himself the right to an "absolute morality" that allowed him to soar above the rest of mankind, whereas others (notably those who had made the commitment to Marxism) engaged in the tough struggle for historical justice and an acceptable social order. Yet a careful reading of Camus' essays and newspaper articles shows that he in fact saw more clearly than anybody else, Sartre included, the delusive condition into which the French were slipping after the war. He understood all that was at stake in the ruthless purge of collaborators. In the pages of *Combat* he warned his compatriots as Gaullists and Communists together created a myth of the Resistance designed to eliminate from memory the complicities of the Vichy regime; he saw the resurgence of venality and opportunism, as if nothing at all had been learned from the war. In the end he became like his character, Jonas the artist, suspended in a cage above the room where daily life goes on with maddening indifference to the truth-teller in the air above who calls out his useless warnings. It was Camus' own delusion, one given up before his death, that fame and success made him an authoritative witness who could persuade his compatriots to change their ways.[1]

I write about Camus as I saw him during my student years, notably in 1948–1949, and as he came to play a role in my own intellectual development. I emphasize the histrionic figure who

1. The chapters on Camus in *Testimony* by Shoshana Felman and Dr. Dori Laub are a powerful reassessment of Camus' contemporary relevance and suggest that his critique of the delusional character of postwar society is equally pertinent today. See *Testimony: Crises of Witnessing in Literature, Psychoanalysis, and History* (New York: Routledge, 1992). With the recent publication of the book he was working on at the time of his death, *Le premier homme* (Paris: Gallimard, 1994), Camus has leaped into prominence again as the great artist-moralist of modern France.

swept us off our feet and into his wake. The progress of the young *pied-noir*, who went from Algerian obscurity to the editorship of *Combat* and the inner circle of Gallimard, is not just a story of personal success; it realizes, in an exemplary way, the French dream of combining political relevance and artistic achievement. The chapters devoted to Camus develop different perspectives, but all cohere around my personal perception of this multifaceted hero who was, for many of us, the antithesis to that other great hero, General Charles de Gaulle. This is the Camus who became exemplary for millions of Europeans and Americans, between 1945 and 1960, as a witness against evil. His heroism lay not only in his passion and personal integrity but also in his persistent effort to rescue certain fundamental values—freedom, moral responsibility, social justice—from the oppressive atmosphere of postwar life under the twin shadows of the Holocaust and the Bomb. This rescue attempt, which can be viewed as a last effort to resurrect liberal humanism, failed; indeed, 1960, the year of Camus' death, marks a pivotal moment in the emergence of the new antihumanism associated with the structuralist movement. Camus' ambivalence toward that very humanism he defended anticipated the antihumanism of Foucault, Lacan, and Derrida, who were, like Camus himself, pursuing the perspectivism of Nietzsche. My debt to Camus is immense. Reading him I began to understand the moral dimension of human life, the weight of my own choices, my responsibility to others, none of which I had been able to learn from my family or teachers.

Part II, titled "No Happy Endings," takes up poet Max Jacob, one of the first French writers I studied in depth. Brilliant, evasive, always failing to meet his own or his family's expectations, Max Jacob typified the black sheep of many middle-class Jewish families. Growing up in St. Louis, I had known half a dozen like him. They were melancholy types, inclined to baldness and prostate trouble, who dropped in once a month to sample my mother's borscht and swap stories with my father over the kitchen table. But none of these men had Jacob's wit, his erudition, or his amazing gift for improvisation. Nor were they afflicted with his spiritual aspirations and his crushing sense of sin, a double burden that made his poetic *œuvre* unique but also scandalous and unassimilable. Jacob's personality fascinated me from the start; unraveling his work took much longer.

My path into Jacob goes through his failure to become a truly dominant figure. In Chapter 6 I have contrasted Jacob's destiny of neglect with the career of the famous Catholic writer, Paul Claudel. As a powerful public figure, Claudel's triumphal Catholicism survived his early sympathy for Vichy. His friends at the NRF forgave him his diatribes against the Third Republic and even the infamous "Paroles au Maréchal" (familiarly known as the "Ode to Pétain"); but Jacob was never forgiven for being a victim. The guilty conscience of post-Vichy France found this distasteful and preferred to repress the poet along with the very memory of French involvement in the Holocaust.

Jacob's spirituality was characterized by a tendency to passivity and abjection. He pictured himself as a toad, as a burnt offering, as a sinner who deserved to fry in hell. Chapter 7 corrects this view of Jacob as passive victim by showing that, in his last poems and his religious meditations, he did in fact meditate on the Holocaust, did protest the infamies of Vichy, and that he was an authentic if muted voice of protest for his people. The misreading of Max Jacob was caused not only by his spirituality but also by his radically innovative aesthetic, which can be described as "pre-postmodern." It was this as much as all the rest that made Jacob inaccessible to his own generation. Chapter 8 is an effort to renew critical dialogue around Jacob by examining his "double postulation" toward modernism and postmodernism.

Chapter 9 draws a parallel between my own search and Jacob's central theme, the transformation of eros into religious devotion. Why, you ask, should we try to make sex into something else—isn't it sufficient to itself? I would argue that there are few enough of us for whom sex isn't problematic in some way; certainly Freud viewed it as the nexus of our deepest confusions if also our greatest source of power. Max Jacob, a homosexual, was never comfortable with his sexuality, in part because of his Catholic moralism; but the very choice of that moralism lay in the traumas of childhood. Jewish boys often find the path to sexual maturity difficult, and Jacob was no

exception. This difficulty drove his mystical urge to transform
sex into another kind of loving, oriented toward the divine. In
Chapter 9 I have used his book *L'Homme de cristal* as a source for
my reflexion on troubled sexuality, his and mine, and on the
possibility of some kind of transcendence.

Simone Weil is the principal subject of Part III, "Broken
Narratives." As much as any single figure of the postward
period, Weil has become a Rorschäch test for critics. She forces
us to face the fact that what we say about a writer may often
reveal more about us than about her. She is a test case for the
narrative critic, whose own story appears in the way he tells
hers. I was drawn to Weil originally because we shared the pain
of migraine headache. Weil's headaches were frequent and
disabling, my own somewhat less so; but I knew exactly what
she meant when she said that, during one of her migraine
episodes, all the pain of the world was driven like a nail into her
head. I spent years pursuing a cure, from chemicals to yoga to
psychoanalysis. In the end I learned that the cures themselves
led to new diseases that needed to be cured. Addiction to pain
medication was one of the hazards of trying to dissolve the nail
in my head. But Weil never tried this easier way out; she
accepted the nail as her destiny. By her life and work, she tried
to atone for the world's pain, taking into her body the misery of
the poor and oppressed, the struggles of the proletariat, the
insecurity of exiles. This theater of cruelty was played out in her
head, in a way that can only be explained as mystical or as
delusive, or perhaps both. Back in the 1950s, at the time I
discovered her, Weil was often called a saint. I found a saintly
compulsiveness in her dedication to the forgotten of this world,
those she called "slaves." She was awkward, fragile, the consummate intellectual; but, in spite of all this, she saw her mission as one of activism in the factory, the unions, the picket
lines—and even the battlefield.

One of the lines of inquiry I followed was to understand
Weil's relation to her body through objects-relations psychology, which was just beginning to become known in the United
States in the 1960s. Using this approach, I began to discern the
affective tragedy she had suffered in infancy, from which came
everything else, including her alienation from her Jewish ori-

gins, her bodily link with humanity. My affinity with Weil gripped me even before I could make sense of her work. Trying to emulate her while studying at Columbia, I began to volunteer several days a week at Friendship House in Harlem, a Catholic interracial community. I taught French, made sandwiches, gave away my coat to a mugging victim, sang, prayed, even made a pilgrimage to the Shrine of St. Anthony to implore cash donations. This was a period of holy histrionics. I see now that, as with Camus and Jacob, I had been drawn to a writer whose inner distress was vented by theatrical gestures aimed at resolving intractable cognitive, psychological, or social problems. From Weil I learned the meaning of suffering, which she saw as the strongest argument for Christian belief. Through her example I came to understand that, if Christianity can be validated in any way, it must be through the infusion of meaning into this darkest aspect of human life, the suffering and oppression of the innocent.

Chapters 10 and 11 deal with various aspects of Simone Weil's life and career, viewed primarily through the lens of my relationship with her. I was struck from the start by the fact that we both had the same birthday, February 3rd, and this suggested that the affinities between us are like those between twin brother and sister. I have pursued this twinning in Chapter 11, which involves a study of Jewish self-alienation, and in Chapter 12, which touches on mystical experience, hers, mine, and Max Jacob's. Chapter 13 is a study of the concept of transgression, as developed by Bataille and Foucault, but also as lived out by Weil. I have focused on a period in Weil's life when she pushed beyond the limits of ordinary thought and experience. When in 1934 Weil took a year's leave from her job as lycée professor to work in a factory, her life took an irreversible turn. At this time she challenged the limits of her fragile body, her sensitivity, and whatever capacity for survival she possessed. Up to that point, her knowledge of suffering had been personal, as she put it "biological," but now she discovered and intimately lived the whole spectrum of sufferings that fall to the oppressed. This transition from her own psycho-biological destiny into solidarity with all those who are oppressed is the key to Weil's life and thought. It informs the notebooks she kept during her four months in New York, prior to her journey to London, notebooks that recount her breakthrough into an authentic spiritual dimension. They define the transgressive act, not as good or bad, not merely as a challenge to social convention but, rather, as a challenge to one's own sense of identity.

Weil remains an essential figure for my book. I see her not simply as "the self-exiled Jew," described by Thomas R. Nevin, but as someone who, in the struggle to become whole, drove herself mercilessly to reconcile various fragmented narratives.[2] She pursued this goal of integration in a way that was not simply conceptual but *material* and contributed to her untimely death. Above and beyond her moral conscience and her intellectual brilliance, I found in Weil, as I did in Camus and Jacob, the pathos of individuals who tried incessantly to rise above the contingencies of their own tormented lives toward some finer goal. From all three, though differently in each case, I learned the appetite for transcendence.

Weil was the most brilliant thinker of the three figures presented here, but also the most delusional. All her adult life she attempted to regulate her behavior as a function of some idealized oppressed group, refusing, for example, to heat her apartment during the winter under the impression that unemployed workers lived without heat. She contributed to her own death through an eating disorder in the conviction that she was atoning for the sufferings of those under Nazi oppression in occupied Europe.[3] In the manner of hysterics and saints, she tried to control the world by manipulating her body; yet, even while in the grip of delusion, she came to realize the delusive nature of power and the hideous triviality of evil.[4]

---

2. Thomas R. Nevin, *Simone Weil: Portrait of a Self-Exiled Jew* (Chapel Hill: University of North Carolina Press, 1991). Hereafter *SW*.

3. Pierre Janet calls eating disorders "delusional." Quoted in Peter Dally, Joan Gomez, & A. J. Isaacs, *Anorexia Nervosa* (London: Heinemann, 1979, 4.

4. Thomas R. Nevin writes: "The evil in oppressors is obvious. Far more engaging to Weil is the psychological mechanism of illusion shared by evil's agents and victims. She speaks of evil in Dantesque terms: it is monotonous, empty, trivial, vulgar, but it is also a false infinitude, a response of illimitable imagination to fill the void God's apparent absence from the world imposes on the mind. . . . It cannot be otherwise in an an existence determined by

Albert Camus, who was responsible for publishing Weil's work at Gallimard, shared her love for ordinary people, as he himself came from humble origins. He shared with both Weil and Jacob the role of witness to World War II.[5] All three were caught in the huge bonfire that, at mid-century, burned humanist Europe to the ground. All were aware of the critical moment at which they lived and tried to cope with the challenge. All three tried to awaken their contemporaries while finding the way out of their own personal delusions.

Camus tried to teach his generation a new moral awareness. Jacob taught the craft of poetry to innumerable young writers, using poetry as a spiritual ascesis that was also a game. Poetry had its delusional aspect, but it also provided a way through delusion, opening on flashes of insight. Weil, the only professional teacher of the three, was famous among her students for departing from the official *programme* to raise questions of workers' rights and social justice. This delusional woman, admirable in her force of will and her commitment to justice, became emblematic of my own Jewish alienation and my strange way back to ethnic and religious self-acceptance through the belly of what she called "the Great Beast," the Church of Rome.

World War II was a period rife with posturing, lies and delusion.[6] Most notably, delusion appeared in the Nazi belief that one can compromise with evil.[7] In his study of delusion,

---

necessity and the illusory wielding of power." In *Simone Weil*, 283. Hannah Arendt has taken up and explored this theme of the triviality of evil.

5. Camus himself insisted on the convergence of views between himself and Weil in his comments on her political writings, which he edited and published.

6. An interesting political example is noted by Seymour Martin Lipset in his essay "Values and democracy": "There is perhaps no more impressive evidence of the deep moral hostility of many French employers toward unions than the systematic effort to demolish all union rights during the period of the 'phony' war, from September 1939 to May 1940. Seemingly both employers and their political representatives in the government put 'teaching the workers and unions a lesson' ahead of national unity and, in the last analysis, national survival." In Jeffrey Alexander and Steven Seidman, eds., *Culture and Society* (Cambridge: Cambridge University Press, 1990), 77.

7. As Elie Wiesel has pointed out, the victims too were subject to delusion: "The general opinion was that we were going to remain in the ghetto until the

James M. Glass has shown how politics begin in the individual mind:

> What is remarkable about delusional knowledge is its refusal to consider any aspect of experience that might involve feelings of ambivalence. Delusion provides a certain, often unbreakable identity, and its absolute character can maneuver the self into an unyielding position. In this respect, it is the internal mirror of political authoritarianism, the tyrant inside the self. The authoritarian regime dominates through the application of terror to the polity's political and social life; delusion terrorizes through the often horrifying scenarios (or spectacles) of an internal regime that takes place in bizarre symbolizations.[8]

Delusion took a new form after the war, when Europeans chose to forget the Holocaust. Delusion may involve the denial of reality, as in the case of the Holocaust, or it may take the less virulent form of a philosophical reductionism, which arbitrarily limits the range of reality. Delusion also appears in the cultural realm of simulacra, as in television, which derealizes life by translating it into images removed from reference or without any referential foundation. Literature holds up a mirror to our delusions and, at its best, shows us how they are embedded within real-time experience. In this book I have tried to show the constant up-down dialectic that connects delusion and awakening in our lives. I have used this dialectic as the unifying link of my own struggle to awake from delusion by that low-cost and widely available praxis known as reading.

Looking for Heroes in Postwar France combines criticism with memoir or personal narrative in a genre that is now coming into its own. Narrative criticism was given impetus by Wallace Fowlie in the books of memoirs that he wrote in the 1970s and early 1980s. A more recent and more elaborately theorized example of the approach is Nancy K. Miller's *Getting Personal*

---

end of the war, until the arrival of the Red Army. Then everything would be as before. It was neither German nor Jew who ruled the ghetto—it was illusion." Elie Wiesel, *Night*, trans. Stella Rodway (New York: Avon Books, 1960), 21.

8. James M. Glass, *Delusion: Internal Dimensions of Political Life* (Chicago: University of Chicago Press, 1985), xiii.

(1991).[9] *French Lessons* (1993) by Alice Yeager Kaplan is a memoir of cultural learning, while Susan Rubin Suleiman's *Risking Who One Is* (1994) is described as "mediated autobiography."[10] The originator of this approach is the great French essayist Michel de Montaigne, who explored his own inner reality in the process of writing about a range of subjects and authors who were separate and distinct from himself. Montaigne's strategy was based on a view current among contemporary theorists of autobiography who hold there is no clear line between self-writing and writing-the-other, not a difference in truth but a difference only in literary conventions. You are your ideas, your words, your fictions as well as your history. Whatever you write about yourself must pass through the relay of other voices, other personalities, and those works of art that have changed your life.

9. Nancy K. Miller, *Getting Personal* (New York: Routledge, 1991).

10. Alice Yaeger Kaplan, *French Lessons* (Chicago: University of Chicago Press, 1993); Susan Rubin Suleiman, *Risking Who One Is: Encounters with Contemporary Art and Literature* (Cambridge: Harvard University Press, 1994).

P A R T

1

Success Story

CHAPTER 1

Becoming Meursault

I don't believe in heroism; I know it's easy and I've learned it can be murderous. What interests me is living and dying for what one loves.

Camus, *The Rebel*

WHEN the Battle of the Bulge began in mid-December 1944, the 97th Infantry Division was hurriedly packed up and rushed from California, where we had been training, to Fort Dix, New Jersey, the traditional port of embarkation. After a fourteen-day Liberty Ship crossing, we arrived at Camp Lucky Strike on the Normandy coast. I was an eighteen-year-old private-first-class in Weapons Platoon, Company F, 386th Infantry Regiment. By the time we arrived in Europe, the Ardennes breakthrough had been contained, and the German army was in full retreat. At Lucky Strike we unpacked our weapons and underwent last-minute training by tough combat veterans.

Before my division went into action, I received a three-day pass to Paris. An Army truck dropped me on the Champs-Elysées and I raced off to explore the city. I crossed the Seine on the Pont Royal and wandered along the Quai Voltaire, stopping to read handwritten signs pasted on bullet-pocked walls where resistance fighters had died. The Germans had been driven out of France, but the horrors of the occupation were fresh and daily life was a struggle for survival. Market stalls displayed wilted vegetables and American canned goods at outrageous prices. People in the streets looked shabby and furtive, still unable to comprehend that freedom had arrived. The biggest shock was the *mutilés de guerre*. Armless, legless, blind, some sporting little tricolor ribbons in their buttonholes, they gave me my first experience of what explosives did to the human body. I stopped at a kiosk to buy a copy of the Resistance paper, *Combat*, and sat down at a café table where I struggled with high school French to read an editorial signed "Albert Camus." At the next table, a man in a worn black raincoat saw my phrase book and asked if he could help.

After translating the editorial, he explained that two days before the liberation Camus and his *équipe* took over a printing plant and openly printed and distributed *Combat* in defiance of the Vichy government. On August 24 a unit of the Second Armored Division of General Phillippe Leclerc marched past the very café we were in to establish the FFI (French Forces of the Interior) headquarters at the Gare Montparnasse. Soon after that the *Combat* office on Rue Réamur became a hub of activity twenty-four hours a day for French intellectuals and for the foreigners who streamed into Paris. Journalists from all over the world turned up at *Combat* to pay their respects to the young author of *The Stranger* who had become the voice of France.

I told my new acquaintance that, after three days in Paris, I would be leaving for the front. He looked at me with a mixture of sadness and gratitude that embarrassed me. I had no inclination to die for anything and the thought of combat was terrifying. His look threatened to turn me into a hero instead of an immature eighteen-year-old American kid. I had already learned about heroes from the combat vets at Lucky Strike. Heroes were the ones who got you killed. I stood up quickly, we shook hands, and I walked away.

Along the windy streets, the sycamores were hacked in skeletal shapes. I tried to erase the man's look, but it hung in my mind like a decoration, probably posthumous. I realized that the French had heroes all over the place. I'd seen the equestrian statue of Jeanne d'Arc on the Place des Pyramides. At every crossroads there was a statue or a plaque. As if the French didn't have enough heroes of their own, they were now annointing us to be the heroes of this war they hadn't wanted and had managed not to fight. From the phony war to the *débâcle*, the French had failed to take the measure of Nazism. This was something I had trouble reconciling with their intense sense of national honor. Still, there was Camus, the hero of the moment. The editorial I'd read had a restrained passion about it that was sombre and moving. It spoke of the need for "intransigeance" and proclaimed that where "shame, lying and tyranny determined the conditions of life, it was necessary to accept death" (*E*, 278).[1] That was the trouble with heroism. It called on you to rise above yourself, to attain some kind of moral superiority. On the eve of going into combat, I resolved to hug the ground when the shooting started.

I walked for hours until there were only taxis, prostitutes, and GIs on the streets. I wandered around the Left Bank and ate a grey *biftek pommes frites* at the Dôme. I knew it was an ordinary night in Paris, but for me it was the first, and every emotion cut like a knife. I had recovered from my attack of antiheroism and felt too alive to consider my own death a possibility. That night I started on a walk through Paris that has been going on for fifty years.

I had a letter of introduction to a French family from friends in St. Louis. Next day, the Bertrands shared their soup of carrots and turnips in a glacially cold apartment, while I shared nylons and cigarettes. Friendship ignited instantaneously. From the Bertrands came a sense of what life had been like under the Germans. It was not just shortages, bread lines, fear, the loss of freedom. The ideological pressure, which corroded their sense of national identity, was almost as bad. Groups turned against each other. The Catholics saw defeat as the wages of sin and campaigned against the unions and the schools, calling on St. Odile to restore national purity. The peasants mistrusted the workers, the Vichyites rampaged against the leftists and the

1. All quotations from Albert Camus in Part I are from *Théâtre, récits, nouvelles*, ed. Rogert Quilliot, Bibliothèque de la Pléiade (Paris: Gallimard, 1962), hereafter *TRN*, and from *Essais*, ed. Roger Quilliot and L. Faucon, Bibliothèque de la Pléiade (Paris: Gallimard and Calmann-Lévy, 1965), hereafter *E*.

maquisards, blaming them for German reprisals on civilians. Suspicion, greed, and self-righteousness: nobody escaped, they told me, anticipating one of the themes of Camus—the complicity of victims.

That afternoon André Bertrand took me to an exhibit at the Musée d'Art Moderne on the Avenue Wilson. I saw several works of French Impressionism that provided a background luminosity for my three-day pass. My long ramble under the *becs de gaz*, the statue of St. Joan, the young whore on whom I practiced my French in the Dôme. It was all etched into my senses under the orange-purple light of Monet.

When my division left Lucky Strike for the final push into Germany, I carried Paris inside me like a cocoon. There was a world, a way of life, there was a mystery connected with "Art" that I had to unravel, to live backward into the past, so that it could carry me ahead into the future. This promise stuck with me as we pushed up through the Westerwald and crossed the Sieg River in assault boats. Anti-radar tinsel decorated the pine forests as we advanced northward toward the Ruhr, meeting sporadic resistance. Lieutenant Wolinsky, prone to heroism, moved the platoon ahead of the rest of the company. On the down slope of a thickly wooded swale automatic weapons opened up from our flank. We returned fire, but there was nobody there. Two men were killed and Tommy Hicall, a Seminole Indian from Florida, was wounded. We lay on the ground nursing our anger until the company commander radioed us to deploy between the other platoons and regroup in a hunting lodge on the edge of the forest. As we slogged back through the forest carrying our dead and wounded somebody at the rear of the column called the lieutenant a dickhead and somebody else yelled for him to watch his back. There was more muttering as we rolled the bodies into their blankets and lined them up next to the door. A jeep took Tommy Hicall away, out of his head with pain.

A single guard was posted and the rest of us fell asleep on a hardwood floor under the glassy stare of elks and boars. At midnight somebody shook me awake and handed me an M-1 rifle with a clip of cartridges. I buckled my boots and went out into the moonlight to stand guard. I stamped my feet in the bitter cold and argued with myself. What was worth dying for? There must be something. But everything beyond life struck me as trivial. Nothing was worth dying for. I had lost friends that afternoon. I tried not to think of them, but their faces crowded my mind. Now other friends were asleep inside the lodge. We had been through a lot together. Maybe they were worth dying for. But death is absolute finality. I believed there was nothing beyond. There was a sense of unreality about being here in this nameless place and I remembered my childhood dream. I was in an elevator with my mother, rising from one floor to the next. Each time the doors opened I hoped it was the real world of dogs and kids and living people, but it was always mannequins with fixed smiles, floor after floor, till I woke up in panic.

This revery was interrupted by the glimpse of a shadow dodging along the high wooden palisades that surrounded the lodge. I grabbed my rifle and swung it to my shoulder calling— "Halt! Who goes there?" There was no answer. I saw the breath in front of my face, then heard a sound as the shadow moved toward me. Twice more I called "Halt! Who goes there?" Still no answer. I sighted along the barrel of the M-1 and squeezed the trigger. The shots made a terrible racket in the night as I emptied the clip. A dark bundle sagged against the fence twenty yards away. I expected my backup to come running, but nothing happened. No sergeant of the guard. No platoon leader. I was out of cartridges. The dickhead had shared a bottle of schnapps with the sergeant of the guard and both were asleep inside the lodge. I left my post and went inside, stumbling over sleeping bodies till I found my squad leader. When I shook him he mumbled and pulled a blanket over his head. I searched and found a handful of clips for the M-1. It was deathly silent outside and the moon had gone behind a cloud as I rushed back to my post. An hour later somebody came to relieve me and I stumbled inside to my blanket and pack. I fell asleep in a moment but had horrible dreams. In the morning, we found the body of a German teenager. His face was chalky, his teeth veined with blood. He was in uniform and carried a knapsack full of grenades. I stared down at him, feeling nothing in partic- ular. Guilt would come later. The order came to move out and I went over to the column where I shrugged into my gear and picked up the .60-mm mortar. My friends closed in and there was a rush of solidarity that drove the feeling of emptiness away. After that, I had no more internal debates. I was in the war to stay.

When the Ruhr pocket was cleared we moved east and joined the army of General Patton for the liberation of Czechoslovakia. We fought our way into the city of Cherb and then rode tanks to the outskirts of Pilsen, where our column was ordered to a halt. General Eisenhower ordered Patton to hold the line there and allowed the Russians to capture Prague. A few days later the much-decorated First Cav bypassed the lowly 97th Division and pushed past us to the outskirts of Prague for the honor of meeting the Russians. Our war was over. On the long train ride back, we traversed the devastation of Germany with an indifference we hadn't felt on the way out. When we crossed into France it was like coming home.

I had taken the first step in my bildungsroman. I had seen Paris and I had bonded with the French people. When the time was right, Paris would reveal my own personal identity and some broader truth—I hoped. When the war ended, I felt a surge of relief and turned to inventing my future. The big question was how to get back to Paris. I thought more about Camus and at the first opportunity read *The Stranger*. The novel's call for an uncomplicated sensuality had an obvious attraction, but I found something even more appealing. Camus' hero, Meursault, was the mirror of my own choiceless indeterminacy, my own emotionless emotion. I was told that I showed nothing, concealed everything, that I wore the mask of the impassive young American who has never learned to express his feelings. If it is through emotions that we relate to the world, then, like Meursault, I was in abeyance. Beyond this negative identification, *The Stranger* voiced a call to rise above the morass of our guilt-ridden society, to cast off inhibitions and reinvent life without the impediment of tradition. It is what all young people want to hear. There was another key to my identification with Meursault: we had both changed our lives by an act of violence. Both of us had killed—Meursault an Arab and I a German soldier. This set us apart, giving us a destiny that could never be justified. Judged and sentenced to die, Meursault became emblematic of all the guilt I carried inside me. Meursault was my mirror, my alter ego, and Albert Camus became my first French writer. I loved him the way you love a movie star or a saint. The person who shows you life's path, who brings you in out of the cold. André Malraux has described the way I felt about Camus: "What interests me in any man is the human condition; in a great man, the form and essence of his greatness; in a saint, the character of his saintliness. And in all of them, certain characteristics which express not so much an individual personality as a particular relationship with the world."[2] By studying Camus, I could discover the reality of the world at a particular moment of history in a particular place— my own. I was prepared to believe what he told us about our society, that it had emerged badly corrupted from the war, ready to compromise the ideals for which so many had died. I was ready to let Camus lead me out of the cave of philosophical blindness into the Mediterranean sun. I hadn't yet learned that, as Nietzsche saw it, behind every one of a philosopher's caves is again a deeper cave.[3]

My determination to learn more about Camus, made in 1945, had a certain fundamental rightness. Albert Camus towered above most other writers of the postwar period. Struggling up out of poverty in a North African tenement, struck down repeatedly by tuberculosis, he had the gifts of a literary artist and the mind of a moralist. Tall, rangy, with the feistyness of a street kid, he grew up in the racial melting-pot of Belcourt, where Berbers and Arabs mixed with Europeans and North African Jews. The rude moral code of the working-class ghetto, its idiom and sense of humor, were his birthright. When Sartre first met Camus he described him as a combination of intellectual and Algerian thug. The French found that combination irresistible, and they lionized Camus, thrusting him into the limelight while he was still struggling to formulate his vision.

When we visualize Camus, it is the clandestine editor of

2. André Malraux, *Anti-Memoirs*, trans. T. Kilmartin (New York: Holt, 1967), 8.

3. Friedrich Nietzsche, *Beyond Good and Evil*, trans. Helen Zimmern (New York: The Modern Library, 1917), 227.

Combat who comes to mind. Coat collar raised, cigarette butt dangling from the corner of his mouth, he looks ironically into the middle distance. This aloof man with his dark good looks has not succumbed to fame nor been daunted by evil. His face is elongated and somewhat angular, showing his Spanish heritage.[4] The answer to life's riddle hovers on his lips. But there was another Camus. A Camus who loved contact sports and swam in the warm Mediterranean until the winter day, early in 1931, when he started vomiting blood. The boy was rushed to the hospital, where his right lung was found to be affected with tuberculosis. The hospital terrified him, abruptly his life changed. No sports, no reading, no school, absolute immobility. In those days, in fact almost until the time of his death in 1960, the only treatment for tb was artificial pneumothorax, an injection of air to collapse the lung. All his life Camus underwent such treatments, first for the right lung then, beginning in 1942, for both. This was a crushing blow, the eruption in his life of "the irreparable," an absolute with which there was no negotiation or compromise. At this moment Camus' sense of the absurd was born, his obsession with death, and the sensitivity to "natural evil," any affliction that comes not from the moral sphere but from the natural order. He realized that things are not what they seem, that under the smooth illusionary surface of life there is the indifference of nature. He discovered the reality of death and hated it. Lottman quotes his anguished words to his uncle at the time of his attack: "I don't want to die!"[5] This was the time when Camus began to learn the courage that set him apart and to take risks with the calm lucidity of a man who knows he is going to die.

The Stranger became the allegory of my own awakening and I ignored the book's limitations. It did not bother me that the moral order described was simplistic or that Meursault was a saint of the perverse. I saw him rather as an exemplary hero who awakens from the rote behavior of everyday life to communion with nature and a kind of religious ecstasy.

---

4. Camus' mother was Spanish. His father's family lived in Algeria after migrating from France, probably from the Alsace region.

5. Herbert R. Lottman, *Albert Camus: A Biography* (Garden City, N.J.: Doubleday, 1979), 45. All further references are given in the text as *ACB*.

This reading of Meursault stands in opposition to one proposed by René Girard, who explains the character's appeal in terms of his "innocent criminality."[6] Meursault is the narcissist who speaks in each of us, insisting that we are exempt from the moral rules. Girard was probably right, but the narcissist listens only to what he wants to hear. My awakening, like Meursault's, was all I was capable of at the time. Each of us finds the mentor he is ready for at any given time, and, in the early postwar, Camus was mine. I found his philosophy appealing precisely because it hovered between alternatives. It was a philosophy that remained in the *entre-deux*, the space where moral choice is suspended.

"A King in Exile"—de Gaulle

I returned to Paris in 1948 with an AB degree and a patchy knowledge of French history, including Charlemagne, Louis XIV, Napoleon Bonaparte, and General Charles de Gaulle. My earlier visit to Paris as a GI had come six months after the General's triumphal appearance on August 26, 1944, at the Arc de Triomphe, where he was welcomed by a sea of citizens shouting his name. He wrote in his memoirs: "*Ah! C'est la mer!* A tremendous crowd was jammed together on both sides of the roadway. Perhaps two million people. The roofs too were black with many more. At every window were crowded other groups waving flags. Human clusters were clinging to ladders, flagpoles, lamp-posts. As far as the eye could, there was nothing but this living tide of humanity in the sunshine, beneath the tricolor." He adds, "I myself, at the center of this outburst, I felt I was fulfilling a function which far transcended my individuality, for I was serving as an instrument of destiny."[7] de Gaulle's apotheosis at the Arc de Triomphe was followed by the liturgy of the Magnificat in the Cathedral of Notre Dame, which could not help being taken as a coronation. Because he considered that he was de facto president of a republic that had never been

6. René Girard, "Camus's Stranger Retried," *PMLA*, XXIX (1964): 519–33."
7. Charles de Gaulle, *The War Memoirs of Charles de Gaulle*, trans. Richard Howard (New York: Simon & Schuster, 1955), II, 349–50.

dissolved, de Gaulle set up house in the Ministry of War offices and governed by decree as head of a provisional government reluctantly recognized by the allies.[8] He had agreed to call elections after the total liberation of French territory and to organize the election of a constituent assembly. In the referendum of October 21, the French people set the process in motion. In November 1945 the new constituent assembly met and elected de Gaulle head of government. But he could no longer rule France as if it were "a sort of monarchy."[9] In the divided government that took over the task of creating a new constitution for the Fourth Republic, the General was shunted aside. He could express his personal opinion but could not exercise power. The electorate was drained by the war, outraged by inflation and food shortages, and in no mood to support the General in his campaign for broader powers. In January 1946 he assembled his ministers and informed them of his decision to step down. He describes this meeting in his memoirs: "I came in, shook hands all round and before anyone sat down, spoke these words: 'The exclusive regime of political parties has reappeared. I disapprove of it. But apart from establishing a dictatorship by force, which I do not desire and would certainly end in disaster, I have no means of preventing this happening. I must therefore withdraw.' "[10] De Gaulle devoted the next two years to building the RPF (Rassemblement du Peuple Français), a new party based on Gaullist principles. Stanley Hoffmann writes: "In his vision of the world, nations were like peers whom the aristocrats' code of values expects to perform acts of individual prowess, but for the common good." These "acts of prowess" included "the fight against totalitarianism and the new battles against underdevelopment in much of the world, against 'enslavement by the machine' in the more advanced part of the world, against foreign hegemonies all over the world. . . . Another idealistic aim was the restoration of Europe, which de Gaulle considered the center of civilization."

8. Jean Lacouture, *de Gaulle the Ruler, 1945–1970* trans. Alan Sheridan (New York: Norton, 1991), 14.
9. Stanley Hoffmann, *Decline or Renewal? France since the 1930s* (New York: Viking, 1974), 188.
10. de Gaulle, *War Memoirs*, III, 285.

The role of France was crucial to these goals, which required as a first step that France be restored to her *grandeur* of earlier times. *Grandeur*, Hoffmann states, "was an attitude rather than a policy."[11] *Grandeur* meant that France must cease to be passive vis-à-vis the great powers. It meant also that the Fourth Republic, which de Gaulle viewed with disgust, could never realize the restoration and regeneration of the nation and her people. During this period de Gaulle experienced his ultimate temptation—to have done with the confusions and machinations of democracy. Léon Blum had noted earlier, in a comment on de Gaulle's famous Bayeux speech of June 14, 1944: "between the General and democracy, one notes something like an incompatibility of temperament."[12] The General's biographer, Jean Lacouture, observes: "So the Bayeux speech, that appeal to republican effectiveness, was to be received, on account of its grandiose style and the climate of the time, as a threatening order and a challenge to democracy."[13] The grandiose and autocratic image, which had been so inspiring when France was defeated and the General rallied his people from exile, was something he could not shake and did not want to. In 1947 and 1948 only absolute dedication to the ideal of *grandeur* promised a remedy to the chaos brought on by France's return to parliamentary democracy. The communists had broken all ties to a government in crisis. Strikes raged everywhere and brought a spirit of insurrection. There was feverish talk about a communist coup. The General's associates urged him to seize power. At the Marseilles Conference in April 1948 André Malraux called for a return to chivalry and the resurrection of the ancient conquerors: "O French faces, which I see around me and on which I see again those Gothic faces beside me in captivity . . . let the Stalinist journalists laugh! An immense honor is given to you: this great body of France, groping in the shadows, watched by a world so often fascinated by it, it is given to you to raise it up with your perishable hands. France is like those great iron statues buried after ancient conquerors pass by and which

11. Hoffmann, *Decline*, 190–94.
12. Lacouture, quoted in *de Gaulle the Ruler*, 130
13. Ibid., 131.

suddenly, in times of cataclysms, are unearthed by a flash of lightning.[14]

I admired de Gaulle the soldier and recognized all he had done to salvage the French nation; but I was convinced that he suffered from "megalomania," witness his call to *grandeur*. Léon Blum, Raymond Aron, and other liberal thinkers had reached the conclusion that de Gaulle could not be a true democrat, despite his denial of any break with republican traditions and values. In the cafés where we met to discuss art and politics, we instinctively shared this view. Most of us were ex-GIs. We mistrusted authority and had no use for kings in or out of exile.

The Anti-de Gaulle—Albert Camus

As for Camus, the word *grandeur* was one he could only use ironically. His values were expressed in an unsigned editorial that appeared in *Combat* on August 21, as the fight for the liberation of Paris began. Frenchmen, Camus wrote, had begun the war "with the simple reflex of humiliated honor." Now, as resistance turns into revolution and a new society begins to emerge, they must "place the highest value on intelligence, courage, and the truth of the human heart" (*ACB*, 331). For a short time, Camus (who had belonged to the Communist Party for a time in Algeria) bent his efforts toward a socialism that would realize his highest aspirations. It was through this concept of a clear-sighted socialist consensus that he sought to dispel the waves of delusional thinking already building in postwar France. At this stage, his mission seemed clear: to use his literary ability in the service of the public good. This was the path followed by many French intellectuals—diplomat/artists such as Giraudoux and Perse, journalist/artists such as Mauriac and Sartre. The need for Camus to speak out now was especially urgent, when the literary scene was dominated by communist Louis Aragon and his paper *Les Lettres françaises*, which had assumed the mantle of the Resistance.

14. Quoted in ibid., 146.

The slogan in 1948 was "Neither Marx nor Coca-Cola!" Europe must make its own way independent of both the USA and the USSR. One of the big political events of the year was the formation of a new political party, the RDR (Le Rassemblement Démocratique Révolutionnaire). A friend took me to the kickoff meeting in the Salle Pleyel on December 13. With supreme *culot* she shouted, "Friends of Albert Camus!" as we crashed the stage-door and found front-row seats in the packed auditorium.

There they were, all the great figures of our day, men and women who, under the driving influence of socialist David Rousset and with the participation of Sartre, Camus, and Merleau-Ponty, were going to give Europe another chance. Richard Wright (whose words were translated into French by Simone de Beauvoir) spoke passionately of the plight of people of color and their thirst for liberty. André Breton invoked imagination, which could only attain its goal of total autonomy in a free society. Sartre (who, like Breton, would become an ally of the communists) argued passionately for a third way that would be neither right nor left, neither capitalist nor communist. He was seconded by de Beauvoir, who had become an advocate for oppressed women everywhere in the world. Then it was Camus' turn. A hush fell over the auditorium as this gaunt man with his Bogart toughness and dark good looks rose to his feet. Camus spoke with contained passion about the artist's role in the contemporary world:

> We are in an era when men, moved by mediocre and ferocious ideologies, become used to being ashamed of everything. The writer is made to feel responsible for the misery of the world. . . . In an era in which the conqueror, by the very logic of his attitude, becomes executioner and policeman, the artist is forced to be insubordinate. . . . In the face of contemporary political society, the only coherent attitude of the artist . . . is refusal without concession. . . . By his very function, the artist is witness to freedom. (*ACB*, 456)

His ambivalence toward the sartrean notion of "engagement" was evident in his speech. His exhortation to "refusal" foreshadowed the violent rejection of all parties that made him such a solitary figure toward the end of his career. Already there

were clashes of temperament and differences of opinion with
Sartre and especially de Beauvoir, who found Camus' moralis-
tic literary persona in conflict with the human being underneath. As for Camus he found it hard to adjust his views to those
of his colleagues. He was a loner, the "stranger" of the novel
that made him famous. He felt uncomfortable in the limelight
and protected himself by his surly demeanor—or was this
simply part of his role? None of this detracted from our adula-
tion. We admired Sartre and de Beauvoir, we were awed by
Breton, but we loved Camus. If we romanticized him, it was
because he was a romantic figure. He shared the same good
fortune as General Philippe Leclerc, to whom de Gaulle said on
the eve of the Battle of Paris, "How lucky you are!" Both men
were young, capable, given great responsibility.[15] That night in
the Salle Pleyel, Camus wore the winner's aura, the look of a
man who is in the right place at the right time. More important
than luck, Camus was one of the few men who saw with lucidity
the condition of contemporary France. He saw a move toward a
Europe of concentration camps, a Europe where freedom was in
retreat. He was one of the few who understood that the French
were not dealing with what had been done during the Vichy
period. Vichy had been expunged from the record, turned into a
legal phantom. Until that was faced, there could be no clear
conscience in France. Much of the blame, as he saw it, fell on the
shoulders of leftist intellectuals like Aragon, hypnotized by the
mirage of Stalinism. This was in his speech that night in 1948,
but most of it went over our heads.

The Nietzschean wake-up call to a new awareness was implicit even in Camus' early journalistic work, assuming greater
amplitude in the years after the war. Camus came out of Algeria
into the shadow of war, thanks to the energy and vision of
Pascal Pia, then editor-in-chief who, in 1943, recruited him for
Combat. The first issue of a newspaper with this name appeared
in December 1941 after the fusion of two previous resistance
journals. Clandestine *Combat* was composed in Paris, then

15. There is another parallel between Camus and Leclerc. Appointed
Inspector-General of French forces in North Africa, Leclerc was killed in a
plane crash in the desert on November 28, 1947.

printed and distributed from Lyon. When Pia left to assume other duties in 1944, Camus replaced him as editor-in-chief, bringing in other writers, Sartre among them. It was in Camus' apartment on the rue Vaneau that the first numbers of the liberation *Combat* were assembled after the Allied debarkation in Normandy. As with the other resistance papers, *Combat's* mission was to correct the lies of the Vichy press, report Nazi atrocities, and publicize messages from de Gaulle's government in exile in England. By 1943, *Combat* was appearing once or twice a month with a press run of about 120,000, though since each copy was passed from hand to hand the actual readership was double or triple this number. Camus' writings for *Combat* covered a wide range of topics, Algeria, theater, Franco Spain, as well as daily life in occupied France.[16] Significantly, the volume published by Camus as *Actuelles I: Chroniques, 1944–1948* is preceded by a quote from Nietzsche: "It is better to perish than to hate and fear; it is better to perish twice than to make oneself hated and feared; this should be one day the supreme maxim of any politically organized society." The first of these essays, entitled "The Blood of Liberty," was published on August 24, 1944, and evokes magnificently the liberation of Paris. Even at that explosive moment, Camus did not lose sight of the goal of a new society to emerge from the ruins of the old. He and his colleagues wanted to create a newspaper in the service of a new democracy, free from all obligations to vested interests. He attacked the servility of the press and the venality of those who saw the end of the war as a chance to return to their pleasures: "Those men who don't like it when the world changes have the impression today that they were tricked. The liberation of France for them only meant the return to traditional dinners, the motor car and to *Paris-Soir*.[17] Let freedom come quickly, so we can at last be mediocre and powerful at our

16. Only two articles from the underground pre-liberation *Combat* have been positively identified as by Camus though others bear his stamp. His other proven *Combat* writings are post-liberation. See *Between Hell and Reason: Essays from the Resistance Newspaper "Combat," 1944–1947*, ed. and trans. Alexandre de Gramont (Hanover, N.H.: University Press of New England, 1991), xviii.

17. *Paris-Soir* was a mass-market tabloid where Camus had worked as a clerk.

ease!" (*E*, 1542). Then and later, Camus used his role as a public figure to speak out against oppression and corruption, leading to the charge of mandarinism by certain of the existentialists. There were several major shifts in Camus' thought after the liberation. Though he had been for the purging of collaborators, and engaged in a polemic with François Mauriac on this subject, he became disgusted with the killing and took a stand against the death penalty.[18] Camus' greatest struggle came over Mauriac's petition asking de Gaulle to commute the death sentence of Robert Brasillach, a talented writer who had been a frank supporter of the Nazis. Brasillach had written for the collaborationist newspaper *Je Suis Partout*, denouncing the enemies of Vichy and supporting German invasion of the unoccupied zone in November 1942. He had also written: "We must get rid of the Jews as a whole and not keep the children." Camus reluctantly signed Mauriac's petition, but de Gaulle made no move to save the writer, who was executed on February 6, 1944.

Though Camus had leaned toward socialism after the Liberation and during his participation in the RPR, he eventually turned against Stalinist communism. He wrote in *The Rebel*, the book that led to his break with Sartre: "the history of Russian Communism constitutes the denial of its principles" (*E*, 629).[19] Camus was more North African than European and had done extensive research on French abuses in the colony, yet when civil war came in Algeria he refused to take sides. Through these changes, there was a sometimes nuanced dedication to humanist values, as in this editorial printed on December 14,

18. In the fall of 1944 Camus wrote in *Combat*: "Let us first say that the purge is necessary." When Mauriac remonstrated in *Le Figaro*, Camus replied: "We have chosen to accept human justice with its tremendous defects, careful only to correct it with a desperately maintained honesty." See Herbert R. Lottman, *The Purge: The Purification of French Collaborators after World War II* (New York: Morrow, 1986), 143. By the time of Brasillach's trial in January, 1945, Camus' position had changed.

19. At the time he published *The Rebel*, Camus believed that Sartre would never reject him. He told Octavio Paz: "I have three friends in the literary world, André Malraux, even if I no longer see him because of his political positions, René Char, who is like a brother to me, and Jean-Paul Sartre." *Le Nouvel Observateur*, June 9–15, 1944, No. 1544, p. 13.

1944: "it seems to me that there is more in man to admire than there is to scorn. Our society until now was designed to emphasize especially what was worthy of scorn in man. Thus, we had no taste for such a society and that was in order. But now we must recognize what is admirable. Today, we feel that France needs grandeur and man needs victories. A victory a day, over the world and over oneself, this is the only command that can be meaningful in the great adventure in which we are engaged" (*E*, 1546). Implicit in what he was saying was the message that humanism was exhausted. Knowingly or not, Camus was undermining the very values he claimed to promote. This points to the conclusion that Camus' complicated positioning, always on the outside looking in, always hedged about with caveats and conditions, helped undermine the core values of the liberal humanist tradition, even as he struggled to defend and sustain them. In this respect, his ambivalence on the Algerian question is definitive and explains his subsequent marginalization.

Charles de Gaulle was the unequivocal hero of the ideal. Although he had periods of depression, he never wavered in his convictions. His pursuit of *grandeur* and the glory of French civilization represented an absolute that we Americans (and also a large number of Frenchmen) could never accept. Camus, on the other hand, was an idealist whose pursuit of "intelligence, courage and the truth of the human heart" struck an immediate resonance. What none of us understood at the time was that it is easy to enunciate ideals; the hard part is to give them content. For Camus these were not abstractions, and he struggled to make them work. There were obstacles enough in the social order; but perhaps the greatest obstacle Camus encountered was internal—the anguish of trying to act while remaining in the ambivalence of the *entre-deux*.

CHAPTER 2

Camus as Hamlet

The time is out of joint; O cursed spite,
That ever I was born to set it right!

Shakespeare, *Hamlet*

W E talked about Camus as we stood in the crowded staircases of the Sorbonne waiting to see our academic advisers, exchanging tips on restaurants, bars, and the hangouts of the literary giants we were all eager to meet. We also talked about Garry Davis, an American who lived down the block from me in the Hôtel des Etats-Unis and had declared himself the first "Citizen of the World." I met Davis about a month after he gave up his American passport and held his famous sit-in at U.N. temporary headquarters at the Palais de Chaillot. Camus had joined a board of solidarity that supported the sit-in. He called Davis "this lean Sancho with the madness of his master." Camus was also the organizer of a rally attended by some three thousand people where André Breton and other celebrities defended the first Citizen of the World. Davis was a quiet, reserved man who had been a bomber pilot. His courage inspired respect, although many called his act sentimental and ineffectual. None of us who knew Davis felt inclined to imitate him.

We went out for drinks at the Sélect and shared information on the Sorbonne, the literary scene and, of course, Camus.

Janine, who had taken me to the kick-off meeting of the RDR, cut her classes at the Sorbonne to collect petitions. One was for the French Communist Party to condemn the Russian blockade of Berlin; another, to support Camus' drive to allow refugees from Franco Spain to settle in France; and still another calling on France to recognize the newly founded state of Israel. We were sometimes joined by an editor of the expatriate literary magazine *Zero*. He got wind of Camus' new play about five Russian anarchists who in 1905 carried out a string of bombings after deciding that murder was "necessary and inexcusable." He wanted to publish an excerpt from *Les Justes* but never got through the ring of watchdogs that surrounded Camus.

Those of us who were ex-GIs were puzzled by Davis, who was playing chicken with the U.S. government. We had learned to be suspicious of heroes and idealists such as Davis; but Camus was an exception to this rule. He had both courage and style, an unbeatable combination. Camus also had that something a little "mad" about him necessary for an authentic hero. Like de Gaulle, he had been caught up in the tide of events, and, in a totally different way, he had not been overwhelmed by them. This "madness" contributed to his great charisma. He stood up for lost causes, he put his career and even his life on the line. We knew he suffered from TB, but he always found energy to speak out against injustice and to explain the hidden meaning of events, which other leaders tried to conceal. From Camus I learned what it meant to have a moral conscience, although it would be a long time before I could actually exercise moral judgment. I learned from him that life continually presents us with alternatives, that what we choose defines who we are. I learned also—the hardest part—that if you choose out of convenience or immediate pleasure, you are giving up the very thing that gives you a claim to self-respect. The other thing I learned was that politics was not simply a kind of sideshow, designed to entertain us; it was also a moral ground, just as important as private life and maybe more difficult.

With all this, Camus had the final attribute, success with women. Hearing reports of his conquests, we admired his machismo and tried to copy his hidalgo bearing, both tender and proud. We could imitate him, but he always remained just beyond our grasp. He was "in-between" all possible definitions.

Binarity (the *entre-deux*) takes on a paradisal form in one of Camus' earliest essays, "Between Yes and No," in the book *L'Envers et l'endroit* (1937). In the essay, which evokes his mother, Camus sits looking out over the sleeping Belcourt quarter of Algiers and finds a momentary peace in the interval between yes and no:

> Simple, everything is simple, in the lighthouse lamps, a green, a red, a white; in the cool of the night and the odors of the city and the slum which rise toward me. If this evening it's the image of a certain childhood that comes back to me, how can I not welcome the lesson of love and of poverty that is to be drawn from it? Since this hour is like an interval between yes and no, I leave for other hours the hope and the disgust of living. Yes, collect only the transparency and simplicity of lost paradises: in an image. (*E*, 28)

The French speak of twilight as *entre chien et loup*, the time when one form wrestles with another; but then comes night, and the tug of war is suspended. In the passage quoted above night signifies a moment's relief from the torments of childhood. Peace (which is only momentary) comes with the acceptance of life's utter lack of meaning. This is Camus as a young man, lulled by the delusion that it is possible to remain suspended between yes and no. This is his initial position, one that he struggled to maintain as long as he could, that he did in fact retain to the end whenever he functioned in the theatrical mode.

Camus' philosophy of the *entre-deux* or "in-between" is an early version of the neo-Nietzscheanism that would later be promoted in a more systematic way by Foucault. His cultural position was similar to that of Nietzsche, whose portrait hung on the wall of his office at Gallimard. For Nietzsche, the great delusion was Christianity, the great awakener, war. Nietzsche trained as an artilleryman during the Franco-Prussian conflict, but his military service was brought to an abrupt halt by an accident followed by five months of painful recuperation. Discharged from the service at the start of his twenty-fifth year, he was nonetheless marked by this intense experience of physical challenge and illness, just as Camus was marked by his life-long struggle with tuberculosis. For both thinkers war became the matrix from which a new consciousness might emerge. Though both valued the aesthetic life and oscillated between poetics and philosophy, both finally recognized that only a profound moral awakening could revalidate the terms of discourse and revitalize society. Like Nietzsche, Camus sought to awaken his generation. Just as Plato called humanity out of the cave, Nietzsche called the people of Europe to emerge from the philosophical shadows of the nineteenth century. Camus' wake-up call was explicitly based on the writing of Nietzsche. Nietzsche's warning about delusional thinking in *The Birth of Tragedy* foreshadows the entire reach of Camus' own philosophical career:

> It is an eternal phenomenon: the insatiable will always find a way, by means of an illusion spread over things, to detail its creatures in life and compel them to live on. One is chained by the Socratic joy of knowing and the delusion of being able thereby to heal the eternal wound of existence; another is ensnared by art's seductive veil of beauty fluttering before his eyes; yet another by the metaphysical consolation that beneath the whirl of appearances eternal life flows on indestructibly—to say nothing of the more common and almost more forceful illusions the will has at hand at every moment.[1]

The main thrust of Nietzsche's critique of European thought, especially in his later works, was directed against the notion of truth and the hegemony of traditional ideals. As he came to see it, concepts and ideals were mere constructs, designed to allay the pain of "the eternal wound of existence," that realization of total emptiness that only the thought of the East had ever adumbrated in an adequate way.[2]

---

1. The English text is taken from Alan White's, *Within Nietzsche's Labyrinth* (New York: Routledge, 1990), 26–38. He gives an excellent discussion of the passage.

2. Nietzsche found much to admire in Asian thought: "I hope that my condemnation of Christianity has not involved me in any injustice to a related

The Nietzschean strain in Camus' work is expressed primarily in his two major essays, *The Myth of Sisyphus* and *The Rebel*. In those works he argues explicitly against conceptual truth, whether as dogma, ideology, or construct; but the point is made more forcefully within the plays and novels, most notably in *The Misunderstanding* and *The Fall*. Simultaneously, Camus' career shows his own fierce struggle with questions of truth. As a public figure he was committed to truth-telling. Yet to tell the truth as he saw it brought enemies, often those who had earlier been his friends. And the Algerian conflict made it apparent to him that there was no position of truth from which to dispense a solution to irreconcilable constituencies.

Camus' battle with delusion can be seen as an effort to shed all forms of "metaphysical consolation" that seeks some kind of eternal substrate (deity, nature, life) beneath the veil of appearances: the adored Mediterranean seascape was as close as he came to an "eternal principle." He abandoned the early belief that Sisyphus (his image for mankind) can achieve happiness and that "the eternal wound of existence" can be healed.[3] As the years passed, he deepened his Nietzschean commitment to *amor fati*, the affirmation of things as they are. His belief in humanism disappeared, leaving a corrosive emptiness, a dark night of the mind and senses that his Mediterranean ecstasy could not displace.[4]

This stoic indeterminism attracted me to Camus at first, but it was also this that made me turn away from him. Without ever

religion with an even larger number of adherents: Buddhism. Both belong together as nihilist religions—they are religions of decadence—but they differ most remarkably. For being in a position now to compare them, the critic of Christianity is profoundly grateful to the students of India. Buddhism is a hundred times more realistic than Christianity. . . . Buddhism is the only genuinely positivistic religion in history." *The Antichrist*, in *The Portable Nietzsche*, trans. and ed. Walter J. Kaufmann (New York: Viking, 1954), 586–87.

3. *The Myth of Sisyphus* concludes with the words: "We must imagine that Sisyphus is happy" (*E*, 198).

4. Jean Grenier, Camus' teacher, strongly influenced him during his formative years. Grenier propounded a kind of humanistic nihilism, influenced by the teachings of Lao Tzu. The first section of Grenier's book, *The Islands*, is titled "The Attraction of the Void."

having been taught any eternal truths, something in me refused to give up their possibility. This may have been because my father, whom I loved and admired but finally pulled away from, was very much the same kind of self-made nonconformist as Camus. Like Camus he had known poverty, struggled to educate himself, and remained deeply suspicious of all forms of authority. Men like these hate and mistrust institutions, so much so that they fail to understand that institutions, even when corrupt (as they always are), provide a necessary continuity in social existence. Camus was a child of the public schools, a beneficiary of the system; and, because of this, he mistrusted the state, while showing a deep gratitude to individuals within the system who had helped him.[5]

The army had taught me something about the tyranny of the system; but it didn't affect my need for certainty and for order. Temperamentally, I needed some kind of conceptual anchor, something to give shape to the turmoil of my inner life. I had a yearning for truth that I began to be aware of only when I began to assimilate and adopt Camus' philosophy; at that point, I realized that it could never be my own.

Camus' philosophical position involved a dualism born of his Mediterranean experience: the fragile beauty of the world compromised by the fact of evil.[6] He experienced an intolerable tension between the ideal (love, justice, beauty, existence) and the irreparable (disease, injustice, cruelty, egoism). This insight was articulated in *The Myth of Sisyphus*, published in 1942 just after *The Stranger*. Camus' first major philosophical work turns on the great locus classicus of modern thought: the opposition between Socrates and Christ, between reason and emotional impulse in respect to evil. The book posits a diminished rational power that must respond to the enduring human need for meaning, order, and stability, yet do so in the absence of any possible belief system or coherent moral framework.

5. He dedicated his Nobel address to Louis Germain, the primary school teacher who had been a substitute father in his early childhood.

6. Camus was a forerunner of the Green Movement, an environmentalist who never foresaw how the Mediterranean coast would be devastated by pollution and indiscriminate building.

Camus had initially explored this basic cultural tension (which has proved so productive for thinkers such as Renan, Nietzsche, and Heidegger) in his thesis for the Diplôme d'Etudes Supérieures, entitled *Christian Metaphysic and Neoplatonism*.[7] His choice of the subject was influenced by his teacher, Jean Grenier, as well as his philosophical studies with René Poirier, a man of conservative views; but the issues involved were also of great personal importance to the young Camus. These were *his* needs, *his* emotions, *his* rage for order struggling against his own absolute disbelief. Camus thus chose to thematize his most deeply felt emotions and use them as a basis for philosophical reflection, an approach that places him in the tradition of Augustine and Kierkegaard. This personal dimension is obscured by the scholarly apparatus of the thesis but becomes apparent in the muscular dialectic of *The Myth of Sisyphus*.

In the thesis, Camus argued that for the Greeks man was self-sufficient. The justification for their existence was found in the aesthetics of their temples and the athletic cultivation of their bodies. Camus saw the Neoplatonism of Plotinus as the apex of Greek thought. Despite various efforts at reconciliation, Christianity could never coexist with Greek culture. It brought a terror of death, a scandalous doctrine of incarnation, and an equally scandalous belief in redemption and life after death. While the Greeks believed in a reasoned approach to the problem of evil, Christians, as exemplified by Augustine, tried to overcome it by a leap of faith that distorts man's ability to know and love the world in which he lives.

The Myth of Sisyphus was a reprise of the fundamental issue raised in the thesis on *Christian Metaphysic and Neoplatonism*. A vital link is found in Camus' discussion of the Kierkegaardian leap of faith. He writes: "So it is that, by a tormented subterfuge, he [Kierkegaard] has given the irrational the visage, and to his God the attributes, of an absurdity which is unjust, inconsequent and incomprehensible. Intelligence alone in him tries to stifle the profound complaints of the human heart. Since noth-

7. Translated and commented by Joseph McBride, *Albert Camus, Philosopher and Litterateur* (New York: St. Martin's Press, 1992).

ing is proved, everything can be proved" (*E*, 127). Camus has done in *The Myth of Sisyphus* what he attributes to Kierkegaard: he has renamed God as the absurd. The emptiness and malignity that we attribute to the devil are, in fact, the consequences of our own invention of God. Though he feels a personal resonance with the anguish of Augustine, Camus' overwhelming commitment is to Greek thought, which loves the world and its creatures. He then squarely faces the challenge to reinvent for his time the encounter of reason with a landscape of sun and sea, where the light plays incessantly across the surface of the water in an endless dance of forms.[8]

In his thesis Camus brought together two great thinkers, North Africans like himself, who confronted the spiritual life with the harsh reality of the irreparable. This was always Camus' problem, but he could accept neither the Greek solution (beauty) nor the Christian (faith). The third solution he considered was that of Nietzsche and, in fact, Nietzsche's "yes and no" comes closest to Camus own way of dealing with the problem.

When we live this tension between beauty and the irreparable, he claims, then we have fully entered the human condition. This binarity was first expressed in the 1937 essay "Between Yes and No" and continued to characterize much that Camus wrote. Meursault awakes from the rote behavior of everyday life to communion with nature and a kind of quasi-religious ecstasy. For Camus, like Nietzsche, was a "religious" writer: their anti-Christian polemics were the sign of their commitment to awakening mankind from delusional thinking. Both tried to use the reality of human suffering as an instrument of social and personal transformation. The ecstatic moment *entre chien et loup*, between yes and no, this moment outside of time implies a mystical dimension in Camus' work, something rarely attained but there as a possibility until the last years of his life. Embittered and exhausted, he knew in his last years the tempta-

---

8. Camus chose as epigraph for his essay the same lines from Pindar that Paul Valéry, another Mediterranean, had used for "Le Cimetière marin": "O my soul, do not aspire to immortal life, / but exhaust the domain of the possible" (*E*, 93).

tion to abandon it all and rush into exile, like Clamence, or into solitude, like Jonas, the artist figure in his story of that name. But even under great stress, Camus retained his lucidity. There could be no Nietzschean flight into madness, no delirious identification with the Antichrist.

Two quotations illustrate the parallel in Nietzsche's and Camus' views of what was needed to remake history. Nietzsche wrote in *The Will to Power*: "I teach the No to all that makes weak—that exhausts. I teach the Yes to all that strengthens, that stores up strength, that justifies the feeling of strength."[9]

Compare this to Camus in *The Myth of Sisyphus*: "I thus draw from the absurd three consequences which are my revolt, my liberty and my passion" (*E*, 145). Camus' revolt is Nietzsche's "No"; his liberty and his passion are Nietzsche's "Yes."

The Myth of Sisyphus explicitly takes up the double argument of Nietzsche: that Christian civilization has reached its end but that a new vision of life is possible. Nietzsche's heroic pessimism is renewed in the famous opening lines of Camus' essay: "There is only one truly serious philosophical problem: that is suicide. To judge whether or not life is worth living is to reply to the fundamental question of philosophy" (*E*, 99). Suicide was the new and dramatic element that Camus introduced into the dialectic between reason and faith that had been at the core of his university thesis. Whether to live or to die, whether to choose the indifferent beauty of the world or the sterile rationality of self-inflected death, this was the problem of Kirolov in Dostoevsky's *Possessed*. Camus argues that, rather than the abdication of faith or the renunciation of suicide, there is another alternative, consciousness and revolt:

> Consciousness and revolt, these refusals are the opposite of renunciation. All that is irreducible and passionate in a human heart animates them against the very grain of life. It is a matter of dying unreconciled and not willingly. Suicide is a misunderstanding. The man of the absurd cannot exhaust everything, and exhaust himself. The absurd is his most extreme tension, that which he constantly maintains by a solitary effort, for he knows

9. Friedrich Nietzsche, *The Will to Power*, trans. and ed. Walter J. Kaufmann and R. J. Hollingdale (New York: Random House, 1968), 54, 33.

that, in his consciousness and in his day by day revolt, he witnesses to his only truth which is defiance. (*E*, 139)

The jerky and disconnected quality of the prose, through which certain keywords return like drumbeats (absurd, revolt, consciousness), shows that Camus is writing a manifesto rather than a philosophical essay. He is calling on his contemporaries to awake and accept their responsibilities in the harsh light of "truth." Better this conditional and partial truth than the slow suicide of inaction or the delusion of religious belief. Though he denied any validity to religious thought, Camus was obsessed by the problem of evil. The existence of evil and the necessity to deal with it in some adequate way became for Camus the ultimate challenge. This was especially hard for a man whose own moral stance involved constant role changes and the epistemology of the *entre-deux*.

As the years passed Camus moved increasingly out of the public arena, looking for consolation in his first love, the artistic life, which is Nietzsche's second form of delusion.[10] At the very end, he was planning a return to the theater, though he had been "onstage" since 1935 and Algier's *Théâtre du Travail*, when he made his official entry into the domain of theatrical self-representation.

During those interminable discussions of Camus at the Sorbonne or the Sélect or our favorite restaurant, Chez Raffy, we tried to understand the man and what he stood for. We could not reach agreement on that point. The one thing we concluded was the necessity to take a moral stand; but we also learned that morality becomes difficult when you cannot ground it in some kind of eternal principle. As the year went on, I felt the growing attraction of Catholicism, whose "eternal principles" inspired

10. During his infatuation with Wagner, Nietzsche extolled art and, even after his break with Wagner, continued to pursue a Schopenhauerian view of the aesthetic mode as a form of metaphorical liberation from the pain of truth. His view of art remained ambivalent. In his later writings, there is an alchemical play of metaphors in which necessity is both accepted and overcome. See Henri Birault, "Beatitude in Nietzsche," in *The New Nietzsche*, ed. David B. Allison (Cambridge Mass.: MIT Press, 1977), 219–31.

no fear since I had never suffered their tyranny. This was a kind
of pre-honeymoon, in which I focused only on what I might
receive from the Church, not on what I might have to give up.
Feeling at times as though I were betraying Camus, I opened
myself to the possibility of some kind of truth, if only what we
would now call "truth effects," truths that are local and provisional within a given context. I put off until later the hard,
perhaps impossible, struggle to reconcile Catholic absolutism
with some form of perspectivism.

If it was difficult to parse Camus' philosophy, it was equally
difficult to place Camus as an artist. One grey November afternoon I took refuge from the rain in "Les Amis des Livres,"
Adrienne Monnier's bookstore on Rue De l'Odéon. I began to
read a section of Rilke's novel *The Notebooks of Malte Laurids
Brigge* that had just come out in translation in a literary review.
It began with Brigge's perception of Paris: "So, then people do
come here in order to live; I would sooner have thought one
died here. I have been out. I saw: hospitals. . . ."[11] Suddenly my
mind flashed back to lines written by Camus in 1940: "What is
hateful in Paris: tenderness, feelings, the hideous sentimentality
which sees only what is pretty and finds the pretty beautiful. . . . What is exalting: the terrible loneliness."[12] Camus
shared with Rilke a compulsion to see things as they are, that
beauty which is in horror, and which Rilke considered to be the
fundamental insight of modernism.
    There are striking affinities between Camus' *Notebooks* and
those kept by Rilke from 1903 to 1910 and incorporated in
Brigge. Both Camus and Rilke were lacerated by the scenes they
witnessed in Paris. Camus hated the degraded poverty of
northern cities. Rilke's Brigge falls ill and experiences the cal-
lous promiscuity of public hospitals. Camus wrote in his *Notebook* for August 1937: "On the way to Paris: this fever beating in
my temples. The strange and sudden withdrawal from the

11. Rainer Maria Rilke, *The Notebooks of Malte Laurids Brigge* (New York:
Capricon, 1958), 13.
    12. Albert Camus, *Carnets, mai 1935–février 1942* (Paris: Gallimard, 1962),
205. Subsequent quotes from the *Carnets* are to this volume.

world and from men. The struggle with one's body." Rilke was horrified by the mute suffering of the sick and deranged. Both had an affection for animals. The poet and the future novelist used the city to train their powers of observation and sharpen their use of language. In Camus as in Rilke we find the inner feelings and sensibility of a poet. Camus' writing in the *Notebooks* has a richness of color and tonality not found in his later, more astringent works. At moments he equals Rilke's ability to fuse emotionally with a place: "Florence! One of the rare places in Europe where I have understood that dormant at the core of my rebellion lies an assent. In its sky, in which tears and sun mingle, I learned to give my assent to the earth and to burn in these somber flames of its feasts" (*E*, 88). The *Notebooks* share with Rilke's novel an obsession with death, though each writer deals differently with this recurrent issue. For Brigge, death is the ultimate reality. Each human is fated to undergo a death of his/her own, terrible in its uniqueness. He collects deaths, assessing them, evaluating them, storing up models for his own. When he sees a man faint and die on a city bench, Brigge writes: "he was already far beyond fear: then I had his fear."[13]

Reading those lines, I recalled my own experience of death. Twisted corpses of German soldiers frozen in the fields. Putrefied horses with great swollen bellies. A German boy lying alongside a wooden fence with a sack of grenades. "And where we had thought to slay another, we shall slay ourselves."[14] Camus too had seen death close up. In 1930 and 1942, when he had surgery for acute tuberculosis, there had been the chance that he would not recover. He had seen death closer than Rilke; his grasp of it was both conceptual and emotional:

> Djémila . . . and I sense clearly now that the true, the only progress of civilization—which a man from time to time attains —consists in the creation of conscious deaths . . .

13. Rilke, *Notebooks*, 143.
14. Joseph Campbell with Bill Moyers, *The Power of Myth* (New York: Doubleday, 1988), 151. In his Nobel address Camus made a similiar if less grandiose argument for universality: "the man who, as often happens, chose the path of art because he was aware of his difference soon learns that he can nourish his art, and his difference, solely by admitting his resemblance to all."

The creation of conscious deaths reduces the distance which
separates us from the world, enables us—without joy—to achieve
conscious remembrance of the exalting images of a world lost to
us forever. And the sad song of the hills of Djémila embeds the
bitterness of this lesson more deeply in my soul. (*E*, 64–65)

Camus' posthumous novel, *A Happy Death*, echoes many of
Rilke's ideas about "a death of one's own." Standing there in the
bookstore on the Rue de l'Odéon, I grasped the link between
Camus and the great poet of German modernism. It involved,
among other things, an ability to look honestly at death, in a
way that would be impossible for many who followed them.

Camus can be linked to another major figure of modernism,
Franz Kafka.[15] Just as the German-speaking Kafka lived sub-
merged in Prague, so Camus in Algeria was surrounded by an
alien Moslem majority. There is an element of detachment and
alienation even in Camus' most deeply felt pieces on Algeria. It
has been argued that Meursault's murder of the Arab expresses
the repressed aggression of the *pied-noir* against the indigenous
population.[16] In any event, Camus' Algerian rhapsody is never
without its undercurrent of terror. The celebration of the wind
at Djémila brings him face to face with death. Everything gives
way, stone, idea, earth. The absurd is born. That is Camus'
absolute, his core identity, the absurd. The name of Kafka is
never mentioned in Camus' essay on Prague, though he speaks
of looking for "a certain Jewish cemetery" during his brief visit
to that city. Kafka, in fact, is not buried in the Jewish cemetery in
central Prague, with its tilted clusters of weathered stones. He
lies outside the city in a suburban cemetery. In any case, there is
a striking affinity between Camus and his great predecessor,
whom he wrote about at length some years later in an adden-

15. Lottman writes: "He read and reread Kafka, whose work seemed to
him prophetic, one of the most significant of our time. And the reporter for the
New York French-language newspaper *La Victoire* . . . contributed the
thought that Camius himself was 'our Kafka without dreams'" (*ACB*, 379).

16. Kafka's story "Jackals and Arabs" prefigures Camus' position between
the Arabs and the *pieds-noirs*. The last line is spoken by an Arab about the
menacing jackals: "Marvellous creatures, aren't they? And how they hate us!"
Franz Kafka, in *The Penal Colony: Stories and Short Pieces*, trans. Willa and
Edwin Muir (New York: Schocken, 1948), 154.

dum to *The Myth of Sisyphus*. The bleak atmosphere and the desolation of spirit depicted in Camus' essay (entitled *Death in the Soul*) echo the tonalities of the German-Czech fabulist: "For days, I hadn't spoke a single word and my heart was bursting with cries of repressed revolt. I would have wept like a child if someone had opened his arms to me. Toward the end of the afternoon, broken with fatigue, I stared fixedly at the lock of my door, my empty head echoing with a popular accordion tune. At that moment, I could not go on" (*E*, 36). The experience of Kafka's Prague reprised the first experience of Paris. The city produced a vertigo of loneliness, alienation, and despair. It did not take much to throw Camus into the kind of dissociative crisis that seems to have been chronic in Kafka, who might have written the paradoxical statement: "Living consists of keeping the absurd alive." Camus' *The Stranger* is a modernist fable in the manner of Kafka, a work of elegant clarity that uses seemingly "realistic" notations to convey an ambivalence that can neither be deciphered nor explained.

The essay on Kafka in *The Myth of Sisyphus* gives special emphasis to the combination of a realistic use of detail with the symbolic method. Camus first makes the point that, "nothing is more difficult to understand than a symbolic work. A symbol always transcends its user and causes him to say more in reality than he is conscious of expressing" (*E*, 201). He sees Joseph K. of *The Trial* in a way that suggests his own presentation of Meursault: "By a singular but obvious paradox, the more extraordinary the character's adventure the more natural the story will be perceived: it [naturalness] is proportional to the gap that one can feel between the strangeness of a man's life and the simplicity with which that man accepts it. It appears that this is the naturalness of Kafka" (*E*, 202). Allegory has been assimilated to include any form of criticism or commentary, any use of one sign to double another. Unlike symbol, which conveys the essence of its referent, allegory is seen as fragmentary— repetitious, incomplete, and structually weak. Worst of all, it is ontologically deficient. But the new type of allegory, which begins with Kafka and of which Camus is a practitioner, is based on a different premise from the Coleridgean view that art must voice the secret life of things. This new allegory mimics appearances in an apparent realism that is no realism at all. Objects are seen in an unwavering, Medusa-like stare, such as Fredric Jameson has identified as the schizophrenic aspect of postmodern art. We look so intently that objects blur, fusing into strange new forms. This new allegory presents incompatible meanings that, as Craig Owens has said in another context, "are engaged in blind confrontation in such a way that it is impossible to choose between them."[17] Other works by Camus, notably *The Plague* and *The Fall*, also reach toward an allegorical dimension, indicating that the Kafkaesque fable was the genre within which he worked most effectively. Despite the restraint of Kafka's manner, the Czech ironist had a visionary side. His fables contain fables, his mysteries open on other mysteries. There is, for instance, the mysterious door mentioned in the priest's sermon toward the end of *The Trial*. The priest speaks of a man who has spent years waiting before a closed door. When finally he summons courage to address the gatekeeper, he is told: "The door has been open all this time. Now I am closing it."[18]

Camus opened doors to those who followed him but never went through the door himself. To go through the door (i.e., to make a choice that excludes all other options) requires a self-definition that Camus was not prepared to accept. Instead, as his career unfolded, one role merged imperceptibly into another. The poet of the *Notebooks* became the moralist of *The Fall*. Kafka's modernist allegory (as used by Camus, Sartre, Beckett, Kosinski) has become the vehicle par excellence for giving absurdity its literary shape. It is this special use of allegory that served Camus in his two definitive works, *The Stranger* and *The*

---

17. Craig Owens, "The Allegorical Impulse: Toward a Theory of Postmodernism," part 2, *October*, 13 (1980): 59–80. 61.

18. A different version of this episode occurs in the story "Before the Law," in Kafka, *The Penal Colony*, 149–50. Here it is the door of the Law that stands open. For years the man waits. The story ends: "The doorkeeper recognizes that the man has reached his end, and to let his failing senses catch the words roars in his ears: 'No one else could ever be admitted here, since this gate was made only for you. I am now going to shut it.'" The fundamental paradox applies to Camus: How can there be a system (the "Law") made only for one individual?

Fall, the first of these as an allegory of delusion, the second of awakening. Camus' personal narrative can be seen as the itinerary between these two books.

Camus' "in-betweeness" is the fundamental key to both his writing and his historical role. Sometimes his ambivalence brought him dangerously close to delusion, which is inevitable if you deny all forms of truth; but Camus had a clever way of shedding delusion. This was his theatricality, which insists that the actor's intensity of purpose is all that matters. Underneath the severity, the pride, the moral elevation there was a histrionic personage, an actor-writer who played the role of the literary *cabotin* with the consummate skill of a Voltaire or a Victor Hugo.

CHAPTER 3

The Roles of Albert Camus

As for me, I want to be that perfect actor.

Camus, *Notebook*

"I grew in the sea and poverty was my wealth, then I lost the sea, then all luxury seemed grey, poverty intolerable. Since then, I wait. I wait for the return voyage, the house by the sea, the clear light of day. I wait, I struggle to be polite. People see me pass in elegant cultured streets, I admire the views, I applaud like everyone else, I shake hands, it's not really me speaking. People praise me, I daydream a little, I'm offended, but show almost no surprise. Then I forget and smile at whoever insults me, or I greet those I love too courteously. What's to be done if I can only remember a single image? Finally they urge me to say who I am. 'Still nothing, still nothing'"

Camus, *La Mer au plus près: Journal de bord*

I became a fabulous opera.

Rimbaud

THEATER was Camus' first love, theatricality his vocation. He liked to clown around for his friends or entertain them with ribald songs. He was in some respects a *cabotin*—not merely an actor-director-playwright but someone who dealt with life's crises as performances, to be resolved by gesture and eloquence after argument and negotiation had failed. His childhood, as portrayed in *Le premier homme*, shows a family ruled by an authoritarian grandmother, where the family members play out their assigned roles. You did not argue or talk back in this family. The dominant emotional figure for Camus was his beloved mother who seldom spoke; but he converted his mother's muteness into its opposite. The theater gave him his voice and held out the promise of escape from the dilemma of *chien et loup* and the metaphysical binarity of good and evil that threatened him throughout his life.

There is no single key to Camus such as the one my friends and I searched for around café tables in 1948–1949; but his theatricality comes the closest to explaining what is obscure about him. A theatrically compressed, disguised as its opposite —sobriety, restraint, ethical severity. In this perspective, his philosophical ambivalence becomes transparent: an actor is always changing roles.

In November 1948 I attended a performance of Camus' *State of Siege*, considered a disaster by the critics. It was my first experience of total theater, and I was caught up in the bravura of the *mise-en-scène* and moved by the acting of Jean-Louis Barrault as well as the dark beauty of Spanish actress Maria Casarès, known to be Camus' lover. Camus' credentials as playwright, *homme de théâtre*, and friend to the quivering young Casarès gave him added prestige in my eyes. I understood what it meant to achieve reality by multiplying your masks and by speaking lines somebody else had invented. I would learn that Camus felt most at home when he was in the theater. In the time of his bitterest disillusionment, after Sartre's attack on him in 1952, he turned back to the theater for consolation. But theater wasn't merely a refuge; rather, it was a deeply vibrant way of being alive. Roger Quilliot emphasizes Camus' theatricality in his notes for the Pléiade edition: "Camus was a spontaneous actor;

not only capable of replacing an ailing colleague at a moment's notice, but also an actor in daily life . . . his friends know how he delighted to mime a scene, to read a text aloud, in short, to act. This was so because acting represented for him a fundamental form of existence" (*TRN*, 1687). It is important to see the actor behind this man whose hallmark was his consummate sincerity, for sincerity is itself a role. The actor gives himself over to the delirium of being other. He puts on other faces, speaks with other voices, lives other lives. Camus confided to a friend: "It seemed to me that I could have been an actor and that this profession would have satisfied me."

The theater provided Camus with "that friendship and that collective adventure which are necessary to me and which are still one of the most generous ways of not being alone." (*TRN*, 1711). It also provided a means for self-discovery and self-appropriation within a unique community in which the sacred once again gives meaning to life.

In his essay entitled *Why I Do Theater* Camus writes: "the theater is my convent," and he contrasts the production of a play to other forms of social activity, such as marriage, politics, or academic life (*TRN*, 1720). He finds them inferior, because they do not provide the same sense of mutual dependence in a supreme task.

In the long passage quoted in epigraph, Camus pretends that his only claim to selfhood lies in the initiatory experiences of sun and sea that he knew as an adolescent, before his illness, before his maturity and his exile into the adult world of Paris and World War II. His early writings indicate some kind of dissociative problem, a sense of estrangement brilliantly captured in *The Stranger* and harshly reemphasized in *The Misunderstanding*.[1] Throughout *The Plague* there is repeated reference to "abstraction" and "detachment" as conditions brought on by

---

1. The concept of "dissociation" was introduced into psychology by Janet as a way to describe the ego's failure to integrate the psyche. It was replaced in Freudian psychoanalysis by the associated notions of "repression" and "splitting." Without making a case one way or the other in respect to Camus, it is clear that this kind of defense mechanism can be used by the actor/playwright to deal with conflict in real life as well as in the projected or symbolized life of theater.

various types of psychic overload. Camus' long refusal of alle-
giances can be seen as the public dimension of an underlying
emotional incapacity at whose origins we can only guess. Theater brought him to life, awakened his sense of reality, gave him
the polyphony of a fabulous opera. It was in the theater that he
first constructed his cultural identity and found his calling. A
colleague recalled his participation in the Théâtre de l'Equipe in
Algiers: "Amid that animation, a tall young man, strikingly thin
and pale, his eyes very bright, seemed to direct everything, as if
burning with an interior flame: Albert Camus" (*TRN*, 1691).
Camus was an actor both inside and outside the theater. During
his brief career he invented many roles and played them to the
hilt. The first role was that of the writer who conceives his goal
as the bearing of an honest witness to history, both in his
journalistic essays and in *The Plague*. This was his finest role.
Despite his eventual retreat from the delusiveness of public life,
he will always be remembered as one of the century's most
articulate champions of justice. Of Camus' many other roles, I
will discuss two additional ones that became especially significant to me: the secular saint, represented by Tarrou and Rieux
in *The Plague*; and the judge-penitent, represented by Jean-
Baptiste Clamence, bizarre hero of *The Fall*, the work where
Camus recounts his awakening from the delusive hell of public
life. The point of this discussion is to show how role-playing,
which is akin to story-telling, simultaneously creates and dis-
pels delusion, both on the stage and in the domain of "real-
world" action.

The Honest Witness

At the end of *The Plague*, Dr. Rieux avows that he is the author of
the chronicle we have just read. He states that he has "expressly
made a point of adopting the tone of an impartial observer."[2]
Reviving a central motif of the Camus canon, that of the trial,
Rieux states of himself in the third person: "Summoned to give
evidence regarding what was a sort of crime, he has exercised

2. *The Plague*, trans. Stuart Gilbert (New York: Random House, 1948), 301.

the restraint that behooves a conscientious witness. All the same, following the dictates of his heart, he has deliberately taken the victims' side and tried to share with his fellow citizens the only certitudes they had in common—love, exile, and suffering."[3] If mankind is the victim of a crime, who is the perpetrator? When Camus worked as a journalist, first in Algeria, then in occupied France, the identity of the enemy was clear enough— the enemy forces, be they German or Vichy French.[4] But when the victim/perpetrator dyad becomes a parable of the human condition, then the role of the honest witness becomes more difficult. If Camus rails at God, at life, at the human condition he risks appearing paranoid, in the manner of those magnificent victims, Antonin Artaud and Louis-Ferdinand Céline. Perhaps he will seem obsessed with the "absolute morality" of which Sartre accused him in 1952. It is to Camus' credit that he dismissed these dangers, sensing from the start that he was a privileged witness to a decisive moment in history and that he would be judged in the end by the fidelity and the austerity of his account. The deliberately understated style of *The Plague* is designed precisely to avoid the appearance of that intoxication that leads to self-righteousness and judgment. A further prop to the impartial moral stance derives from the fact that the principal speaker throughout the novel is Dr. Rieux, a man of deliberate action, who does not fall victim to the eccentric acts that threaten so many minor characters in Camus' novels, for example, the robotic woman in *The Stranger* or the old asthmatic and the man who spits on cats in *The Plague*. In a world where no activity can be entirely justified, compulsive activity appears as a distorting mirror of socially acceptable action. Yet eccentricity as a means of self-stabilization is not to be disdained. Joseph Grand in *The Plague* constantly writes and rewrites the first paragraph of a novel. Grand, the humble clerk, who does the bookkeeping for the sanitary squads, is, we are told, the true

    3. Ibid., 301–2.
    4. Shoshana Felman and Dori Laub argue that *The Plague* can also be read as the Holocaust. They base this on the "resonance of a few quotations" (97). More cogently, they argues for history itself as holocaust. *Testimony: Crises of Witnessing in Literature, Psychoanalysis, and History* (New York: Routledge, 1992), hereafter *T*.

hero of the epidemic: "Yes, if it is a fact that people like to have examples given them, men of the type they call heroic, and if it is absolutely necessary that this narrative should include a 'hero,' the narrator commends to his readers, with, to his thinking, perfect justice, this insignificant and obscure hero who had to his credit only a little goodness of heart and a seemingly absurd ideal."[5] Grand is a hero because he helps his fellow citizens, but also because he keeps alive (if only in a derisory way) that disinterested artistic ideal that is the hallmark of our humanity in a degenerate time. He copes with the trials of the human condition, and his way of coping is no more absurd than that condition itself. Grand, Rieux, Tarrou, all of Camus' characters bear witness, just as he did himself, to the effort to dispell delusions of all kinds and the struggle to live as an ordinary man at a particular moment of history.

The Secular Saint

"Sainthood" was not a current word in my vocabulary in 1948. I had seen paintings in the Louvre—Saint Teresa in ecstasy, St. Sebastian bristling with arrows. In the dark recesses of Saint-Sulpice hung portraits of fleshy women with too many clothes, gazing morosely past my head at the sanctuary light. In college I had read about the temptations of St. Anthony, but "temptation" was as foreign as sainthood. Still, as the result of my encounter with the writings of Georges Bernanos and Max Jacob, I realized that the term encompassed a range of experience that had some historical and cultural importance. Saints were men and women who went against the grain, who defied their families and humbled their desires, all for the love of God. I began to frequent dubious bookstores around the squat rococo church of Saint-Sulpice, where Djuna Barnes had set many scenes of her novel *Nightwood*. These shops, full of what the French call *bondieuseries*, were viewed as places of ill repute by my intellectual or left-wing friends, but to me they conveyed an unknown world. Trite, sentimental, reeking of piety, yet repre-

5. *The Plague*, 137.

senting something I wanted to know more about: the love of God, whatever that might be.

That winter I read an article in *Le Figaro* that called Albert Camus "a secular saint." I found this astonishing. If saints humbled themselves for the love of God, how could an atheist be a saint? There was, I realized, an entire conceptual world connected with religion about which I knew nothing. That there might also be a range of authentic religious experiences, which could cause people to drastically reform their lives, was now something I had to consider.

Not long after reading the *Figaro* piece on Camus, I went to lunch in the restaurant Raffy at the height of the noon rush. There were no empty tables, and I sat down opposite a priest to eat. I had never spoken to a priest before and viewed all clergy as aliens. This man was tall and gaunt, his courtly manner at odds with the noisy restaurant. I brought up the subject of Camus and my perplexity about a "secular saint." He listened seriously, then assured me that true saintliness had little to do with belief in God. He told me that he admired Camus. After all, when Camus joined the Communist Party he told Grenier that he had done so to reduce the misery of mankind. Camus, the priest said with sudden intensity, stood shoulder to shoulder with the saints in his struggle against evil. "It must be especially hard," he said, "to wage war against evil when you have no faith. It takes a special kind of grace." He looked me straight in the eyes with a hint of a smile on his long gaunt face. "What do you think?"

I explained that I had gone to war against the Nazis, by compulsion not by choice. I had seen the devastation of Europe brought about by Hitler's megalomania, yet I had never really thought about evil. A look of pain crossed his face."You must think about evil. There is so much of it!" He paid his bill and was gone.

That afternoon, following the priest's suggestion, I bought Camus' new book, *The Plague*, and met his diffident hero, Dr. Rieux. Rieux devotes himself tirelessly to fighting the disease that is sweeping Oran. When, at the end of the ordeal, Rieux loses his wife to the plague, he has also lost any vestige of egoism or personal concern. He and his associates represent all men who struggle against evil and oppression, their struggle itself giving meaning to an absurd and senseless world.

Camus was one of the great protest-atheists of his day, a man who rejects the idea of God because he believes that no God could have created the world we encounter in our daily lives. The world where children are abused and dictators kill at random to maintain regimes of terror, but also a world where earthquake and famine wipe out entire populations. Rieux is not simply the chronicler of the plague. In his restrained and "objective" way, he paints a terrifying picture of the human condition: "that stupefied populace of which each day a portion, crammed into the jaws of a furnace, dissipated in greasy smoke, while the others, shackled with the chains of helplessness and fear, waited their turn" (*TRN*, 1463). This image simultaneously evokes Malraux the atheist and Pascal the Christian.[6] For both of Camus' great predecessors, man exists in a condition of absurdity and terror. Camus' commitment to the resistance, his anguish at being separated from his wife who remained in Algeria while he was in France, his struggles of conscience, his decision to oppose the death penalty—all this was distilled into the characters of Rieux and the eccentric moralist, Tarrou.

Late that night, I closed the book and pondered the question of my own personal morality. I had never received any moral education. I had certain moral reflexes, inculcated by my family and environment, but I had never truly struggled with right and wrong, never truly worked my way through a moral issue. I remembered that night of guard duty in the Ruhr when I had found nothing worth dying for, then killed a German soldier. Once again I felt my unwelcome solidarity with Camus' Meursault, compelled to a murder he could neither justify nor explain. I remembered waking up that morning on the floor of the Ruhr hunting lodge, after a few hours of sleep. I was assailed by questions without answers. Why were we killing and being killed? The evil of Hitler was still an abstraction, but the dead German boy with staring blue eyes and a trickle of blood at the

6. In Malraux's novel *La Condition humaine* the captured Communists are burned alive in the boiler of a locomotive. Pascal writes about men chained together and executed one by one.

corner of his mouth was a reality. All I could do was shrug the
questions away and follow the back of the GI marching in front
of me. My only rationale was commitment to my buddies. I saw
myself as an amoral being, a puppet whose strings were pulled
by events. But that was during a time of war; now, if I was going
to become fully human, I had to begin to learn what it meant to
be a moral being.

Slowly, I brought myself back to my room in Paris, to the
book I was reading. It seemed a long trajectory from being
Meursault to being Rieux. *The Plague* was both a transparent
book and a difficult one. Transparent because everything was
spoken, explicit, on the surface—the evil of disease, human
weakness, courage, and the search for a response to evil. Difficult because Europe had gone through a terrible convulsion that
lay beyond my twenty-two-year-old understanding. Camus'
novel represented evil in the remoteness of allegory. I had seen
the hulks of shattered cities across Germany. I had helped
liberate a slave-labor camp where starved prisoners crouched
like animals in the shadows of their barracks; but history must
be lived, in the body as well as the mind, to be truly grasped. My
experience as an American suburbanite was too remote to allow
an imaginative leap into the life of Dr. Rieux. What I did possess
was faith in Camus' own experience of history. He was a witness who could be believed. This tentative moral awakening is
something else that I owe to Camus, and it began in that whitewashed room under a slanted roof where I stayed up all night
reading *The Plague*.

In the months that followed, I made the effort to learn more
about Camus. In particular, how he had struggled with the
question of reprisal against the collaborationists. He wrote in
Combat: "We have chosen to accept human justice with its
terrible imperfections, careful only to correct it through a desperately maintained honesty" (*ACB*, 339). I admired his ability
to change when he decided, only months later, that state-
sponsored death was intolerable and undertook his long campaign against the death penalty.

Retrospectively, Camus' argument for the purge (acceptable
in a period of stress but not after) lifted the burden of what I had
done from my shoulders. So long as I thought about it with "a
desperately maintained honesty," it was okay to kill a German

teenager who was trying to blow up my platoon. Through Camus, I came to realize that life was a matter of choices and that morality was nothing more nor less than the quality of reason one brought to those choices. But the choices weren't easy. It helped if you had a point of reference, a religious doctrine or ideology; but we were taught to be sceptical of such things. The Church—with its liturgy, its intellectual complexity, and its artistic marvels—fascinated me, but I was wary of its embrace. You don't just walk into the arms of a ten-thousand-pound gorilla. Besides, Albert Camus, my role model, had steered clear of involvement with all institutions.

In the 1930s and 1940s, Communism and Catholicism were communicating vessels, but Camus never made that transit. He was, as Grenier points out in the preface to the Pléiade edition, not so much an atheist as an "antithéiste" opposed to a certain conception of God: "An all-powerful God, should He exist, could not be forgiven for having allowed the unmeasurable evil which submerges the world He created and which without Him could not endure" (*TRN*, xii). Grenier concludes: "If his opposition to faith was radical, it must not be forgotten that it constituted an homage to faith itself, and that it took seriously, or rather tragically, as it must be taken, this problem posed by suffering and death."[7] This was Camus' long and painful struggle with theodicy, the question of the righteousness of a God who allows evil on a monumental scale in the world he is reputed to have made. As David Hume put it for all atheists before and since: "Why is there any misery at all in the world? Not by chance, surely. From some cause then. Is it from the intention of the Deity? But he is perfectly benevolent. Is it contrary to his intention? But he is almighty."[8]

Camus' joust with theodicy occurs in *The Plague*, where Fa-

---

7. Poet and Christian mystic Charles Péguy seems to anticipate Camus when he makes a distinction between "revolutionary atheism," in which there is great hope, and "bourgeois atheism," the atheism of those who choose comfort, materialism, and the status quo. "From reactionary atheism, from bourgeois atheism, one can expect nothing but ashes and dust, because there all is death and ashes." Péguy, *The Modern World*, in *Men and Saints*, trans. Anne and Julian Green (New York: Pantheon, 1944), 97–99.

8. David Hume, *Dialogues Concerning Natural Religion* (New York: Hafner Publishing Co., 1948), 69.

ther Paneloux addresses the problem of the epidemic in two
sermons. In his first sermon, Paneloux is confident of his
ground. He tells his congregation: "Calamity has come on you,
my brethren, and, my brethren, you deserved it." The plague
has come as a punishment because the people of Oran have
sinned. He delivers the argument of traditional theodicy: "This
same pestilence which is slaying you works for your good and
points your path."9

By the time of his second sermon, Paneloux is a changed
man. He has worked with the sick and is himself carrying the
plague bacillus. His message now is that plague is a mystery as
is God's love for man: "the love of God is a hard love. It
demands total self-surrender, disdain of our human personality. And yet it alone can reconcile us to suffering and the
deaths of children, it alone can justify them, since we cannot
understand, and we can only make God's will ours."10

In his first sermon Paneloux uses arguments that are flawed,
arguments from the theological tradition that believes that evil
can be explained. These include such views as the following:
suffering will be transformed into joy at the end of time when
God's plan is revealed in ultimate harmony; our heavenly re-
ward will be commensurate with our suffering here below; and
the familiar argument that only free beings, capable of sin
as well as heroic virtue, are worthy to know and love an infinite God.

Such arguments seem meaningless to Rieux and his outspo-
ken friend Tarrou who remarks: "When an innocent youth can
have his eyes destroyed [reference to an incident in the war], a
Christian should either lose his faith or consent to having his
eyes destroyed."11

Behind Tarrou stands Ivan Karamazov, the greatest protest-
atheist in literature, who maintains to his brother Alyosha:

> But then there are the children, and what am I going to do with
> them? That is the question I cannot resolve. For the hundredth
> time I repeat: there are hosts of questions, but I've taken only the
> children, because here what I need to say is irrefutably clear.

9. *The Plague*, 94, 98.
10. Ibid., 228.
11. Ibid., 229.

Listen: if everyone must suffer, in order to buy eternal harmony with their suffering, pray tell me what have children got to do with it? It's quite incomprehensible why they should have to suffer, and why they should buy harmony with their suffering. Why do they get thrown on the pile, to manure someone's future harmony with themselves? . . . and therefore I absolutely renounce all higher harmony. It is not worth one little tear of even that one tormented child who beat her chest with her little fist and prayed to "dear God" in a stinking outhouse with her unredeemed tears! . . . And if the suffering of children goes to make up the sum of suffering needed to buy truth, then I assert beforehand that the whole of truth is not worth such a price.[12]

Camus too was an Ivan. The suffering of one single child irrevocably denies the existence of God. Later, I was to learn that, despite his atheism, Camus was deeply moved by the work of a young Jewish woman named Simone Weil, who saw the terrible reality of human suffering as a compelling argument for the reality of a crucified God. Before he left for Sweden to receive the Nobel Prize, Camus went to the Weil apartment and meditated in the room that had been Simone's as a girl. Camus did not simply reflect on the "problem of evil" with the detachment of some cloistered theologian; he struggled with it in the turmoil of his heart, he clashed with it in the ultimate wickedness it assumed in his own time. He never left off worrying that he, perhaps, had it wrong, that he did not see all of the picture.

Judge-Penitent

Albert Camus, moralist, resistance hero, secular saint—it was too easy. Respect for my hero demanded that I work harder to define him. Whatever he was, Camus was not a saint. You couldn't play the literary game and be a saint. Being lucky wasn't enough. You had to master the skill of the literary polemic, you had to walk the high moral road but know when to cut your adversary down to size. Literary gamesmanship forced Camus to invent a new role for himself in the mid-1950s.

---

12. Fyodor Dostoevsky, *The Brothers Karamazov*, trans. Richard Pevear and Larissa Volokhonsky (San Francisco: North Point Press, 1990), 244–5.

This was the role of the judge-penitent. There were crucial issues here, as Camus assumed the Cassandra role with an historical acuity that set him above everybody else.

When *The Plague* was published in 1948, Camus insisted in articles and interviews that he was not Rieux any more than he was Meursault. He was a man who refused definition, just as he both enjoyed and disdained the homage of the Paris literary world. Camus considered himself an artist, but an artist who tried to do the right thing in the muddle of contemporary life. He was a man of refusals. He cultivated the exclusionary pride of the hidalgo and constantly practiced "refusal without concession."

His refusal of revolutionary violence and Stalinist Russia with its prison camps brought on the break with Sartre.[13] The editorial board of Sartre's journal, *Les Temps modernes*, handed over the review of *The Rebel* to a relatively unknown writer, Francis Jeanson. The review was harsh. When Camus replied, Sartre stepped into the fray. Camus was devastated by the epithet "the High Priest of Absolute Morality" and by Sartre's reproach: "A violent and ceremonial dictatorship has taken possession of you, supported by an abstract bureaucracy, and pretends to rule according to moral law" (*ACB*, 505). As we now understand, Sartre & Cie attacked Camus not because his book had some philosophical flaws but because he had dared to speak out against communist totalitarianism, in which they had unwisely placed their own dogmatic faith. That was the one thing they could not tolerate.

Following these events, Camus underwent a period of self-examination, during which time he wrote *The Fall*. In this book

13. "It is a similar suppression that is enacted by the systematic deafness of *Les Temps modernes* and by Sartre's reasserted silence on Stalin's oppressions, a similar censorship both of the victim's cry and of Camus' own outcry as a witness, in the concerted muffling of his dissident voice, crying in the desert against Soviet concentration camps. In *this double suppression of the cry of both* the victim and the witness, what is particularly grave and particularly rich in implications in the vision of *The Fall* is that Sartre, or the *fellow intellectual*, has betrayed the testimonial task, *betrayed, precisely, as a fellow witness*, since he chose not to acknowledge Russian concentration camps and not to look at history from hell." Felman and Laub, *T*, 186.

he presents a new kind of individual, the judge-penitent, who is both innocent and guilty in equal amounts.

Shoshana Felman and Dr. Dori Laub have renewed Camus criticism with their brilliant reading of *The Fall* as allegory of the world's silence before the Holocaust. This reading is one of the ways in which we must understand the book from now on. But the nature of allegory is to have multiple meanings. By its simplest definition allegory "says one thing and means another" (from the Greek *allos* = "other" and *agoreuein* = "to speak"). How does this apply to *The Fall*? First, it has that apparent ontological deficiency and lack of dynamism associated with allegory. Its powerful message is masked by a talky and arbitrary form. Second, its various meanings seem to conflict. Is the private or public meaning more important? Who is Clamence, Camus, Sartre, or Everyman? And why has Camus chosen this devious form to spell out his most crushing polemic?

The Fall is a counterallegory to *The Stranger*. In the later book Camus is no longer the neutral apologist for a guiltless antihero who is sentenced to death for failing to cry at his mother's funeral and whose true guilt lies in the fact that he is a man "who refuses to lie . . . who does not play the game." Jean-Baptiste Clamence, the narrator-protagonist of the 1956 novel, is a man aware of his bad faith, who faces up to the moral illusions on which his previous career as a "generous lawyer" had been based. Once a public figure, he has now become intensely private. He is a penitent whose confessional is a waterfront dive and whose confessor is a nameless bypasser. Clamence, once a world-class player, is now a "judge-penitent" who shares the guilt of others and judges himself more harshly than any of his former adversaries or clients. The guilt of Clamence crystallized when, returning home one night, he witnesses a suicide, hears the victim cry for help, but turns his back and goes home. The obsessive monologue spoken by Clamence develops around this kernel event. But there is no attempt to dramatize events, because such an aesthetic strategy is itself a lie. Felman and Laub write: "Because what has been witnessed cannot be made whole and integrated into an authoritative telling, *The Fall* has lost at once the narrative consistency of *The Plague* and the claim of the former novel to historical monumentality" (*T*, 171). Because true witnessing is no longer possible, we have allegory rather than a realistic fiction. Realism is surreptitious in its lies; allegory parades its fictionality. Felman and Laub claim that the age of narrative has given way to an age of testimony and see *The Fall* as emblematic of this shift: "Encompassing uncannily the story of de Man as well as that which separates Camus from Sartre, *The Fall* turns out to be—beyond the personal and beyond any reductive psychological trivialization—the fated and ill-understood story of the baffling fall of an entire generation, a story (and a history) from whose bewildering complexity and from whose chaotic implications we have not as yet emerged" (*T*, xix).[14] But along with testimony we need interpretation. The Kafkaesque allegory conveys the inner meaning of history, but only a new breed of postmodern interpreters, represented by Felman and Laub, can tell us what the allegory means.

The honest witness, the secular saint, the judge-penitent are the most important of Camus' roles. There were others attributed to him, most of which he denied in spite of their apparent relevance. Like Nietzsche, with whom modernity begins, Camus defined himself by what he was not. He denied even the most obvious literary influences, for instance, the stylistic influence of Hemingway on the clipped sentences of *L'Etranger*. Was Camus a humanist? We have his 1937 remark that humanism is inadequate. Was he a Marxist? He joined the Party in 1934 and quit after two years,[15] in protest against the withdrawal of support for the Arab cause. Camus broke all alliances—no cause seemed pure enough for him. He broke with the Comité

14. They see de Man's transformation from journalist to theorist as parallel to that of Camus. "The failed confession of *The Fall* could thus stand in the place of de Man's missing confession: insofar as it belatedly accounts for the aftermath of the trauma—and for the belated transformation—occasioned by the war, *The Fall* indeed can be read as de Man's unspoken autobiographical story." Felman and Laub, *T*, xviii.

15. The length of time is in dispute. Lottman gives it as one year (*ACB*). Jean Daniel gives it as two in his *Nouvel Observateur* article on Camus. Jean Daniel, Czeslaw Milosz, Octavio Paz et al., "La Revanche d'Albert Camus," *Le Nouvel Observateur*, 1544, 9–15 June, 1994.

National des Ecrivains, which had spoken for the writers of France during the war, he denounced UNESCO for allowing Spanish participation. Perhaps he had, as Grenier put it, *la nostalgie de la grandeur*. Though he spoke on behalf of the RDR, he never again joined a political movement after his short involvement with the communists.

He rejected existentialism: "I do not much relish the celebrated existentialist philosophy and, to put it candidly, I believe its conclusions to be false."[16] Through Jean Grenier, Camus began a correspondence with Max Jacob, who read and admired *The Stranger*. The poet wrote to Grenier: "M. Camus seemed to me a young man with a future; he demonstrates a faith in art which could well transform itself into other faiths" (*ACB*, 56). The judge-penitent, the man who is both guilty and innocent, is a kind of secular parody of the Christian position. It is a Christianity without hope or the expectation of forgiveness. Instead of forgiveness, there echoes through *The Fall* the derisive laugh heard first in *The Plague*. It is Nietzsche's laughter at "the eternal comedy of existence," it is the laughter of the devil, who knows he will win in the end. Though Jean-Louis Barrault called Camus "a secular monk, all streaming with a God he dared not name,"[17] Camus made atheism his most unremitting rejection. Camus was a twentieth-century Nietzsche who chose the Christ of organized religion as his adversary and condemned Christianity because it separated man from the only ultimate reality—the material world.[18] The multiple meanings of Camus' allegories reflect the irreconcilable pluralisms of

16. Originally an article in *Combat*. Quoted in Henri Peyre, *French Novelists of Today* (New York: Oxford University Press, 1967), 316.

17. Originally in a special number of the *NRF* on Camus. Peyre, 312.

18. Felman and Laub (*T*, 185) see Camus' Jesus as archetype of all those who enter into unwilling complicity with history by bearing witness to it: "Paradoxically, the allegorical figure of Christ appears in the arena of *The Fall* not as a saviour, but as a witness to the fact, and as a bearer of the knowledge of the fact, that human history precludes any salvation. Since the witness is a dissident by definition, since the witness can, by definition, have no ally, Christ in turn is betrayed by his own allies, and his testimony, met by deafness and repressed by silence, is ironically denied by his own apostles. Christ's canonization and his transformation into God henceforth insures the deafness to his testimony and the impermeability to his 'seditious cry.'"

modern life, which are themselves a determining condition of the contemporary absurd. Here again, Camus was prophetic, since he defined the way we would be living at the end of the century, in a world of electronic delusion, where we use material comforts to shield us from the irrational oscillations of history.

Was Camus in fact a hero? There was only one hero in postwar France. He was an aristocrat, a professional soldier, a patriot, and a believer named Charles de Gaulle. Camus was the anti-de Gaulle, the hero for the rest of us. His irony and his silence offset the General's rhetoric. He wanted to disenchant France from its myths, not restore them. Camus repeatedly stated his suspicions of heroism. Rieux replies to Tarrou in a contemplative moment: "Heroism and sanctity don't really appeal to me. . . . What interests me is being a man."[19]

Although the chemistry of war formed both Camus and the General, one was the mirror image of the other. De Gaulle, the hero of action, could point to his rallying of the French after their defeat and the restoration of French national dignity and purpose. For an antihero such as Camus, his cause was his person, the books he wrote, the aura that surrounded him, the life he lived. On the other hand, the moral stand that Camus took as editor-in-chief of the postwar *Combat* was decisive and raised public consciousness to a unique intensity. But there was something single-minded and intense in the man himself that lifted him above the public arena. Despite their reservations about Camus, even the hard-bitten existentialists were susceptible to Camus' aura. Sartre wrote:

> It was in 1945: we were discovering Camus, the Resistant, as we had discovered Camus, the author of *L'Etranger*. . . . You were almost exemplary. For you bore within yourself all the conflicts of our time and went beyond them because of the ardor with which you lived them. You were a real *person*, the most complex and the richest, the last and the most gifted of the heirs of Chateaubriand and the scrupulous defender of a social cause. You had all the luck and all the merits, bringing to a sense of

19. *The Plague*, 255.

greatness a passionate love of beauty, to the joy of living, the sense of death. . . . How we loved you then.[20]

The war in Algeria was Camus' ultimate test. The event that made revolution inevitable took place at Sétif in 1945, when French troops killed thousands of people (Algerians sources put the number at 45,000) during a demonstration that had begun as a celebration of the Allied victory over the Germans. From that time onward, all partial solutions failed. France poured 40,000 troops into its colony and violence increased. When de Gaulle took power he made ambiguous promises to both sides. Camus tried to maintain his commitment to both the Algerian people and the *pied-noir* community, from which he himself had come, but in doing so he alienated himself from both. Maybe he should have spoken out strongly for Algerian independence, but even here he remained *entre chien et loup*, the man of the *entre-deux*. In retrospect, his vacillation betwen a French Algeria and his belief in freedom and self-determination seems not just understandable but commendable, given his fierce love for his mother, forever identified with the land of his birth.

Camus had a strongly defined personality, but his intellectual position was one of fundamental ambiguity. He enters the twilight of history like the Orpheus of Cocteau's film, floating into an indeterminate zone, the *entre-deux* where our terrible daylight questions become irrelevant. There are other great figures in this twilight zone. Oscillation between affirmation and doubt defines the human condition for a lineage of famous sceptics that includes Hume and Nietzsche. The view of man as something "in-between" involves a concept of human contingency that takes us back to Plotinus and St. Augustine, the authors Camus wrote about in his university thesis. It was while reading the *Enneads* of Plotinus that Augustine came face to face with the contingency of human existence, man's incompleteness and imperfection vis-à-vis the totality of God. He wrote in

20. Jean-Paul Sartre in *Les Temps modernes*. August 1952. Quoted in Germaine Brée, *Camus* (New Brunswick: Rutgers University Press, 1961), 48–49.

Book VII of his *Confessions*: "And I looked at other things below You, and saw that they neither were nor were not absolutely. They *were*, indeed, since they came from You, but they *were not*, since that which You are, they were not." Man, as portrayed by Camus, is a direct descendent of Augustinian man, trapped on the ladder of existence—except that for Camus the ladder leads nowhere whereas for Augustine it leads to God.

In the mid-1940s Camus relished the fame and recognition that he received. By the early 1950s he had reached a period of utter disillusion. His ironical story, *Jonas or the Artist at Work*, shows an artist who is undermined by love of his wife and children, devoured by his friends, then abandoned by a capricious public. In 1951 Camus' philosophical book, *The Rebel*, was under attack. Weakened by tuberculosis and desperate for a sustained period of rest and meditation, he found himself solicited from every side, unable to think or work as he desired. He wrote in his *Notebook*: "Everyone pounces, on me, destroying me, ceaselessly demanding their share, never extending a hand, helping me, loving me for what I am and so that I can remain what I am" (*E*, 2945). Jonas is Camus, delivered to the dogs of fame, but also caught in the drama of ultimate doubt. Jonas ends his career suspended on a platform, staring at a blank canvas. Camus too lived suspended between earth and sky. The deepest wish of such a man was not to be acclaimed but to be left alone. *The Fall* voices this hatred of the literary world and the deeper uncertainty that arose from his lacerating indeterminacy. By this stage in his career Camus had pushed his sincerity to the point where it seemed the opposite: duplicity. We are all duplicitous, he seemed to say, our only identity is doubt. After years of fighting against delusion, Camus seemed to bow to its inevitability. It was this painful decision to live in proximity to opposing belief systems while denying them any validity that distinguished Camus and defined his unique position.

Through a succession of literary personae Albert Camus performed, in the theater of our collective minds, the great historical *agon* of the first half of the century, the struggle between various forms of good and evil that came to be represented, finally, by Hitler and that we codify under the name of Holocaust. He saw the hope of twentieth-century history in the challenge to find a pivot from which evil can be turned away and delusional thinking dispelled; but, inexorably, events overwhelmed him. In his brief moment as a public figure, he tried to call us out of the shadows into the Mediterranean sunlight, his symbol for a new European community based on civility and moral responsibility. In the light of current events, such a community appears almost as much of a dream (if not a delusion) today as it did in 1945 or in 1957 at the time of his Nobel Prize address.

CHAPTER 4

Death of a Nobel Laureate

The last act is bloody, no matter how charming the rest
of the play.

Pascal

F R O M California I watched Camus receive the Nobel Prize
for Literature on December 10, 1957. What a drama—the
poor kid from a family of illiterates in an Algerian slum
recognized as the greatest writer of his time! It was the conclusion of a fairy-tale, and I wondered how Camus was taking it.

Nobody was as surprised as Camus himself when he received the Nobel Prize. In the manner of all great honors, it
awoke conflicting emotions. And it propelled Camus to reveal
his true character in a way that he had never done publically
before. His speech was dense but full of emotion, gratitude for
the award, but also profound humility. As I read and reread his
Nobel speech in the *New York Times*, I realized how truly extraordinary this man was. Camus insisted that the award belonged not to him but to all those who had worked to defeat
Hitler: the partisans, the murdered hostages, the Holocaust
victims, the invading armies, and, especially, the poets and
artists of the Resistance. Because I was included in my own
small way, I tried to understand what he meant by his call to
"rebuild with all men the ark of the covenant." It came back to

what he had said at the meeting of the RDR in the Salle Pleyel that night of December 13, 1948. Only by a tremendous act of solidarity and commitment, joined to unsparing compassion for others, could a new society be built. It involved a repudiation of the forces of death, especially the despairing nihilism that had led many to throw in their fate with Vichy or with Moscow. There was something lonely and grand in this appeal, sent out to all of us across the world who were of the postwar generation, called to rebuild our human community in a difficult and violent time. I felt intensely the character of the man; or rather, for the first time, I understood what it was to have character. Camus' trajectory meant that you did not have to think of yourself simply as a victim, responding to whatever chance sent your way; but, at every moment, you had the freedom and the obligation to choose what to do or not do, what to say or not say. Camus proved that any individual could rise above the circumstances of his origin. This included both the genetic and the economic facts of life.[1]

Applying this to myself, I realized that most of what I had done in life up to this point had been reactive, driven by neurotic imperatives or by sudden impulse rather than reasoned choice. What I had always taken for a love of risk was really a compulsion to behave irrationally, just because I felt like it. When I was a GI at Camp San Luis Obispo, on guard one night at an ammo dump, I took a live .60 mm mortar shell apart, to send home as a "gift" to my parents. My marriage had come about in the same irrational and compulsive way, in 1951 after a year spent teaching French at St. Louis University and trying to write a novel. Myron Schwartz, my father's oldest friend, said ironically, "He spends the year in the attic, then comes down and says he's getting married."

My involvement with the Church was equally compulsive and unexamined. Despite the expected magic, it had not made

---

1. He speaks of the nineteenth-century pioneers in Algeria: "And their children and grand-children had found themselves in this land just as they had, without a past, without morality, without a lesson, without religion but happy to exist and to to live in the light, anguished by night and death." *Le premier homme* (Paris: Gallimard, 1994), 178–79.

me a moral being, because I had only substituted a rigid grid of prohibitions for the work of my own conscience. Reading Camus, I found a new perspective and was able to look at myself with something approaching objectivity. I had tried to seize an identity. I tried to replace the partial identities that I had been born with (Jewish, Midwesterner, middle-class) with something off the shelf of the cultural supermarket (Catholic, scholar, novelist). But that wasn't how it worked. If you wanted to be *other*, then you had to make a commitment; you had to spend years learning new reflexes, new mentalities; you had to mobilize your passion and put it into that choice. I was an authentic member of the Camus generation, but I was trying to put that indeterminacy to work in the service of some kind of program. It was a quixotic program, involving liberal politics and religious awareness. Years would pass before there was any kind of fusion between the two. Meanwhile, I was teaching Camus, Sartre, and de Beauvoir at UCLA. *The Stranger* was the foundational text of that time. SDS, the Black Power movement, the new liberalism were all influenced by the ambiguous persona of Meursault and, behind him, the towering figure of Albert Camus.

Soon after his Nobel celebration, the old adage came true: "The gods first elevate those they intend to destroy." Camus became a tragic hero, first lifted to the heights of celebrity, then annihilated. Simone de Beauvoir tells how she learned the news:

> I was alone in Sartre's apartment one January afternoon when the telephone rang. "Camus has just been killed in a car crash," Lanzmann told me. . . . I put down the receiver, my throat tight, my lips trembling. "I'm not going to start crying," I said to myself, "he didn't mean anything to me anymore." I stood there, leaning against the window, watching night come down over Saint-Germain des Près, incapable of calming myself or of giving way to real grief. Sartre was upset as well, and we spent the whole evening with Bost talking about Camus. . . . I got up, threw on the first clothes I found, and set out walking through the night. It wasn't the fifty-year-old man who'd just died I was mourning; not that just man without justice, so arrogant and touchy behind his stern mask . . . it was the companion of our

hopeful years, whose open face laughed and smiled so easily, the young ambitious writer, wild to enjoy life, its pleasures, its triumphs, and comradeship, friendship, love and happiness. . . . Camus as I had loved him emerged from the night about me, in the same instance recovered and painfully lost.[2]

I had been in Paris in 1945 when Camus achieved star status. I was also there in 1960 at the moment of his death. By that time, I had moved on to other heroes and heroines but nevertheless felt a stinging sense of personal loss. On the morning of January 5 I went out to the bakery to pick up some croissants and passed a newsstand on my way back. There I saw the familiar face looking at me from the morning editions. I fumbled for change and read the news standing there in the cold. Camus had planned to take the train from the Midi back to Paris but, instead, changed his plans and decided to drive with Michel Gallimard, his wife, Janine, and her daughter, Anne. They left Provence on the third, spent the night in Thoissey where they celebrated Anne's eighteenth birthday, and left around 10 A.M. on the morning of the fourth. It was chilly, and a January drizzle had dampened the road. Gallimard's Facel-Vega skidded out of control on Route Nationale 5 just north of Sens, eighty miles south of Paris. The car bounced off one plane tree and crashed into another. Camus' skull was fractured and his spine was snapped, killing him instantly. Michel Gallimard, Camus' long-time friend, was still alive though badly injured. He died some days later. Gallimard's wife and step-daughter survived. It was reported that the police found an unused railroad ticket in the writer's pocket.

Again the irreparable intervened. It appeared as if some terrible process, unleashed during the war, was still going on. Camus had born witness against absurdity, and now absurdity had killed him. I said earlier that facing death is the ultimate antidelusional act, but not when it takes you by surprise. There has to be at least a moment for the scales to fall, for the past to click into focus, for the final calculus of reality. Camus did not

2. Simone de Beauvoir, *Force of Circumstances*, trans. Richard Howard (New York: G. P. Putnam's Sons, 1964), 484.

have that moment. Still, he had been preparing for death ever since his first pneumothorax in 1931. In a way, he had anticipated death by fighting against delusion both in his personal life and in the public sphere *before* the fatal event. He spoke out against the Nazis, against Franco Spain, against Vichy and the collaborationists, against French oppression in Algeria and the Russian labor camps. He struggled within himself and with a range of opponents, both friends and enemies, taking a public stand whenever moral evil in some form or another threatened ordinary people. More than any other figure in twentieth-century France, Camus demonstrated what it was to have character and, based on a powerful inner sense of conviction, to take a stand against evil.

Ironically, it was not moral evil that killed Camus. It was neither the Nazis nor the Algerian terrorists nor the right-wing OAS. As if in proof of what he had always believed, it was a slippery road and a moment's distraction on the part of his friend that killed him. The theologians call it natural evil and see it in fire, earthquake, flood, and disease. But like moral evil it calls forth a condemnation of the order of things. To the protest-atheist, natural evil, though in a different way from moral evil, flagrantly contradicts the idea of a just God. For Camus God becomes the absurd. And the absurd is that willful murderer, Caligula, who kills to pass an idle hour. Camus' death seemed to confirm the pessimism in his Nobel speech, when he said that his generation had inherited "a corrupted history where mingle failed revolutions, crazy technologies, dead gods and exhausted ideologies, where mediocre powers can destroy everything but no longer know how to convince, where intelligence is debased into becoming the servant of hate and oppression" (*E*, 1073). There had been hope in the Nobel; but now evil had reasserted itself as our greatest witness of the postwar period was reduced to silence.[3]

Camus' absurd death can be viewed as the foundation of a

---

3. The manner of Camus' death lends support to the idea advanced by Simone Weil and Hannah Arendt that evil in our time is impenetrable, not because it is so monumental in scale but because it is banal.

new metanarrative associated with the postmodernist perspective and with a different kind of nihilism from that which he denounced in his Nobel address. Seeing human thought as delusional, postmodernism thematizes delusion itself through a range of verbal, conceptual, and political self-reflexive strategies. We stand within this radical critique of culture like a cell block. There is no appeal to reason or to nature that can release us. Still, there were voices in the cell block that denounced evil, notably that of Michel Foucault, for whom delusional thinking and moral evil were explained by the repressiveness of the social order. The evidence of Camus' death reinforced the structuralist attack on philosophical thinking by rethematizing the absurd. In 1984 Foucault's death from AIDS did the same thing. Their exemplary lives and deaths demonstrate that you can bypass the truth dilemma by entering history as a narrative that attains the condition of myth, so that truth becomes possible again in a new and different way—truth as what happens, truth as fiction, truth as (Camus says in his Nobel speech) what we use our freedom to seek, if never to attain.

This tragedy, which resonated around the world, marked more than the death of a resistance hero who had become the matinee idol of French existentialism. It marked the end of a passionate attempt to renew certain traditional values of French culture. This rescue attempt, humanistic in intent if not always in name, was doomed to eventual failure. For all its splendid achievements, humanism was inadequate to the full truth of the human condition and could neither account for evil nor offer an adequate resistance to it. The disenchantment of the 1960s, which culminated in the events of May 1968 and their destructive aftermaths, served as coda to the death of Camus and the demise of French humanism. When Camus died in 1960, Sartre was recovering from a period of exhaustion and depression brought on by overwork and the use of amphetamines. In a tribute to his one-time friend and associate, Sartre struggled with his own pessimism and loss of faith: "I call the accident that killed Camus a scandal because it suddenly projects into the center of our human world the absurdity of our most fundamental needs. . . . The Absurd might be that question that no

one will ask him now, that he will ask no one, that silence that is
not even a silence now, that is absolutely *nothing* now."[4] The
ending of Sartre's tribute speaks of victory over defeatism, yet
the tone is sombre. Sartre implies the futility of the courageous
project that the two men shared during their ten-year-long
friendship. In spite of the bleakness of this tribute, Sartre was
not pessimistic enough. He refused to recognize the extent of
the new absurdism that was already at work with a nihilism
that only Camus had foreseen. Sartre was wrong: the death of
Camus was not an absurdity but rather a decisive juncture of
change. It signaled a massive shift along the fault line that
divided the powers and dominions of the French cultural establishment.

This "Pascal without Christ" would never again urge his
fellowmen to wager on the possibility of happiness. The face
that looked out at Frenchmen from every corner newsstand on
January 5, 1960, was no longer simply enigmatic and remote. It
was obliterated. Camus had considered the alternatives one by
one—Christianity, Communism, humanism, art—and found
possibilities of regeneration in each even as he refused them.
His most sustained intellectual, moral, and artistic battle had
been with the question of evil. He had shown how far an artist
can go in placing the ultimate metaphysical question at the
center of his work. He is close to Dostoevsky and to the Catholic
novelist Georges Bernanos, with whom he shared both a sense
of history and a focus on the question of evil. There is also a
literary kinship with Simone Weil, whose work he discovered
and published in his *Esprit* series at Gallimard.[5] Because of his
in-betweenness, Camus had a unique ability to live in proximity
to the opposing belief systems of his contemporaries. It was an
uncomfortable position, and, for those of us who looked to him
for guidance, cold intellectual comfort. Now even that was
gone. An entire moral and ideological structure had come
crashing down. We had only to open our eyes and face the fact

4. Quoted in Germaine Brée, *Camus* (New Brunswick: Rutgers University
Press, 1961), 174.
5. His tribute to his mother in *Le premier homme* identifies her as one of that
race of "slaves" whom Simone Weil saw as the moral pillars of the world.

that humanism was a discredited fallacy and that high art was a cadaver.

The few great modernists still alive—Picasso, Matisse, Eliot —were frail with age. By 1960 the political dream of a "third force," neither capitalist nor communist, appeared unworkable. Europe was rebuilding, but the aftermath of World War II was grim. The full weight of what had been National Socialism was not yet documented, and the French had already begun to forget the crimes of Vichy, their own creation, which was now considered a fiction with no legal existence.

It was not a good time for heroes. But then it is never a good time for heroes, and the hero appears because he is needed to deal with crises that are by definition unresolvable. The greatest heroes always fail. This includes the heroes who bring meaning into the world, the "signiferous" heroes, as well as those whose mission is to change the tide of events, the heroes of action. Camus was the first kind of hero. General Charles de Gaulle, the official hero of the day, was the second kind, the hero who moves men and events. De Gaulle's goals have been described as "resurrection, reconstruction and renovation." The goals of Albert Camus were the goals of August 21: "intelligence, courage, and the truth of the human heart" (*ACB*, 331). These were the qualities that Camus pursued against all odds. They were deeply etched in both his work and his life. Yet even these outstanding moral qualities could not give Camus' narrative a happy ending: he had precluded that by his own actions and choices made by or for him early in his career. It was, in large part, his in-betweeness, his refusal to say yes in preference to no. But it was also because history itself precludes any happy endings, any simple Gestalt of insight and resolution.

During his last years Camus cut himself off from a literary world he despised and drove himself to write his way out of the impasse of his personal philosophy. He died before completing the task, at a moment when French culture was negotiating a tricky and complicated change. Liberal humanism had collapsed and a group of brilliant strategists was taking over the cultural scene. Michel Foucault, the moralist of the structuralist movement, claimed that the concept of man prolonged essentialistic forms of thought that were responsible for centuries of oppression. Foucault embarked on his own search for meaning by passing through delusion, looking for a narrative version of truth in the history of cultural and linguistic forms.

Camus had stood at a crossroads of French cultural history. With one arm he pointed back toward the modernist movement and the aesthetic humanism in which it was grounded; with the other he pointed forward, toward postmodernism and the "death of man" movement with its systematic undermining of traditional cultural values by Lacan, Derrida, and Foucault. Actor and juggler, he achieved a kind of equilibrium, which those of us who survived him found it more and more difficult to sustain.

P A R T

No Happy Endings

CHAPTER 5

Taking Risks

WHEN I went to Paris on the GI Bill in 1948 I found a room in a fin-de-siècle atelier on Rue Joseph Bara, one of the great bohemian streets of Montparnasse. This atelier at Number 7 had been the famous Académie Ranson, founded in 1908 by painter Paul Ranson and taken over at his death in 1909 by his wife, France. Ranson was an original member of the "Nabis" group, artists inspired by Gauguin, active in theater and the decorative arts, with a penchant toward occultism. The most celebrated Nabis were Bonnard and Vuillard, though Paul Sérusier, Maurice Denis, and Félix Valloton were the only ones who taught regularly on Rue Joseph Bara. My new home was a two-story building forming an L around a garden with a stunted apple tree and some low sheds with a tin roof. Kisling had worked in the whitewashed rooms on the ground floor. My landlady, Madame Bouisseau, herself a painter, claimed that Modigliani had holed up here for a time when he was under contract to the dealer Zborowski.

Jill Dent helped me find the room and carry over my belongings from the Acropolis hotel on Rue de Buci, where I had lived for several months next door to a Spanish poet who composed his *canciónes* aloud in the middle of the night. Jill was spending a year in Paris, trying to decide between life as an artist and marriage to an English businessman. Her father was a doctor in whose London clinic many celebrities, among them William Burroughs, dried out from drugs and alcohol. Jill was a student at the Grande Chaumière, and together we discovered the ghosts of Montparnasse. Victor Hugo had lived around the corner on the Rue Notre-Dame-des-Champs and Hemingway on the same street in 1925. Apollinaire, Max Jacob, and Alain Fournier were only a few of the great names who had walked these streets, banqueted at the Closerie des Lilas under the aegis of Paul Fort or met for lunch Chez Rosalie on the Rue Campagne Première. My room was upstairs under the slanted ceiling with a window that looked across the street into a convent garden— the perfect place for the aesthete I was trying to become.

Through her half-open door I took my first look at Professor Marie-Jeanne Durry of the Sorbonne. She spoke the best French I'd ever heard, telling the man ahead of me he would never master Flaubert, that his French was only up to Georges Sand. With her permed hair, her jewels and red lipstick, Durry was the Joan Crawford of scholarship, one of the first women to attain a professorship in Letters. For GIs she was a gate-keeper whose approval was based on our French, the way we dressed, and grace under the fire of her wit. Durry and I chatted while she gave me a long look. "Eh bien, Monsieur Nil, what do you want to pursue for the Doctorat d'Université?" My answer: "Poetry!"

She tapped a long red fingernail while I stared at a row of leather buttons running down her worsted suit to her tummy. "At your age, Monsieur Nil, that is natural. I suggest that you work on Gérard de Nerval."

That was an order, so I signed up to study the mystical madman. I memorized his sonnets, *Les Chimères*, as I walked the night streets:

> Je suis le ténébreux, le veuf, le prince d'Aquitaine à la tour
> abolie,
> Ma seule *étoile* est morte et mon luth constellé
> Porte le *soleil* noir de la *Mélancolie* . . .

> [I am the tenebrous, the widower, the Aquitanian prince of the
> abolished tower,
> My only *star* is dead and my spangled lute
> Bears the black *sun* of *Melancholy* . . .]

Nerval achieved notoriety by leading a lobster on the end of a dogleash, but his insanity took a tragic turn. He hung himself on a lamppost in Rue Vielle-du-Temple. Often I crossed this street of sinister memory, thinking about Nerval and the confused yearnings that drove him to madness. I was going through a period of sexual confusion and felt an affinity for this tender schizophrenic. All the doubt and anxiety would be worthwhile if, like Nerval, I could write eight memorable sonnets.

Vielle-du-Temple was in the Marais, a part of the old Jewish quarter called the Pletzel or "little square." This was a warren of streets with bakeries and koscher delis where Jews had lived since the thirteenth century in spite of numerous expulsions. Once a week I changed my travelers check in a small café where there was a special blackmarket rate for Jews.

The café was small with steamy windows and a coal stove where a copper kettle was kept at the boil. There was always an intense group of ravaged-looking men arguing politics, eating herring off newspaper, and swallowing tiny glasses of schnapps. Several were waiting for paperwork to be completed that would allow them to emigrate to Israel or the United States. Often they invited me for a glass of tea. Although I was drawn by the friendly atmosphere and the familiar smells of the café, I was deeply into denial and didn't want to be part of the Jewish Catastrophe. Usually I found an excuse to change my dollars and leave, unless Oskar was there. This big powerfully built machinist reminded me of my maternal grandfather, Leon Lutsky, called "Leo the bullshitter" by his coworkers at the Pontiac plant up in Michigan where we used to vacation every summer. I loved my grandfather for his size, his manual skills, and his gift for story-telling. From him I learned about the family's exodus from Europe. As my grandmother's young husband, he was in charge of the six girls and, once in the New World, played their protector. Or so he told the story.

Under the grid of wrinkles biting into Oskar's face, I saw that he was a young man aged by the war. He'd used false papers to get a factory job in central France. "Built munitions for the boches," he said, "slipped in many a dud round." Oskar was full of questions about the United States. How many dollars to buy a car? Was it okay to buy a Ford even though Henry was anti-Semitic? How much could a machinist earn in Brooklyn? What if they found out he was a socialist? I was taken with

Oskar, my French *landsman*. We looked forward to seeing each other. Then one day he was gone. "His papers came through," one of the others explained, "he's on his way to New York." Oskar had a second cousin who'd agreed to sponsor him, he'd shown me letters from the cousin, asked me where Brooklyn was, and would he like it. I told him he'd fit right in.

"He left this for you," the other man said. He pulled a cloth bag out of his pocket, handed it across the table. Oskar knew I'd been a mortar gunner; this was a fragment from an American mortar round. "His good-luck piece," the man said, "he got it when the *Amerlauds* blasted the factory in Lyons." On the steel Oskar had inscribed: "*A mon pôte Nil.*"

In Oskar's bitter humor I heard my paternal grandmother, who for fifteen years supported her family with a deli in a St. Louis slum. Their voices held the same inflections I heard on the occasions whenever my relatives congregated at the synagogue or at our house. Often, as they talked, I heard them mention the name "Drancy."

The poet Max Jacob died on March 5, 1944, in the concentration camp at Drancy, a suburb to the north of Paris near Le Bourget airport. The camp was installed in a housing project called Résidence La Muette, still uncompleted at the time the Juden-referat (Jewish Affairs Office) first pressed it into service on August 20, 1941. From that time on, Jews were systematically rounded up in the Paris area and taken to this new camp, where, in unspeakable conditions, they were kept behind barbed wire under guard of the French police and a handful of S.S. From Drancy, prisoners were taken by bus to Bobigny or Le Bourget railway station where they were loaded onto buses or cattle cars for the trip to the German frontier. At that point French police handed them over to German guards for the trains to the death camps. Sixty-seven thousand Jews made this trip before the liberation. I had arrived in France with the 97th Division only ten months after the poet's death.

A few weeks after Oskar left, I stumbled onto the traces of Max Jacob. As with so many important events in my life, it began in a bookstore. I had spent the day going in and out of Left Bank bookstores looking for works on Nerval. My last port of call was Le Minotaure on Rue des Beaux-Arts, a shop belonging to my friend Roger Cornaille. There, I noticed a man I had seen earlier that day in another bookstore on Boulevard Saint-Germain. We nodded, and Roger introduced me to Jean Denoël, friend and editor of Max Jacob. A month after encountering Denoël, I told Madame Durry that I wanted to change my thesis topic. "Ah," she said,"le pauvre Max!" Then after a moment's thought, "He was *un grand comédien*, you know. But he could not get out of his *fard* (greasepaint). It was said that even at Drancy he played the clown." She gave me a penetrating look. "Are you *israélite*?"

"No," I said, "I'm not Jewish. I'm just interested in his work." I knew I'd told a lie that would haunt me for the rest of my life. Not just any lie, the denial of my deepest identity. In some eerie way I was imitating Simone Weil, who argued to the Vichy Minister of Education that she should be allowed to teach because she was not really a Jew. My denial was a pathetic wish to be other than what I knew myself to be, always had been, and always would be. I came out of Durry's office feeling sick. The lie had been growing in me for a long time, but now it had taken over. That was the day I cut loose from my past and went prospecting for new identities, ethnic, religious, sexual—as if you could walk into a cultural supermarket and pick out who you wanted to be. To put a more positive face on it, this might eventually turn out to be a way of testing who I was, what I could become, and where the limits of my selfhood were really planted.

The Experiment

There was another kind of self-testing going on. It had to do with my sexual identity. I had my first homosexual experience with Michel at the University of Chicago in 1948. Meeting this brilliant teacher was the most exciting thing that happened in my years on a campus where politics, the arts, and the intellectual life were in ferment. I went to hear Michel read Rimbaud and came away hooked on French literature. Later, I took his courses. Under his look of a Scotch clergyman there was a subversive and seductive Socrates who understood the dreams of young men who left home to discover the world of literature and the arts. Above all he held the key to France, to that wonderful culture I had briefly tasted as a GI; his knowledge of it seemed inexhaustible, and, to my amazement, he wanted to share it with me. There was a slight inconvenience in the fact that I did not measure up to his passion; but I was willing to make myself over, to become a gay man, if it meant that the treasures of French culture would be mine. This was analogous to what happened when I encountered the Church, which also was a conduit of French reality; but it led to a makeover that was more lasting, though also not without doubts, anxieties, and physical strain. This plasticity must be some weakness of character, but it is the same trait that has made me a good reader of poets, able to pour myself into the skin of many writers who seemed at first alien; and, I think, it has also contributed to my success as a teacher, since I am usually able to identify with the problems and anxieties of my students. There is a certain light-headedness that comes with this tendency, a feeling that I could be carried off by the next wind of change, but, in fact, that has not happened. I stretched myself in various directions, found the limits, and settled back to live within them. Back during the time I consorted with Michel I felt a kind of amoebalike giddyness, a willingness to let events happen however they might, a sense of what André Gide called *disponibilité*, which was one of my first efforts to make life ressemble art.

The relationship was intense, but it didn't last. My problem wasn't with his charms but my own sexuality. My fantasies, once things settled down, still revolved around a blonde *shikse*, the Muriel of my twelfth year. There was very little emotional component to my homosexual experiments, it was all rather mechanical. Michel was in France on a Guggenheim in 1948–1949, and we continued our relationship in a desultory way, until I decided once and for all that it could never work out.

This was the time when Ed Field, who later became a major poet, took me to the *cabarets-dansant* around the Bastille with their Jupienesque hosts—"You like the boys? The blonde over there? Or the *poilu*?" I thought of Proust's Jupien, tailor, pimp, sexual entrepreneur every time I came back to these dark rooms throbbing with music and male desire. It scared me and awoke some deep impulse that I would only begin to understand years later in psychoanalysis; but there was none of the sexual vertigo I felt with women. I believed Rimbaud's formula that to every man a thousand lives were due, but I lived my thousand lives through reading. I could relate to the homosexuality of a writer like Proust, Cocteau, or Jacob; but I couldn't share it in real life. Instead of finding myself in gay sex, I seemed to lose my emotional edge, my personality flipped out of focus.

Still, for a while I hung out with a crowd at the Montana Bar on Rue Saint-Benoît. I loved the gossip, the innuendo, the intense sexual theater and spent some one-nighters in different hotel rooms around Saint-Germain-des-Prés; but the experiment wasn't working. Each encounter left me confused and depressed. I felt guilty impersonating a homosexual. I was trying to feel like a gay man when many of the guys around me were (in spite of the *je m'en fiche* bravado) victims of their sexuality. There was Peter ("call me Pierre"), whose Dad handed him a box of condoms when he put him on the train in Kansas City. I didn't know whether to feel sorrier for Peter or for Dad, whose parting words were, "Don't come back till you've used these!" It would be another two decades before young men would learn to accept their sexual orientation, in the manner of Ed Field, as a unique way of being human.

It wasn't the gender panic nor was it the biological part that made the gay life unacceptable, since my body did what was asked of it. It was the mental part, *le petit cinéma dans la tête*. I would leave the Montana at six, long before the real action began, in time to catch the Smith College girls who lived around the corner from me in Reid Hall on their way home from classes. Most were preppy girls from upper middle families, making their break for independence, which meant having at least one affair while abroad. In their tweed skirts and cashmere sweaters, with long hair and innocent faces, they were vulnerable to an approach that went, "Say, have you heard about the Kinsey Report? It just came out this year. It tells you the truth about sex in America, what is really going on in peoples' bedrooms. Don't you agree it's important to be honest about it?"

The Kinsey report was a self-fulfilling prophecy: everybody

was using it to get everybody else into bed, which wasn't hard
in that year of the great swarm, when nature had chosen Paris as
the site to play catch-up for all the death and destruction of the
war. This was our Carthage, and we were in love with love. It
wasn't unusual to have two or three affairs going at once. Paris
was a good lab for testing what was important to you emotionally. After two months, I dropped the Montana crowd. It
had been an experiment that failed. My gay friends wanted me
to confirm the proposition that Genet put to Sartre, "Everybody
is homosexual, even Stalin!" But it wasn't true and I knew it.
Genet's *Pompes funèbres* was published while I was doing my
research on the gay life, and it finished my "cure." All those
scenes of men sucking on Nazi Lugers, of murder, and other
forms of violent penetration scared the hell out of me. That
wasn't going to be my form of transgression.

During the winter of 1949, thanks to the friendship of Jean
Denoël, I got to know Max Jacob in greater detail. Denoël gave
me books, pamphlets, and we had dinner together once a week
at the Restaurant des Ministères. We talked about Jacob from
every possible angle. I began to like the little guy, not the dapper
snapper of the early years in tux and top hat but the "Charlot" of
the Saint-Benoît periods, when Jacob turned his back on Paris
and went to live in the Loire region near a famous Benedictine
Abbey where he tried to lose himself in devotion. He lived there
from 1921 to 1927 and from 1936 until his arrest in 1944. With his
baggy suits, his turned-out shoes, and his yellow star Jacob
made a touching and appealing figure. I identified with something restless and alienated in Jacob's relation to his heritage.
He'd grown up in the shadows of the Cathedral of Quimper and
from his earliest years absorbed the piety of his native Brittany,
with its *pardons*, its liturgy, and its superstitions. Like myself he
came from an agnostic Jewish family, and he lived all his life an
in-betweenness that was more radical than the indeterminacy
of Camus, combining in the panache of a single person Jewishness, Catholicism, and homosexuality.[1]

1. Indeterminacy remains a central theme of current thought, as in this

Denoël never explained Max Jacob. His approach was to tell
me anecdotes about the poet, to give me books and out-of-print
articles. One of these was the illustrated volume, *L'Homme de
cristal*. At our last meeting he gave me a gouache of the Breton
port of Bénodet, painted by Jacob in the 1930s. Bénodet was still
much the same when I visited it later that year: "Brittany is a
miracle—it absorbs cars, Le Corbusier-style houses, lipstick,
without ceasing to be Brittany. . . . Here nobody cares about
tradition but within six months the buildings become Breton,
the garages look like Breton Catholics; peasant girls have permanent waves while remaining real-life Bretons."[2] In early
spring I traveled to Britanny to visit my new friends, Jacques
and Colette Hallez, in the seaport town of Trestel; and there,
discovering Britanny for the first time, I made a commitment to
unravel some of the mysteries of Jacob's life and work. I began
to see that work as a system of ironies for both concealing and
revealing the writer's multiple identities. The determining
event of Jacob's life was a vision, some say a hallucination, that
occurred when he was thirty-three, in his attic room in Montmartre: "I came back from the National Library: I put down my
briefcase; I looked for my slippers and when I lifted my head,
there was someone on the wall! someone was there! there was
someone on the red tapestry. My flesh fell to the ground! I was
undressed by thunder! oh! imperishable second! oh! truth!
truth! tears of truth! joy of the truth! unforgettable truth!"[3] The
event is undermined by its own rhetoric, which includes a sly
reference to Pascal's famous "Memorial," a paper that the philosopher sewed into the lining of his clothes to commemorate a
night of religious rapture. The episode is recounted in *The Defense of Tartufe*, one of several books in which Jacob evokes and
questions his spiritual experience. Tartuffe (with two *f*'s) of
course, was Molière's sinister religious hypocrite. The self-

---

statement by Godard: "As for me, I think that what really exists is always
inbetween." From a TV interview on his film *Sauve Qui Peut (La Vie)*.

2. Letter to Marcel Béalu. In Pierre Andreu, *Vie et mort de Max Jacob* (Paris:
La Table Ronde, 1982), 241. All further references in the text given as *VMJ*.

3. Max Jacob, *La Défense de Tartufe* (Paris: Gallimard, 1964), 101.

deprecatory title is defensive, anticipating the jibes of those (like Professor Durry) who persisted in seeing the poet as a clown.[4] What the title reveals is Jacob's crushing sense of unworthiness, his lack of self-esteem, his obsession with "sin." This experience is focused on the apparition he describes. In a naturalistic sense the apparition is delusional. When I first read Max Jacob, I had no grounds for believing that such an experience might conceivably be grounded in a different order of reality. Still, I left the door open. Although I discounted Jacob's apparition on the basis of its rhetoric, it seemed plausible to think that we normally see only a narrow range of phenomena: both the "infinitely great" and the "infinitely small," as Pascal noted, are off our perceptual scale. Supernatural occurrences could not logically be ruled out.

Inevitably, I sketched comparisons between us. He made Catholicism, which still seemed foreign, much more appealing. I slipped into church with increasing frequency during that Paris year. I visited crypts, became familiar with the reek of incense, and saw the incorruptible remains of saints. I can still remember the smell of certain churches more than forty years later. The memory brings back a momentary joy mixed with the anxiety that for me is inseparable from Catholicism. I wanted Catholicism to relieve the burden of my complicated sexuality as well as my intellectual confusion. These haphazard prospectings into French spirituality began to awaken an appetite for devotion and a need for religious understanding, impulses that I had been aware of for many years without understanding where they were leading me. So ill-prepared and badly motivated, I lurched toward a decision that, in the end, I have found to be absolutely right for me, containing in its paradoxes the best answers to the unresolvable paradoxes of my own life.

4. Picasso's jibe was the cruelest of all. When Max was arrested by the Gestapo in February 1944, numerous old friends tried to intervene. Henri Sauguet and Pierre Colle sought out Picasso to ask his support. Picasso replied: "There's no point in doing anything. Max is an angel. He doesn't need our help to escape his prison" (*VMJ*, 293). Andreu claims that Picasso did not attend the memorial service held on March 21 at the Paris church of St. Roch for his godson, Cyprien Max Jacob. Denoël told me that Picasso came but stayed outside on the steps, smoking.

In late April I caught the flu that was ravaging Paris. After two weeks in bed, interrupted by trips to the pharmacy and quick lunches Chez Rosalie, I decided that only the sun could cure me. A few days before I left, the grey weather lifted and I hopped the bus for a trip down to the Seine. As I strolled along inspecting the offerings of the *bouquinistes*, I discovered a first edition of Jacques Maritain's *Art et scolastique*. The volume was inscribed to literary critic Charles du Bos, who had died recently. The book reminded me of my encounter the preceding year with the neo-Thomist philosopher Yves Simon, who was teaching at the University of Chicago. Thomism held no appeal for me at that time, but I was intrigued by Maritain's ambition to explain art in terms of a coherent philosophical system. When I went South a few days later, I took the book with me. After the complexities of Proust, the ambiguities of Camus, and the ironies of Max Jacob, there was something refreshing in the ordered cosmos of Maritain. Besides the clarity of his exposition, I admired Maritain's sensitivity to modern art. Before the war and his move to The Institute for Advanced Studies at Princeton, he had been in close contact with innumerable painters and poets, including Georges Rouault, Jean Cocteau, and Max Jacob.

I wandered through Provence, stopping at Arles, Les Baux, and Les Alyscans where I experienced the vital, curative energy of the Mediterranean. I found what Camus invoked in his earliest essays and journals: the encounter of reason with a landscape of sun and sea, where the light plays incessantly across the surface of the water in an endless dance of forms. At Les Alyscans, the greatest necropolis in Europe during the Roman Empire, I was struck with the same emotion I felt on my first visit to the Musée de l'Homme. Awe at how the dead outnumber the living. I was thinking deep thoughts at Les Alyscans and tried to imagine what it was like to die, what it was like to float down the Rhône on a wooden raft to be picked up by grave-diggers who would pluck the obole out of my mouth and stick me in a sarcophagus.

Along with these day-dreams of mythic experience came others, which brought me back to my life in the States. Often on that trip through Provence I mused about Jean Romano, a girl I had become involved with midway through my stint at the

University of Chicago. When I first saw Jean, she was acting out Kant's *Critique of Pure Reason* in a game of charades. On her knees, hands joined in prayer to mime the word "Pure," I took her for a boy angel. I pursued Jean for a year without making any progress. She was involved with Walt, handsome, reputed brilliant, and even more mixed-up than I was. I wrote her poems, took her to plays and concerts, but she kept a wall of indifference between us. From this I learned jealousy, the worst passion known to man. On a four-week summer camping trip in the Chapleau National Forest of central Canada I wrote her every day, bummed a ride on a sea plane with some Indian guides to find a telephone, tossed during sleepless nights in my lonely cabin, reading Henry Miller's *Air-Conditioned Nightmare*, cursing and lusting for her. Finally I left early and went back to Chicago, where I spent the rest of the summer sweltering in a Divinity School dorm room. Jean, living nearby with her mother and aunt, remained elusive and unfathomable till my jealousy reached such a crescendo that I knew I would have to marry her if I ever hoped to cure it. I left for France in 1948 with the relationship still unresolved.

Jean was a complicated girl with a pleasant face, frizzy hair, and a look of surprise at the fate that life had dealt her. An orphan, she suffered doubly from the divorce of her adoptive parents, hiding her vast neediness with a gaiety subject to depressive mood swings. When Walt broke up with her, I became her fallback. An artist of some talent, Jean was studying at the Chicago Art Institute during my year in France; later, when I went to Columbia, she followed me to New York and attended classes at The Art Students' League. When I became a Catholic, true to her chameleon nature, she also began to receive instructions from Father John Oesterreicher, an Austrian Jew with a mission to convert the chosen people and their gentile girlfriends. Jean and I were both complicated, neurotic people whose needs did not match up. It had the makings of a disastrous relationship; but that was no deterrent, in fact it added to the lure of a fatal attraction.

In a romanesque chapel at Vence, a shabby little man on the tour bus knelt to pray, to the amusement of two English ladies acting as my guides. This was another opportunity to think deep thoughts. I scowled at my guides, a pair of middle-aged lesbians from Oxford who were giddy with freedom, and tried to remember a prayer but couldn't. Before we separated, the ladies recommended a pension in Beaulieu-sur-Mer. There, among the wisteria and the yellow brilliance of mimosa, I took stock of what the year had taught me. I had read the poets—but what was poetry anyway? Max Jacob called it "invented dream," but I knew it was plain hard work. I felt more affinity with Paul Valéry's assertion that it was doing work with words. Was there anything plausible in Maritain's view that poetry had something in common with prayer? Why conflate the two? They were better separate, the one imagination at play with words, the other a scary dialogue with the unknown.

The major poets of French modernism were Guillaume Apollinaire, Paul Claudel, and René Char, but I was drawn to poets of second rank, whose lives held a certain mystery that I needed to fathom. So I became attached to the elusive figure of Max Jacob. Jacob was just the opposite of Camus, who had won the love and acclaim of the entire world during his vertiginous rise to stardom. Jacob lived out his years in the shadow of Picasso and the great figures of modernism, writing prose poems and religious meditations that did not fit in the canon, just as he himself did not seem to fit. I was attracted to Jacob because he was considered a failure; yet he had left a huge body of work deserving greater recognition than it had so far achieved.

CHAPTER 6

The Destinies of Max Jacob

No doubt the world is entirely an imaginary world, but it is only once removed from the true world. At the door of the hovel where I lie, there stands the plank on which the dead are taken away. The gravedigger Jew has his spade ready. The grave waits and the worms are hungry; the shrouds are prepared—I carry them in my beggar's sack. Another *shnorrer* is waiting to inherit my bed of straw. When the time comes I will go joyfully. Whatever may be there, it will be real, without complication, without ridicule, without deception. God be praised: there even Gimpel cannot be deceived.

Isaac Bashevis Singer, *Gimpel the Fool*

PROFESSOR Durry had divorced me from Nerval, married me to Jacob; now I began to realize what I was getting into. Nerval had been crazy, but Jacob was tormented and bizarre. He had been the victim of delusionary thinking almost as many times as Gimpel the fool. He had seen an apparition on the wall of his room and another on the screen of a Montmartre cinema. Like Gimpel, he believed that he was loved by individuals who betrayed him at the first opportunity. He was snubbed, cheated and hoodwinked, which led to paranoid thinking that was even more destructive than the real (or perhaps imaginary) snubs. While the Nazi net closed around him, he believed himself safe because of powerful friends. I thought that what Durry said about him was harsh, that he had played the fool at Drancy right up to his death. I decided to look into this, to find out exactly how Max had behaved when he got on that train for his last ride. Did his weakness have another side, a hidden strength that, so far, had been unrecognized?

And I would have to start calling him "Max," the way his friends did when they wrote about him, which has now become the convention. Max had been dead for four years when I came to study in Paris. Already a subtle change in the poet's status had begun to occur, the misconceptions had momentarily lifted. One of his *Derniers poèmes*, called "Love for Your Neighbor," attracted special attention:

> Who has seen the toad crossing the street? He's a tiny little man: a doll is not more diminutive. He drags himself along on his knees. He is ashamed, you might say. No! He is arthritic. One leg drags behind and he pulls it along after him. Where is he going that way? He is coming out of the sewer, poor clown. Nobody has noticed the toad in the street. Formerly, nobody noticed me. Now children make fun of my Yellow Star. Happy toad! you don't have a Yellow Star.[1]

Max's self-portrayal as a toad was emblematic of a tendency to abjection, which made him a lightning rod for derision and mistreatment. We know that there are many forms of passivity and that the quietism of a John of the Cross, waiting in a state of psychic emptiness to be seized by God, is radically different from the passivity of the sexual masochist or the passivity of the depressive who has given up the struggle. Among the most terrifying images of passivity are those of the victims of famine whose glazed ascetic appearance mimics the otherworldly ec-

---

1. Max Jacob, "Amour du prochain," in *Derniers Poèmes en vers et en prose* (Paris: Gallimard, 1945), 172. Translation by Gerald Kamber, in *Max Jacob and the Poetics of Cubism* (Baltimore: John Hopkins University Press, 1971), 56.

stasy of the Spanish baroque. These faces and grotesquely distorted bodies are profoundly transgressive, having no place in
our ordinary lives and drawing us back toward moral realities
that transcend our will and our understanding.

Because we cannot separate the strands of these kinds of
passivity in our own mental, emotional, and perceptual life,
it becomes impossible to do so in the life of somebody else.
It seems clear, at any rate, that Jacob at several periods sank
into that depressive state called abjection, where the subject
searches degradation, dissolution, and death as a form of escape from life's terror. Jean Genet has explored abjection, that
flight into self-abasement in which the subject is made object.
But abjection is also the mirror image of the mystic's ecstatic
unification with the divine, as he waits will-less and undesiring
until, in some hidden moment outside of time, he is penetrated
by grace. There are many mansions in the house of abjection,
some chosen and others assigned by the social order. Though
unrecognized as such, abjection dominates the public domain.
Victims of starvation, rape, child abuse, religious fanaticism
pass across the screen as endless figments of hyperreality. We
can make little of this mediaized suffering; so the challenge then
becomes to seek empowerment over our own.

For Jacob the challenge was to transform this downward
impulse to demean himself into a different kind of drive, the
mystic's drive for sanctity and eventual union. This attempt at
self-transformation involved a kind of desublimation, an awakening of the total self that began in passivity. I was learning that
I too had a passive streak, an impulse to accept and submit to
events. It appeared in my homosexual experiences, in the suffering of my headaches, and a deep terror that struck me sometimes, a kind of vertigo that seemed to spiral me into the abyss.

Jacob's passivity came from the fact that he was a born loser.
From the start, he failed to live up to his parents' expectations.
Pierre Andreu writes: "For his father and his mother, his brothers and his sisters, Max was a failure, though they hadn't wholly
given up expecting a return to more suitable careers. He had
been so promising!" (*VMJ*, 43).

The Runaway

In 1901 Max made a definitive break with his hometown of Quimper and left Brittany for Paris where he worked at a series of menial jobs. Shortly after he met Picasso, who became his roommate: "Picasso came to live in my room, Boulevard Voltaire, on the sixth floor. It was a vast room. Picasso painted all night. And when I was getting up to go to work at the department store, he went to bed to get some rest."[2] A few years later, artist and poet were living in the famous Bateau Lavoir on Rue Ravignan, so named by Jacob because it hung out over the Butte Montmartre like a washerwoman's dock. The two men animated an expanding circle of writers and artists that came to be called the School of Paris. Jacob was at the center of the constellation that included, at one time or another, Apollinaire, Cocteau, Juan Gris, Modigliani, André Salmon, as well as art dealers, models, and their hangers-on. Jacob was not the most colorful, but he was the most fantastic, an improviser and role-player, with a Jewish gift for self-mockery and a cutting wit, turned as often against himself as against his friends. Though both he and Picasso could be selfish and cruel, they were held in high esteem. Beatrice Hastings, the English poet, reports of her lover, Modigliani: "He despised everyone except Picasso and Max Jacob."[3] For about a year prior to this Jacob had worked as an art critic, hobnobbing with successful artists and attending the *vernissages* of chic galleries. Why he gave up this worldly career has never been explained; apparently it had something to do with his religious conversion and his decision to be a serious writer. Yet during his years in Montmartre, he published little. He was diffident about his work, which lacked the ebullience of Apollinaire's effortless lyrical production. There was a love-hate relationship between the two poets, marked by public attacks and reconciliations. In a lecture given by Apollinaire on April 25, 1908, the reigning poet of modernism announced:

2. Robert Guiette, "Vie de Max Jacob" (Paris: Nizet, 1976), 12–13.
3. Jeanne Modigliani, *Modigliani: Man and Myth* (New York: Orion, 1958), 79.

"Fame will soon pounce on Max Jacob in his Rue Ravignan. He is the simplest of poets yet he often appears the most strange. That contradiction is easily explained when I tell you that Max Jacob's lyricism is armed with a style that is delicious, cutting, rapid, brilliantly and tenderly humorous" (*VMJ*, 53). Yet it appears that, when he first spoke Jacob's name during this lecture, Apollinaire couldn't repress a guffaw and Jacob, who was grateful for the praise, said later: "Since then Apollinaire often ridiculed me" (*VMJ*, 55). The jibes went both ways. In her book on Picasso, Françoise Gilot tells the story of a dinner at which Jacob read a poem satirizing Apollinaire's affair with Marie Laurencin and a subsequent abortion. By 1909, when Jacob was finally ready to publish his prose poems, his life was changed by the celestial apparition on the wall of his room in the Rue Ravignan. Though a subject of jest by those who refused to take his conversion seriously, Jacob's apparition was, in fact, one of those inexplicable events that turn a man inside out. For the rest of his life, September 22, 1909, was a constant reference point.

In retrospect, it is clear that Jacob's work went against the grain of modernism, dominated as it came to be by the psychological expressiveness of Apollinaire and the Mallarméan orphism of Valéry and Reverdy. Max Jacob only *appeared* to be at the center of the modernist movement because of his association with all the great figures of modernism, from Picasso to Apollinaire and Cocteau. His seclusion in 1921, at the Benedictine Abbey of Saint-Benoît-sur-Loire, seemed to conclusively prove his marginality and his irrelevance to the mainstream of modernist aesthetic production.

All his life Jacob was impoverished, living from hand to mouth. He earned a pittance from the sale of his jewel-like *gouaches*, and there was a monthly annuity paid as the result of an auto accident in 1920 on the Rue Pigalle, when he was knocked down by a car while on his way to the Opera. For a time, he supported himself by selling his manuscripts to the bibliophile Jacques Doucet. Occasionally, he was reduced to begging from his friends. Late in life, he made several lecture tours, giving imitations, talking about the early days of the School of Paris, and reading from his work. Sometimes these

appearances met with success, as during his turn at the Noctam-
bules cabaret in 1936, but too often he returned home depressed, devastated by the knowledge that he'd made a fool of
himself yet again. Until the end of his life, Jacob carried on a
secondary career, that of teacher. Through a vast correspondence he kept in touch with hundreds of young men and
women, instructing them in the art of poetry and the spiritual
life, encouraging them through various life crises, standing as
godfather to their children, scolding, advising, and remembering them in his prayers. His *Conseils à un jeune poète*, published
by Marcel Béalu in 1945, represents the crystallization of this
long and painstaking effort, which may have been his greatest
contribution.

His legendary generosity was extended even to those who
had injured him. Certain bibliophiles, among them Paul Eluard
and Georges Hugnet, who had vilified Jacob during their years
as militant surrealists, brought him first editions to be person-
alized with notes and drawings, thereby increasing their value
many times over. Jacob complied but was not taken in by the
hypocrisy.

John Rodden has written: "One index to a culture is the
figures it exalts."[4] We can add that an equally significant index
is the figures it neglects. The general neglect of Max Jacob tells
us what mattered and what didn't in the culture game as it
developed after the war. To understand Jacob's position, we
need to take a closer look at the literary scene and several of its
dominant personalities.

Martyrdom brought Max to the attention of a broader public,
and the poet's advocates tried to capitalize on this burst of
attention. Jean Denoël began publishing his books, while a
group of friends, themselves struggling to survive in the cena-
cles of postwar Paris, did what they could to promote the cause
of this poet whose work was considered unreadable and remained largely unknown. One of these was Jean Grenier, friend
and teacher of Albert Camus, who had been in correspondence

4. John Rodden, *The Politics of Literary Reputation:* The Making and Claiming of "St. George" Orwell (New York: Oxford University Press, 1989), 4.

with Max for a number of years. Other collections of letters were published by poet and book dealer Marcel Béalu, philosopher Yvon Belaval, and Pierre Andreu, who was later to write the definitive biography of Max Jacob. The important book *L'Homme de cristal* was published in a deluxe illustrated edition in 1946, and there were plans for a series of *Cahiers Max Jacob*, designed to resurrect early or little-known works. Posthumously, this born loser began to have a bit of luck.

The question of how literary reputations are made is of special interest in the case of Max Jacob. John Rodden states in his book *The Politics of Literary Reputation* that little study has been made of "the processes by which writers' images and identities are formed and literary reputations are gained, lost, consolidated, revised, and deformed." Rodden quotes the elder Goncourt: "A book never *is* a masterpiece. . . . It *becomes* one."[5] It becomes one, Rodden maintains, because of the way it is produced, advertised, or presented, received by the public, and, finally, transmitted through time. The "images" of a writer disseminated over a period of years may be valid portraits or the worst distortions. In the case of Max, the revival of interest that occurred after the war did not distinguish between valid portraits and caricatures, such as those published earlier by Maurice Sachs and Hubert Fabureau.[6] Partial responsibility for some of these "forgeries" lay at the poet's own door, since Max contributed to the blurred image that we have of him. It is hard to resurrect any historical figure, but in the case of Max Jacob, it is doubly hard. He was a flagrant mythomaniac and also excessively secretive. An example: his love life has been covered with a veil of discretion that time has rendered impenetrable. We know about his early romance (during the period when he worked as a clerk in the Entrepôt Voltaire) with a woman called "Cécile," but his homosexual attachments are, for the most part, unrecorded. Max's affectivity becomes most explicit in the effusiveness of his correspondence as well as in his devotional writing, yet these "im-

---

5. Rodden, *Politics*, 4.
6. Hubert Fabureau, *Max Jacob* (Paris: *Nouvelle Revue Critique*, 1925). Maurice Sachs, *Alias* (Paris: Gallimard, 1935).

ages" of the man were not designed to enhance his reputation as one of the makers of modernism.

Max Jacob could never be a hero of the caliber of Albert Camus, but his tragic death gave him a new public image and a new lease on fame. Momentarily, the poet who had lived in the shadow of modernism seemed to come into his own. If only as a poet in the line of Alfred Jarry, the creator of Père Ubu, and a precursor of the game-poetry of the young Apollinaire. Beyond that, Max Jacob remained a marginal figure. Neither the literary establishment (represented by the NRF and Gallimard) nor the Catholic mainstream (represented by Claudel and Mauriac) accorded him the recognition he deserved. There was homophobia in this (as witness attacks on him by the surrealists in the early years and scurrilous comments in the right-wing press at the time of his death), but that was not the whole story.[7] Both his poetry and his spiritual itinerary were irrelevant to a world where "making it" was the name of the game. They were dealt with as the Parisian cultural world deals with all matters that are profoundly transgressive: put in the deep freeze indexed for possible rehabilitation. Transgressive figures such as Sade and Artaud have been recognized and become part of the canon, while Max Jacob still waits his turn. Already several books have begun to recognize the radical quality of his literary *œuvre*, which contravenes modernism and points toward a poetics that is authentically postmodern.[8] During his lifetime Jacob was often subject to hostility, scorned or patronized by those in positions of influence, and relegated by the official critics to a position of marginality. The reasons for this were not purely literary. Rather, they involved the transgressive nature of his spiritual commitment, which lay outside the accepted categories and contaminated his literary achievement. This spiritu-

7. The collaborationist journal *Je suis partout* wrote: "Max Jacob is dead. Jewish by race, Breton by birth, Roman by religion, sodomite by sexual preference, he became the most characteristic Parisian figure imaginable, of that decadent and corrupt Paris whose most notable disciple, Jean Cocteau, remains equally its symbolic exemplar" (*VMJ*, 315).

8. Cf. René Plantier, *L'Univers poétique de Max Jacob* (Paris: Klincksieck, 1976), and Sydney Lévy, *The Play of the Text*: Max Jacob's "Le Cornet à Dés" (Madison: The University of Wisconsin Press, 1981), hereafter *PT*.

ality was dissonant both with official Catholicism and with the anticlericalism of the *bohème*. If this were not enough, Max Jacob became a martyr, caught in the maelstrom of the Holocaust. Like all true transgressors, he died outside the categories.

By the time I discovered Max Jacob in 1948, Gallimard had begun (reluctantly and under pressure from Jean Paulhan, Raymond Queneau, and Jean Denoël) to publish his works. The reluctance arose because not only the work was difficult, but also it was also considered too Catholic. This was a strange judgment, since from its inception the Editions de la Nouvelle Revue Française had been the publishers of the ultra-Catholic poet Paul Claudel. In fact, Claudel's *L'Otage* was announced in June 1911 as one of the first three books to be published by the new firm.

Claudel's massive poetic *œuvre* was no more readable than Jacob's, and his work implicitly continued the Symbolist aesthetic that the founders of the NRF rejected. Jacob had rejected Symbolism, in both word and deed, but this did not make him more palatable to the NRF. Despite an editorial board that came to include such diverse figures as Marcel Arland and Jean Cassou, Gide remained the dominant presence. Under his leadership, the NRF was characterized as being afflicted with a "sort of Protestant pseudohomosexuality," not an ambiance that would be welcoming to Max Jacob.[9] Between October 1920 and July 1934, nine selections by Max Jacob appeared in the *NRF*. All but one were short, and he was never seriously associated with the journal. Typical of the attitude to him is this letter from Paul Claudel to Francis Jammes in March 1932: "Poor Max Jacob is struggling along. Yet another one who is a victim of the gross misunderstanding of official critics and of academic ineptitude."[10] Claudel and Gide patronized "poor Max Jacob," never for a moment visualizing him as a player in their own league.

Gide and Claudel continued to correspond until 1926, when

9. Pierre Assouline, *Gaston Gallimard: A Half-Century of French Publishing* (San Diego: Harcourt, Brace, Jovanovich, 1988), 133.

10. Paul Claudel, *Correspondance de Paul Claudel, Francis Jammes, Gabriel Frizeau, Jacques Rivière* (Paris: Gallimard, 1952), 332.

their relations were strained to the breaking point; but by that time, Claudel's niche at Gallimard was firmly established. Even his infamous "Paroles au Maréchal" and his reactionary politics seemed not to damage him.[11] Here is an excerpt from a letter written soon after the collapse of the Third Republic and the installation of Marshall Pétain: "my consolation is in seeing the end of that infamous parliamentary regime [the Third Republic] which for many years has devoured France like a spreading cancer. It's the end of the Popular Front, of the C.G.T. [the principal workers' union], of processions with raised fists, of strikes, of manifestos signed pell-mell by communists and catholics, by the filthy tyranny of the bistrots, of the masons, of half-breeds, of spies and of teachers. At least let's hope so!"[12] Approving Vichy insofar as it defended the Church against the detested Third Republic, Claudel's position during the war was ambivalent, though he never went so far as Cardinal Gerlier of Lyon who said of the Vichy slogan *Travail, Famille, Patrie*, "These words are ours."[13] Claudel also endorsed Vichy's war on Communism, although the communists provided the only sustained resistance to the Nazi invader. Most serious of all, Claudel never recognized the moral failure of the Church during the war, whether in respect to its many highly placed Nazi sympathizers or its silence on the extermination of Jews and other minorities, although to his merit, he turned against Vichy when the persecution of Jews became official policy.

Diplomat, lecturer, representative of Catholic thought and letters, Claudel became as untouchable as any of the great *monstres sacrés* of the Parisian cultural establishment. Gaston Gallimard himself was under suspicion during the Purge, as the result of his transfer of the NRF to Drieu la Rochelle during the war, but there was never any investigation of Claudel. At the time of Jacob's death in 1944, Gide was in Algeria trying out a new sleeping pill and annoyed that Jean Denoël, back at

11. The poem was recited at the Grand Casino de Vichy in 1941 by a performer handpicked by the poet.
12. Quoted in Gerald Antoine, *Paul Claudel ou l'enfer du génie* (Paris: Robert Leffont, 1988), 320.
13. See Jacques Duquesne, *Les Catholiques Français sous l'Occupation* (Paris: Grasset, 1966), 44.

Gallimard in Paris, had reservations about the great man's latest antireligious tract, a dialogue called *The Son of Man*. Max had simply become irrelevant.

After the war, the aestheticism of the NRF gave way to greater militancy. Camus brought philosopher Brice Parrain to the editorial board, and there were other additions, including the first woman, Colette Audry, and novelist Roger Nimier. Gallimard went ahead to publish authors such as Jean-Paul Sartre, Simone de Beauvoir, Raymond Aron, and Jean Genet, while continuing to publish the great modernist authors of an earlier generation such as Claudel. Thanks to the efforts of Paulhan and Denoël, several of Max's works were published under the NRF imprint during his lifetime and others after his death, but there has never been the ultimate consecration of a Pléiade edition.

Claudel knew Max slightly and visited him at St. Benoît. A journal entry for July 16, 1925, transcribes an account of the famous apparition and conversion.[14] The style is as flat as if Claudel were recording the weather. In the same affectless style a journal entry for November 28, 1944, records the poet's death as reported by Mme Yanette Deletang-Tardiff, who interviewed the attending physician at Drancy.[15]

The sole existing letter from Claudel to Max Jacob gives more insight into Claudel's ambivalence toward the poet who was ten years his junior. Claudel wrote, on receiving a copy of Jacob's *Morceaux choisis* (1937): "Thank you, dear Max Jacob, for having superimposed this lozenge of incense [the inscription to Claudel] upon this brazier of beautiful poems and of human flesh that you have sent me. I breathed it all in with delight in that mixture of tenderness and exhilaration that produces at the same time in both the eyes and the nostrils this emanation of fantasy, of love and of smoke."[16] There is no record of how Jacob received this dubious compliment, but he could not have

14. Paul Claudel, *Journal I (1904–1932)* (Paris: Gallimard, 1968), 681

15. Paul Claudel, *Journal II (1933–1955)* (Paris: Gallimard, 1969), 502.

16. Paul Claudel, *Œuvres en prose* (Paris: Gallimard, 1965), 1487. The letter was first published in 1939 in a special number of Aguedall dedicated to Max Jacob.

been pleased by the stereotypical description of his work as fantasy. The "smoke" analogy was a downright insult for a poet too often dismissed as a mere *fumiste*. In fact, Jacob had been anti-Symbolist from his first years in Montmartre, and his works, especially the prose poems, represented a radically new poetics, one that Claudel and the NRF aesthetes failed to recognize.

The image of Jacob promulgated by his friends was not one designed to ignite much interest in a postwar dominated by Malraux, Sartre, and Camus. The Poètes d'aujourd'hui volume, with introduction by André Billy, begins: "Why should I not start with his eyes? Photographs give only a faint idea of them. They were beautiful, with a languorous and oriental beauty." Billy then goes on to describe how Jacob used his eyes: "with a mixture of cynicism and timidity, modesty and desire . . . Malice, ingenuity, lust, melancholy, irony, gentleness, goodness, cruelty, salaciousness, anything you can think of, except innocence, simplicity, lightheartedness, true gaiety, severity, the inability to understand. Except sanctity, I would be tempted to add, if I consulted only my earliest memories."[17] Nothing about the work. The man only under the rubric of appearances. This is the Max Jacob fated to enter the literary manuals (if at all) as a *fantaisiste*, master of the medieval art of *contrepèterie* and *coq-à-l'âne*, but lacking the qualities of decisiveness, leadership, and clairvoyance demanded by the times.[18]

Even Jean Denoël is guilty of the same stereotyping. In his Preface to Jacob's volume of sketches and memoirs, *Le Roi de Béotie*, originally published in 1921 and reedited along with two childrens' stories in 1971, Denoël writes: "In these unexpected and moving pages, black as they are, the fantastical [*farfelu*] Max Jacob has suddenly disappeared. No more pirouettes, the tone is wholly different: the suffering of the world makes itself strangely felt, also its weariness. Perhaps it is this Max Jacob, religious thinker and juggler of sad images, who will assure his

17. André Billy, *Max Jacob* (Paris: Seghers, 1949), 12.

18. *Contrepèterie* involves the inversion of letters or syllables to obtain a burlesque or parodistic meaning. *Coq-à-l'âne* involves apparently arbitrary transition from one subject to another.

literary posterity—the posterity that he sometimes expressed
concern about to his friends."[19] It is not surprising that Jacob
was seen as a marginal figure, since he lived his life against the
grain. But the bizarre fate of his literary reputation constitutes a
special case in the history of French letters, providing a unique
perspective on the cultural politics of postwar France. Those
were the years when tension within the Gallimard inner circle
reflected the intensity of the debate on the outside. The aestheticism that had characterized Gide's dominance at Gallimard
gave way to a new openness, characterized by its sponsorship,
for a time, of Sartre and Merleau-Ponty's journal Les Temps
modernes.[20] Just as the NRF aesthetes had rejected Jacob, now it
was the turn of the ideologues. The intensity of the political
debate made it difficult to take seriously a figure whose poetics
were arcane and whose spiritual obsessions seemed remote
from current events. Beyond this, Jacob character militated
against him. His appetite for failure, his flight into abjection set
him up to be pulverized in the realpolitik of the Parisian literary
and artistic world. Jacob did little to promote himself and everything to undermine his career. His character combined a biting
wit with ostentatious self-deprecation, typical of the so-called
"self-hating Jew." His eventual retreat to the obscurity of St.
Benoit-sur-Loîre completed the picture of a man who chose
failure as both his public and his private roles. Yet there is no
way to measure his influence, whether literary or spiritual. Jean
Cocteau may have been thinking of Max Jacob when he wrote:
"There is no true victory without failure. Whoever does not
understand failure is lost." There are many kinds of failure and
Jacob knew most of them. Unemployed artist, unreadable poet,
exile from the coteries of Parisian life, betrayed by his oldest

19. Max Jacob, Le Roi de Béotie suivi de La Couronne de Vulcain et de Histoire
du roi Kaboul Ier et du marmiton Gauwain, edited with introduction by Jean
Denoël (Paris: Gallimard, 1971), xii.

20. After he was attacked in the pages of Les Temps modernes, André Malraux, then a close associate of General de Gaulle and his chief of propaganda,
compelled Gaston Gallimard to terminate his deal with Sartre, who took the
journal to René Julliard. Malraux had threatened not only to take all rights to
his books away from Gallimard but also to reopen certain files of the Occupation period. Assouline, Gallimard, 328–29.

friend, Picasso, who refused to help at the time of his arrest, dead at Drancy at the age of sixty-eight. He falls between the categories, acceptable to neither Christians nor Jews, a kind of sublime *nebishul*, the perfect scapegoat, companion in misery to Gimpel the fool.

CHAPTER 7

Holocaust as Last Judgment

In this austere place of Jewish martyrdom, the poet
Max Jacob died on March 5, 1944.

Plaque at Résidence la Muette, Drancy

I N April 1942 Max Jacob went to Quimper for the last time to
attend his elder sister's funeral. On his return to Saint-Benoît
he found in the mail that had piled up *The Stranger* by Albert
Camus, which Grenier had sent to him. He read it in the next
few days and informed Grenier that he admired it. This compressed, hard-edged novel represented, in the words of Camus,
"a unique study of a man who is indifferent to present realities,"
which is precisely what Jacob himself could not be under the
circumstances. In June he was forced to wear the yellow star.
Henceforth, most outings and excursions were forbidden him.[1]
He wrote to Béalu: "I've explained to you that it's impossible for
me to travel with the yellow badge without undergoing fantastic accusations by the police. . . . You don't understand because
you don't know how the police behave to us: the raids, etc. and

1. The original "statut des Juifs" had been issued in June 1941. A further
series of drastic measures concerning Jews was handed down by the Germans
on August 31, 1941, and enforced by the French police. All radios and bicycles
were confiscated. Access to all telephones public or private was forbidden.
Jews could not change their address; Jewish lawyers could not practice. There
was an 8 P.M. to 5 A.M. curfew for Jews. On May 29, 1942, Jews were ordered to
wear the yellow star.

to go without the badge is to break the law, hence be in danger" (*VMJ*, 280). Slowly the net tightened around him and his family. In July his brother Gaston was arrested, released after a month, then rearrested in December. Gaston died in a German concentration camp as did Jacob's sister, Myrté-Léa, deported in January 1944. Her arrest was a terrible blow to him. He wrote to Misia Sert: "This is the peak of horror! my youngest sister, the one I loved best . . . has been arrested without cause" (*VMJ*, 286). On February 24 it was the poet's turn. He was arrested that day and sent to the military prison at Orléans, where, for four days, he occupied a small and unsanitary cell with sixty other victims. During this time he stayed busy bandaging wounds, consoling the sick, even singing tunes from Offenbach to raise the spirits of his fellows. From there, on the 28th, already ill with a severe respiratory infection, he was sent to Drancy. His *fiche* shows that he was placed in a room on the fourth floor of staircase 19, with other individuals designated for the next convoy to Auschwitz, No. 69, slated for March 7.

Briefly, a literary cenacle formed around Max, who entertained with anecdotes and reminiscences until he had breathing difficulties and began to vomit. Taken to the infirmary, he became delirious; one of the attending Jewish doctors gave him sulfa drugs. He recovered some strength, becoming once again lucid, but made no effort to fight off his illness. Early on the morning of March 5, he said, "*Je suis avec Dieu*" and died. Dying anonymously in a hostile place was something he expected, something fitting for a sinner such as himself. In a poem called "Death" he visualizes his total anonymity:

> Bref le corps n'est plus qu'un dessin léger, les yeux du nuage aussi sont évanouis.
>
> A peine s'il reste l'étendue d'un beefsteak, une tache de sang et quelques débris de marbre pour rappeler un nom oublié.
>
> [In brief, the body is no more than a sketch, the eyes of the cloud have fainted away.
>
> What's left is barely the size of a beefsteak, a streak of blood and a few marble shards to recall a forgotten name.][2]

2. Max Jacob, *Derniers Poèmes en vers et en prose* (Paris: Gallimard, 1945), 195, hereafter *DP* in the text.

In the rest of this chapter I want to consider, in a way that has not been done before, Max Jacob as a poet of the Holocaust through analysis of texts from his two final books, *Derniers Poèmes en vers et en prose* and *Méditations religieuses*. My aim (both here and in Chapter 8) is to repair the poet's reputation; but, equally, I want to atone for my own inadequacy as a witness. I was someone who came close but never saw. I made no attempt to face the decimation of the Jewish race and did not in any but the most casual way turn my thoughts to events involving Jews during the war years. By this reflection on Max Jacob, I hope to repair that omission and to begin to be a listener, because, as time passes, it is the listeners, for better or worse, who must continue the testimony begun by the survivors. And I have begun to feel, as I write this, that there is even some hope in this for me, because I realize that a part of my psychic disability arises from my surgical self-removal from Jewish life, the Jewish tradition, the Jewish people.

Ever since the start of the war, Max had anticipated an anonymous and dishonored death as, from his perch on the Loire at Saint-Benoît, he saw the invasion and occupation unroll. He wrote of the refugees moving south, while the German convoys traveled north; he wrote of the terrible shortages in wartime: "Il n'y a plus de blé pour le pain. . . . Il n'y a plus de beurre pour les oeufs. . . . Il n'y a plus. . . . Il n'y a plus. . . ." (There is no more grain to make bread. . . . There is no more butter for the eggs. . . . There is no more. . . . There is no more. . . .) (*DP*, 152–53). And he wrote, in a seeming reference to Vichy, of diplomats who negotiate away their country's honor to a pack of demons:

> Monsieur le ministre, vous êtes une sale truie, hurlait le démon Azazel sous les traits du célèbre X. . . .
>
> Je m'en fous! dit le démon Mahazaël. Donnez-moi un million ou je fais dégringoler vos armoires à coup de révolver . . .
>
> Dans la rue le ciel était de plomb et sillonné d'un tonnerre rouge.
>
> [Mister minister, you're a filthy sow, yelled the demon Azazel who looked like the famous Mr. X . . .

I don't give a damn! says the demon Mahazaël. Give me a million or I'll shoot your wardrobes full of holes. . . .

Outside the sky was like lead and furrowed with red thunder.] (*DP*, 148–49)

The last line contains a hint of the punishment awaiting those men no better than pigs who barter their country's honor. If they are not destroyed by the demons they do business with, then the sky will bombard them with red thunder.

There is also a poem that, in veiled terms, salutes the young men who go off to the *maquis* to take part in the resistance:

Au Dieu qui dispense la résistance, je dédie les jeunes gens éminents qui passent dans ma vision et dans la rue des gentilshommes. Aux yeux de la Mort et de la Renommée, ils ne sont plus rien, pas même une figure, pas même un nom.

[To God who dispenses the power of resistance, I dedicate these eminents young men who pass in my field of vision down the street of gentlemen. In the eyes of Death and of Fame, they are no longer anything, not even a face, not even a name.] (*DP*, 189)

Their heroism and death are doubled because they are anonymous, similiar to the fate he expects for himself. These are poems in which Max memorializes the suffering and cruelty of war. He does this deliberately, aware of the clear and present risk to himself. His papers have been searched and may be searched again. These are poems in which he confronts the evil of betrayal and of self-aggrandizement from the war. Elsewhere, he attacks the profiteers. Even this evil on a banal scale can suddenly becoming ultimate evil. So in a poem called "Donnez-moi l'effroi" ("Give Me Fright") he speaks of "the horrors of criminal lust . . . meanness and avarice";[3] but then suddenly it is Judgment Day and all the terrified petty sinners are cast into hell. Here, he is raising the question of how wartime puts an immense weight on the conscience, bringing about

---

3. *Méditations religieuses*, (Paris: Gallimard, 1947), 159, hereafter *MR* in the text.

the loss and redemption of many. In such poems as these, Max is doing what Ponge and Char and many other poets were doing—keeping a chronicle, also an account book in view of a future reckoning. In Max's case, however, this reckoning was not to come in the back-alleys of a liberated France. It wouldn't come as a bullet in the brain of a collabo, it would not even come in the courts. The only place it could come was in the absolute justice of the Last Judgment. Apocalypse, the heavens opening, the dead rising, the writing in the book of life made visible for all to see, the Risen Christ triumphant, calling the Chosen, casting sinners into hell, are the central topoi of Max's imagination in his last years.

In a truly biblical argument with God he cries out: "Puisque Vous êtes Dieu et que vous savez tout, dites-moi quand finira cette guerre!" (Since You are God and since you know all, tell me when this war will end!) (*DP*, 181). He is calling on God to witness, because he believes that God does witness, does understand, although few others do.

Dr. Dori Laub has written that the Holocaust was an event without a witness, that it was in essence untellable: "Not only, in effect, did the Nazis try to exterminate the physical witnesses of their crime; but the inherently incomprehensible and deceptive psychological structure of the event precluded its own witnessing, even by its very victims."[4] Besides having created an untellable event, the Nazis succeeded in making the Jews believe they deserved the fate that was meted out to them:

> Because of their "participation" in the Holocaust they have become the "bearers of a secret" (*Geheimnissträger*) never to be divulged. The implications of this imaginary complicity and of this conviction of their having been chosen for a secret mission are that they believe, out of loyalty, that their persecution and execution by the Nazis was actually warranted. . . . As "subhumans," a position they have accepted and assumed as their identity by virtue of their contamination by the "secret order," they have no right to speak up or protest. Moreover, by never

4. Shosana Felman and Dori Laub, *Testimony: Crises of Witnessing in Literature, Psychoanalysis, and History* (New York: Routledge, 1972), 80.

divulging their stories, they feel that the rest of the world will never come to know the *real* truth, the one that involved the destruction of their humanity. The difficulty that prevents these victims from speaking out about their victimization emphasizes even more the delusional quality of the Holocaust.[5]

Not only did this delusion undermine their will to protect each other and survive, it sealed the event in silence. So terrible was the delusion that many of the survivors interviewed by Dr. Laub could not tell their stories. Even the medical doctor, the psychiatrist, could not be allowed as a witness of their sub-humanity. Dr. Laub's accounts of his sessions with Holocaust survivors help us understand why Max's poems on the catastrophe are so fragmentary, so oblique, so hidden in their reference. There is no question that, even while he repressed full awareness, he knew what was going on. Too many friends, too many family members had disappeared. In one of his last meditations he prayed to "St. Anthony of Padua, patron of prisoners, for my brother and sister" (*MR*, 153). Yet he repressed any more complete elucidation of the Holocaust. He did not dwell on it in his letters or, apparently, in those conversations reported by his friends during the last years. What he did, instead, was turn his repressed grasp of the truth into the circumlocutions of his art, which had always excelled in distorting, refracting, mirroring, inverting events.

This knowledge, at the conscious/unconscious margin, received its best formulation in numerous poems on the Last Judgment. In this process, he tried to do what many witnesses to the Jewish Catastrophe had done through the ages—to testify before God Himself. But he did so with a conscience already inclined to guilt, already inclined to accept responsibility for even those misfortunes of life that were entirely beyond his control—including the Holocaust. In effect, he became doubly a victim, in a way that parallels the statement reported by Dr. Laub, which was made by a psychiatrist to a survivor patient: "'Hitler's crime was not only the killing of the Jews, but getting the Jews to believe that they deserved it.'"[6]

5. Ibid., 82.
6. Ibid., 79, footnote.

The obsessively recreated scene of the Last Judgment has several aspects. There is, first, the theological / cosmological aspect,
in which Max reflects on the general meaning of the apocalypse
for the planet and its people. No single text is devoted exclu-
sively to this; but the earlier meditations are in general the most
philosophical. So this depiction of the Last Judgment in a poem
that imagines the sky darkening, stars falling: a brief celestial
illumination is followed by a chaos of menacing shadows. Only
at one point is the broad generalist tone broken: "Perhaps we
are living these times now, December 1942" (MR, 62). Again, in
a later meditation:

> Tout VA CRAQUER, TOUT CRAQUE. Les nouvelles sont épouvan-
> tables. Les océans se desschent, les continents s'écroulent. Ce
> n'est pas un cataclysme. C'est mille grêles de feu. La colère du
> Ciel foudroie impies et croyants. Ah! tu peux écrire ceci avec ton
> sang. Je te dis que c'est la fin, la fin du monde.

> [Everything IS GOING TO BREAK UP, EVERYTHING BREAKS. The
> oceans dry up, the continents crumble. It's not a cataclysm. It a
> thousand hails of fire. Heaven's anger blasts the impious and the
> believers. Ah! you can write this with your blood. I tell you that
> it's the end, the end of the world.] (MR, 157)

But this is the easy part, this visualization of hail and brimstone,
this sundering of the cosmos as in some Hollywood super-
production. It is too much of a cliché, though one has to admire
the writer's energy, every morning at 5 A.M., dipping his pen,
producing enough rhetoric to fill a page.

The second aspect of the Last Judgment poems is more
serious. It has to do with suffering, the poet's lifetime of miseries, petty and grand, offered now in payment for his sins and
those of all mankind, including those sinners whose ignorance
and avarice contribute to the difficulty of this time of war.
Intense accounts of private anguish appear throughout the two
collections. In "L'Enfer" (MR, 113–15) he recreates the physical
pain and terror of hell by analogizing from his misery as a child
with toothache or being burned by a spilled kettle of soup. He
will be abandoned like a stray dog among the smokes and fogs
of hell.

"L'Enfer" is followed by another "Last Judgment," in which the philosophical reflection becomes allied with vivid memories of the war:

> J'imagine, avec l'expérience de 40, l'isolement des villages sans communication ni approvisionnement pour cause de disette. Oui, je l'imagine et je plains cette génération dernière de la terre mourante.

> [I imagine, with the experience of '40, the isolation of villages with neither communication nor provisions because of shortages. Yes, I imagine it and I pity that last generation of the dying earth.] (*MR*, 117)

In his pity for "that last generation" he asserts his belief in this central but difficult Christian precept, that the grace of one individual can redeem others. Grace is seen as a vast pumping system, in which some contribute and others receive, the virtues of the ones making up for the sins of others. This kind of theological hydraulics is mysterious, open only to the mind of faith. But even if absolutely clear, it would still fail to address the central question of Holocaust. Because whose suffering can redeem such an event, who can relieve God of the burden of what He allowed to happen?

The third aspect of these Last Judgment poems is of rare occurrence, but it signals an important shift in the poet's thinking whereby he fuses his destiny as a sinful Christian with that of the Jewish people:

> Créateur des mers et des ciels, des continents, de tout l'imponderable. . . . Je vous remercie de m'avoir fait naître de la race juive souffrante, car celui-là seul est sauvé qui souffre et qui sait qu'il souffre et offre à Dieu sa souffrance.

> [Creator of the seas and the skies, of the continents, of all that is imponderable. . . . I thank you for having caused me to be born to the suffering Jewish race, for he alone is saved who suffers and who knows that he suffers and offers his suffering to God.] (*MR*, 35)

Identification with the Jewish people marks a turning in the *Méditations religieuses*. Coming gradually but insistently, it is accompanied by a shift in tone and in the position of the speaker. The anguish is more delirious, more intense, the images more grotesque; the speaker becomes depersonalized. This depersonalized voice is almost crazed with the horror of the scenes to which he is drawn in:

> Grille donc, homme immonde! Grille les yeux d'animaux, fixe tes contorsions atroces! Grille comme une bûche que tu as été toute ta vie! Grille et hurle! les oreilles hideuses des démons qui t'écoutent et leurs rires t'insultent. Le vois-tu, le cercle des hyènes qui entourent dans la nuit le feu des bivouacs dont tu est le combustible?

> [Grill then, filthy man! Grill animal eyes, fix your atrocious contortions! Grille like the log that you have been all your life! Grill and yell! the hideous ears of the demons who listen and their laughter insult you. Do you see it, the circle of hyenas who surround you in the night of bivouac fires for which you are the fuel?] (*MR*, 53)

The speaker is beside himself, berserk with the impulse to self-sacrifice, drawn into these fires, this holocaust, which is hell itself. There is a sharp disjuncture between poems that memorialize the common miseries of war and this new condition unique in its horror. These last poems, which anticipate, visualize, prophecy the Holocaust, are of a different order from others that surround them. Explicit in their depiction of horror, they are also strangely distorted, with that displacement and condensation that signify the unconscious and the return of the repressed. They witness to something dreamed and half-represented in a desperate effort to use language to resolve the question of evil in its ultimate form, the destruction of innocent millions to enact the brainstorm of a psychopathic leader. How many thousand million tons of grace need to be exchanged to balance the complicities engendered in this process, involving innumerable others, both German and French, in the force of a shared hallucination?

Dr. Laub and others have documented the posttraumatic terrors of Holocaust survivors, especially the children, those most powerless to understand what was going on. These testimonies reminded me of my own Holocaust-inspired terrors and those of many Jewish-American youths who grew up during the war. While living far from occupied Europe, we became long-distance victims of Nazi oppression. Even before I enlisted in the Army (and for many years after the war ended) I had dreams of running from faceless pursuers in S.S. uniforms, of turning to grapple with them till, half suffocated, I awoke. My wife Judy also had Holocaust nightmares, based mainly on films she saw after the war. I have spoken to Jewish friends and relatives whose unconscious was forever polarized by German atrocities. This is not to compare our experience with those of the survivors, but it puts us in a position to be more competent listeners to the survivors' stories. As Dr. Laub writes: "The listener, therefore, has to be at the same time a witness to the trauma witness and a witness to himself. It is only in this way, through his simultaneous awareness of the continuous flow of those inner hazards both in the trauma witness and in himself, that he can become the enabler of the testimony—the one who triggers its initiation, as well as the guardian of its process and of its momentum."[7] This must apply to those of us who listen at a remove or at several removes, even when we listen to the broken testimony of poems and meditations such as those of Max Jacob. Not that we can make it easier for him to speak; but we can, at last, decode some of the undercurrents, the hints and innuendos, the guarded asides, and finally, the moral power of his testimony. We can do this by paying attention both to what is said and how it is received. For me, these poems and meditations of Max are a maze without center or goal, corridors that open onto other corridors, paths that go nowhere. I get lost here, which suggests to me that the poet too was lost, that his imagination was not equal to the task of expressing a truth that he did not want to know because it overwhelmed him. Yet in my struggle to follow him, even in my confusion, I gain a sense of release from interpreting these poems of suffering, prophecy, and death. This is a worthwhile task, it is a task that needed to be done. If I could continue it, go on from here, there might be a way out of my own prisons. I speculate that so many neurotic

7. Ibid., 58.

Jewish men and women are neurotic for this reason—because they have not adequately attended to the Holocaust. They have not listened, they have not assumed the burden of others, a burden that might lighten their own.[8]

Max was a poet of the Holocaust because it was burned into his mind, because it unhinged him in a way that made connected thought almost impossible. He knew that he was involved in one of those great upheavals that from time to time rumbles across the face of the earth. He knew conceptually that Jews were being deported to extermination camps. But, as a poet, he worked with Holocaust on a different level, as a reality that had to remain unconscious, because it was too terrible to face. This led him to write a new kind of poetry that was driven by a double need. First, there was the need to deal with the problem of evil in a way that made some kind of sense. Second, there was the need to attain release from the emotions generated by the Holocaust. A year before his death Max wrote: "I offer the sufferings of my family, of my race, those of my brother in reparation for their faults, their sins, for their conversion, for my own faults, my sins and my own conversion, for their eternal Salvation and for mine."[9] Here he is appealing to the theologian's exchange of grace—his suffering for their release; but the irony of the situation was far too complex, since he himself became a prisoner while the others stayed in prison and were killed. No exchange took place. This is the bargaining that people, even nonbelievers, do under stress; but its catachistic simplicity is irrelevant to the way evil and grace play out in the world.

At the same time this is the cornerstone of Christian belief: Christ died for our sins. Imitating his sacrifice we can atone for

8. Saul Friedlander has observed that some survivors are unable to attain closure on their camp experiences. "For these witnesses, memory and survival do not seem to entail any cathartic rediscovery of a harmonious self, of a heroic memory, of a unifying moral principle." Saul Friedlander, "Trauma, Memory, and Transference," in Geoffrey H. Hartman, ed., *Holocaust Rememberance: The Shapes of Memory* (Cambridge, Mass.: Blackwell, 1974), 253.

9. Written on the first communion card of Maurice and Bernard Szigeti, March 16, 1943 (*VMJ*, 283).

the sins of others. We may frequently be unsure what Christians mean by sin, but here, where we are talking of the Holocaust, there can be no doubt. Max clung to this rationale because he already had a natural disposition toward it; it came from his sense of unworthiness ("sinfulness"), which was sublime and psychotic in equal parts. It pervaded him, body and mind, staying with him from earliest childhood until the end of his life. So he could make the outrageous connection between his pecadillos as a young man in Paris and the punishment being meted out to the Jewish people. This bizarre distortion, to which he clung until the end, was one of the signs that he had internalized the Holocaust as an unconscious component of his superego. Viewing Nazi oppression as the Last Judgment, allowing himself to be crushed by it, was Max's least successful way of dealing with evil. It is a way that contemporary Jews, looking back on the Holocaust some fifty years later, emphatically reject. The sin was not that of his family, his race, his past life; the sin was that of a political-military-industrial system, administered by men and women who had let themselves be hypnotized by a psychotic leader. All that can be said about this psychological position was that it offered a mechanism for conceptualizing events that went far beyond his capacity to influence in even the most minimal way. As Cocteau wrote, "Since these events exceed our power, let us pretend to be their organizers." In the Last Judgment poems, Max was able to maintain his grip on some kind of coherent conceptual structure, while he struggled with the problem of Dostoevsky and Camus, the wholly inhuman dimension of evil. This brings us back to the discussion of evil raised in Chapter 3 à propos of Camus. There we saw an atheist who rejected God because of human suffering. Here, we are dealing with a believer whose approach has a terrible pathos and leads to an unacceptable paradox: Evil exists, God cannot have caused it, therefore we have brought it upon ourselves.

Max found himself in a dilemma, facing two things that had to be done if he were to keep his sanity. First, the redemption offered by God had to appear on a scale to make it compensate for the evil of the Holocaust. Second, as a human individual trying to live without going crazy, he had to abreact the negative emotions, such as rage, terror, loss, associated with the carrying out of the Final Solution.[10] These were two opposing processes. The first involves the effort to materialize the Holocaust, to see and experience it as it was lived by its victims. This was a necessary first step, before he could invoke God's transcendent power to bring good out of evil. But this was at cross-purposes with the effort to transform the Holocaust's emotional effect. You cannot let go of horror if you are constantly trying to evoke it. Further, the results of unbinding or "abreacting" emotion can only be partial at best and its effect can only be temporary, since nothing in the real world has changed.[11] Still, it is certain that the daily writing of the meditations was deeply cathartic, that it allowed him to live with an unconscious already struck by the vibrations from the Holocaust that reached him in Saint-Benoît. And that daily release allowed him, the next day, to get more deeply into the unimaginable thing, usually masked as the Apocalypse, as in the poem quoted earlier "Donnez-moi l'effroi."

Abreaction sometimes occurs in a violent or distorted poem, dealing with hell, judgment, or death. Even here, the poet may recover his equilibrium and reenter the world of daily life. He does it brilliantly, yet almost casually, in the untitled second-to-last poem of the *Derniers Poèmes en vers et en prose*. Here, we have a basic tension between the bound and the unbound, the finite and the infinite, between life and spilled blood:

> La rivière de ma vie est devenue un lac. Ce qui s'y reflète n'est plus que l'amour. Amour de Dieu, amour en Dieu.

---

10. "Abreaction is the process of discharging pent-up emotions (unconscious affect) through the recall and verbalization of repressed memories." Ludwig Eidelberg, M.D., *Encyclopedia of Psychoanalysis* (New York. The Free Press, 1968), 8.

11. Eidelberg adds that Freud later recognized "the insufficiency of abreaction as a real cure for neurosis," substituting for it "the analytical goal of a fundamental reorganization of the personality." Still it was not wholly discarded: "However, one feature of abreaction is still incorporated in analytic theory, the aspect of *working through*. It is also utilized in other forms of treatment and in sublimation (play and aesthetic experience among others) which afford spontaneous means of release from tension."

Un mur! une montagne est un mur dont la racine se perd dans une terrible nuit. Le mur est couvert de peupliers centenaires aux racines étrangères. Un feu d'artifice ou quelque incendie illumina la grande ombre et les peupliers de la gloire furent ensanglantés.

[The river of my life has become a lake. What is reflected there is only love. Love of God, love in God.

A wall! a mountain is a wall whose root gets lost in a terrible night. The wall is covered with centenary poplars with foreign roots. Fireworks or some blaze illuminated the great shadow and the poplars of glory were bloodied.] (*DP*, 196)

This too is an apocalypse, a prediction of the last days; but there is no anguish here, just the peace of love. The fires and shadows are a light show, but life persists in the roots of the trees. If vision momentarily sees blood, the speaker's peace is undisturbed. Best of all, there is no judgment here. He will let God make the final call. The sane thing for him is to go back to the old poet's game, watching images play themselves out against the night.

CHAPTER 8

Setting Things Right: Jacob as Postmodernist

> Hence, once again, pastiche: in a world in which
> stylistic innovation is no longer possible, all that is left
> is to imitate dead styles, to speak through the masks
> and with the voices of the styles in the imaginary
> museum. But this means that contemporary or post-
> modernist art is going to be about art itself in a new
> kind of way . . .
>
> Fredric Jameson

IN 1959 John Lapp, who had recruited me to the UCLA
faculty and had become a close friend, arranged the pur-
chase by the University Library of some letters of Max Jacob
to an obscure poet named Jean Fraysse. Between December
1935 and January 1937, Jean Fraysse had edited a literary review
called *Les Feux de Paris* to which Max had been a frequent
contributor. When the Nazis invaded France, Fraysse, who had
government connections, panicked and left for Spain. He disappeared into the Pyrennees, where he was probably killed by the
men he had hired to guide him, and was never heard from
again. The Jacob / Fraysse letters seemed, at first, no more than a

scholarly windfall. But, working with them, I became convinced that they were a key to the conspiracy of silence that, for so many years, had obscured the importance of this wonderful poet. It was a golden opportunity to "set things right" by renewing the reputation of a writer who had been misunderstood by his friends, while being disparaged and defamed by the rest of the Parisian literati. Max wasn't simply a *fumiste* or *fantaisiste* but a poetic genius, whose work adumbrated an aesthetic radically ahead of its time.

Galvanized into action, I began to contact those *Feux de Paris* collaborators who still survived, notably poet Roger Lannes. Lannes was an invalid, living in a rest home in Lausanne. Our letters and telephone calls took on the form of a ballet. Lannes was interested, wanted to help me, but suffering from a terrible illness that made it impossible for him to see visitors. Visitors gave him vertigo and headaches, casting him inevitably into fits of depression. Under no circumstances could he see me. He wrote, "It would take me a month to recover from your visit, *cher Monsieur. Je regrette. . . .*"

In 1960 I visited France to document the correspondence and to begin writing an introduction that would convey a sense of the poet and his milieu.[1] I was able to see many friends of the poet, notably Marcel Béalu and Yvon Belaval; but Lannes was the linchpin to the *Feux de Paris* circle. His refusal to meet me was unwavering, but I announced that I was going skiing in Zermatt and would stop in Lausanne on my way back to Paris. He could make up his mind once and for all when I knocked at his door.

I spent five days on the Gorner Grat, skiing with my old Army buddy Ernest Schneider, who was working with the Voice of America in Munich. When Schneider's wife broke her leg, he left abruptly, while I spent one last day with a guide skiing over the top of the mountain into Italy. Exalted by that experience of the heights, I packed up and headed back via the Swiss railway system to Lausanne, a gloomy provincial city. Why Lannes had chosen this place for his debacle I could only

1. Published in 1964 under the title *Max Jacob and "Les Feux de Paris"* (Berkeley: University of California Press, 1964).

guess. Probably he was hiding out from friends who had known him as a glamorous young poet of great promise. Later, when I met him, I decided he had chosen Lausanne as a setting to match his deep depression. Unshaven and wearing a ratty bathrobe, Lannes received me in a small room that smelled of propane and chocolate. Loose brown drapes filtered the papery afternoon light of the overheated room. Lannes' face was drawn with the effects of some devastating mental disease, his hands shook. This was an unrecognizable relic of the handsome young poet who had charmed Jacob and Cocteau back in the 1930s.

We talked disjointedly at first. Then I came to the point of my visit.

"Max wrote that you and your friends represented a new direction in poetry. True?"

"Max called us the *nouveau mouvement poétique*, but it was *boursouflage*; he was the only real avant-gardist."

Lannes shuffled from his chair over to a black trunk with iron straps at the foot of his bed. Shoving up the lid, he pulled out a handful of letters. He leafed through them, chose one, and handed it to me. In it Max thanked him for a poem and said that the members of the new movement were *his* posterity, wholly separate from the genealogy of Apollinaire. He wrote: "I began in 1898 and I had already finished in 1905 when I heard the name of Apollinaire and saw his dear face for the first time."

Max meant that he had already ended his modernist period in 1905; that something else was in the works. He liked to attribute his own intentions to the young men around him, investing them with his ideas and discoveries. "I was one of the first," Lannes said, "to grasp the originality of Max's aesthetic. I saw in that cacophony of discourses an obliteration of reality, the creation of a void which Max filled by *le déchaînement du vocabulaire* (the unleashing of vocabulary)."

"He was an amazing ventriloquist," I observed, "he could imitate a thousand voices. Often in the same poem."

Lannes, who was becoming exhausted, sank back in his chair.

"That was why they called him a *pasticheur*. But he could be tiring too, *le pauvre Max*; in fact, sometimes you wished he would just be simple, straightforward, say *Merde* when that was what he meant. Now, *cher Monsieur*, I really must ask you to excuse me. . . . I feel an attack coming on, please, as you leave, ask Madame Simmonot to bring me my medicine."

I was back in California, thinking about Jacob's new way of writing, when I came across some of the first references to postmodernism by Ihab Hassan and others. It struck me then that this might be a way of characterizing Jacob, not as a modernist or representative of the School of Paris, but as the forerunner of a new school, not yet invented in his day.

In 1961 I returned to France. This time I tried to contact Lannes through his sister, who ran a bookstore near the Eiffel Tower. She took a somewhat dim view of Roger's literary friendships but gave me his phone number, still in Lausanne at a new address. He would not speak on the phone, and his landlady relayed the message that a second meeting was out of the question.

But I found another and equally well-informed source, poet Marcel Béalu. We had several long conversations at his bookstore, Le Pont traversé, next to the Latin Quarter church of Saint-Séverin. He was interested in my theory of Jacob as a postmodern and passed on to me a book that he thought might be helpful. It was a French translation of Walter Benjamin's essay on Baudelaire. It was in reading Benjamin that I came to the conclusion that there was a "double postulation" in the work of Max Jacob. The first postulation is toward modernism, with which he was associated through his friendships and a significant but limited strand, in his work; the second is toward postmodernism, which he anticipated and helped to shape.

Modernism

Exemplified in *Le Cornet à dés* (1917) and *Le Roi de Béotie* (1921), this strand presents the author as *flâneur* or poet of the streets in the manner extolled by Benjamin in his essays on Baudelaire.[2]

2. See Walter Benjamin, *The Paris of the Second Empire in Baudelaire* (London: Verso, 1983). Max wrote: "I left the Rue Ravignan every morning at daybreak,

Benjamin visualizes the poet strolling beneath the glittering superstructure of commercial arcades past the phantasmagoria of commodities or, conversely, as ragpicker, collecting the detritus of capitalist surplus value to transmute it with the help of alcohol into images of power as in the poem "Le Vin des chiffoniers." Baudelaire's drunken ragpicker embodies the degradation and dehumanization resulting from commodity fetishism but also recalls the popular heroism of the Commune.

Implicitly acknowledging a link with Baudelaire, Max wrote a ragpicker poem entitled "La Rue Ravignan," which shows the poet at his window, observing the traffic in the street below:

Rue Ravignan

"You never bathe twice in the same stream," the philosopher Heraclitus used to say. And yet, it's always the same ones who come back up! At the same time of day, they pass by, gay or sad. To all of you, passersby of the Rue Ravignan, I have given the names of History's defunct! Now here comes Agamemnon! and here's Madame Hanska! Ulysses is the milkman. . . . But you, old ragpicker, you, who, in the fairylike morn, come to collect the still living scraps as I put out my good stout lamp, you whom I do not know, mysterious and poor ragpicker, you, ragpicker, I have named you with a noble and celebrated name, I have named you Dostoevsky.[3]

The inebriation and vertigo of Baudelaire's bacchanalian ragpicker contrasts with the pathos of Jacob's more reflective poem, which achieves a subtle identification between the poet, collector of words, who is just now putting out his lamp, and the ragpicker, whose misery he elevates by calling him Dostoevsky.

I went on foot to the Place de la Nation, from there to the waterfall in the Bois de Boulogne and came back home to bed, drunk with fasting, meditation and fatigue. These were my exercises: I had to find an idea for each postcard seen in one or another shopwindow. If I couldn't invent an idea, I had to stand motionless until the idea came. So I slowly filled with my cheap pencil my cheap one sou notebooks. . . ." The poet's explanation of how, in 1907, he wrote Le Phanérogame, published at his own expense in 1918. In Le Roi de Béotie (Paris: Gallimard, 1971), x.

3. From Le Cornet à dés, trans. Judith Morganroth Schneider, in Lévy, PT, 140–1.

No doubt the ragpicker had a wild and disheveled look, like Baudelaire's anarchist, but the literarity of the name uncannily anticipates Benjamin's theory. The bourgeois poet joins the poet of the streets and together they become subversives, in the way that Marx attributed to the *bohème*: "The social position of this class predetermined its whole character. . . . Their uncertain existence, which in specific cases depended more on chance than their activities, their irregular life whose only fixed stations were the taverns of the wine dealers—the gathering place of the conspirators—and their inevitable acquaintanceship with all sorts of dubious people. . . ."[4] Although he admits that Baudelaire was incapable of sustaining any nonconformist position for more than a few days, Benjamin saw him as the agent of the secret unhappiness of his class. The ragpicker-poets, the addicts and social pariahs who constitute the *bohème* exemplified for Benjamin the degradation and falseness of modern experience. Baudelaire, Benjamin, Jacob—all three were avant-garde outcasts from bourgeois society, *flâneurs* who transmuted the stuff of everyday experience into images. All three were malcontents, emotional vagrants looking for a home. As such all three (and Benjamin also for ideological reasons) expressed sympathetic identification with the working class. Max's *Le Roi de Béotie* is one of several works in which the poet appears as a *flâneur*. This is essentially a book of acid-tipped portraits drawn from life, enriched by dialogues that have the immediacy and color of the streets of Paris. It is filled with brief descriptive snapshots and the minutiae of overheard conversations. Everything is lovingly recorded, yet there is always a vein of satire, a revulsion against the grossness of ordinary people. This is implicit in the title of the collection, since Boeotia was a state of ancient Greece where people were reputed to be fat and vulgar.

The first part of *Le Roi de Béotie* consists of sketches from city life like the one just quoted; the second consists of experiences in hospital, the outcome of Jacob's accident in 1920 when he was knocked down by a car while on his way to the opera.[5] In Chapter 2, I commented on the use of the hospital by Camus

4. Quoted in Benjamin, *The Paris of the Second Empire in Baudelaire*, 12.
5. Jean Denoël gives 1919 as the date for this event. So far as I can ascertain, the date of 1920 given by Pierre Andreu is correct.

and Rilke as a microcosm of human suffering. For Jacob, the hospital is a museum of the varieties of human experience, but it is also the place where the cruelty of modern industrial society is seen in its harshest light. The second part of his book begins with this letter to Pierre Colle:

> My dear Pierre,
>
> Your letter made me cry. A little anemia: bed, nerves, night fears, or rather your exquisite tenderness and the elevation of your character made me feel the inequalities of society. These men, so like you, like me, and so badly treated by men like you and me. I know well the causes of hatred! and if I were not Max Jacob, ah! how much joy I would feel to be Brieux.[6] Why discharge from the hospital people who are not cured and have nowhere to go? why send them off with scornful familiarities [des tutoyements de mépris] and words of hate? Why send without God with words without God from a hospital without God men without God and who without God don't know where to go?[7]

The social protest motif sounds in Jacob's sketches of hospital life with the same intensity that we find in Camus and Rilke. He rejoins them by his savage reflections on suffering and death:

> Animality, madness, screams. Pain gives ax blows in the chest to hasten the coming of the Sacred Heart of Jesus. Animality, madness, screams, pain is divine, for death is divine, but pain is animal hence. . . .
>
> Editor's note: The divine element here is the welcome given to pain. . . .
>
> Close your eyes . . . the portrait of . . . in the lamp-tinged mirror, it is I, minus my fever which doesn't exist, but I call fever what you call sickness. I have seen you again, I see you, you my second, my double, you no longer look like the old me. . . .
>
> I will never get into this coffin, it's not built for me; it's not for me. . . .
>
> My eyes already close to begin understanding life, as much of it as one can in understanding death.

6. Eugène Brieux, author in 1914 of Les Avariés, a successful play about venereal disease.
7. Le Roi de Béotie (Paris: Gallimard, 1971), 139.

Remarked by the audience: a dog's death-rattle, a bird's death-rattle, a comedian's death-rattle which is after all mine.[8]

This is Max Jacob the modernist *flâneur*, poet of social protest, a writer who meditates on the themes of suffering and death. Thematic content, however, is in constant competition with word play or logophilia. One example: in the "animality" passage, the rhyming of *poitrine* (chest) with *divine* underscores a compulsive rhythm. This kind of device often signals the beginning of a combinatory, but here he cuts it short with a self-conscious "Editor's note."

Jacob was deeply involved with cubism and critics have described cubist elements in his work,[9] yet neither this nor any of the other movements that made up the modernist collage—expressionism, futurism, dadaism—were decisive influences. There is, however, an important modernist element in Jacob's aesthetic theory as opposed to his practice: his emphasis on beauty and emotional impact. In the 1916 Preface to *Le Cornet à dés* he writes that the goal of the prose poem is to give us "the emotion of the beautiful."[10] Emotion is one of the most contested notions in literary theory and it is not clear how Jacob is using it here. Presumably, he means "aesthetic emotion," the impact of a beautiful form; yet he is also referring to a central theme of modernist expressivity, since he declares earlier in this same Preface: "Style is the will to externalize oneself by chosen means."[11] That is, the poet externalizes his deepest experiences by a verbal construct which produces an emotional effect on his reader. This is a view of poetry that applies to Baudelaire, Apollinaire, and most modernist writers. Sydney Lévy rightly argues that, in fact, Jacob's desire to "externalize" himself was undermined by his logophilia, notably his use of punning and *contrepèterie*, which "had a negative effect: his punning was not taken seriously . . . it conveyed no information, it was

8. Ibid., 149–151.
9. Notably Gerald Kamber in his *Max Jacob and the Poetics of Cubism* (Baltimore: John Hopkins University Press, 1971).
10. *Le Cornet à dés*, 14.
11. Ibid., 11–12.

merely 'noise' in the informational as well as sensational sense" (*PT*, 11).

Modernism is a secondary strand in Max Jacob's *œuvre*. His work was overall *anti*modernist because it was disruptive of what Lévy calls (in speaking of Jacob's puns) "efficient communication." Lévy writes: "the pun arrests attention at the signifier, and thus, by its sheer presence, prevents or obstructs so-called efficient communication. In other words, it functions as a film either without substance or as one that fashions another substance, itself ambiguous and unstable, and thereby proclaims the lack of reference and representation. The pun is therefore not only a sign of disturbance, but is itself that disturbance; it disrupts the very communication that a text is supposed to accomplish and thus puts the texts into free play" (*PT*, 11). Modernist aesthetic writing aspired to achieve "efficient communication," not by discursive or conceptual discourse but through the organic relay of metaphor. The resistance offered by metaphor (which can be visualized as a fold or thickening in the text) is productive of the emotive effect. Emotion in turn tends to the development of a community of shared feeling—a consensus. This is the consensus of the concert hall or the art gallery but also involves the broader perception of a shared culture. But after World War II disruptive and dissociative forms of art, of which Max Jacob had been a precursor, came to the fore. Modernity began to lose its power to move and energize artistic and social movements. Jürgen Habermas, who assumed the mantle of Benjamin and Adorno as theorist of modernity, saw its failure in a splitting of the cultural sphere, with the result "that the life-world, whose traditional substance has already been devalued, will become more and more impoverished."[12] Having lived through the trauma of World War II in childhood, Habermas sought to find new modalities for achieving the goal of "communicative rationality," which he saw as the intersubjective relationship into which speaking and acting individuals enter in order to reach reciprocal understanding based on a valid use of reason. Against current forms of scepti-

12. In Foster, ed., *The Anti-Aesthetic: Essays on Postmodern Culture* (Port Townsend, Washington: Bay Press, 1985), 9.

cism arising from structuralism and deconstruction, he argued for "the comprehensibility of the symbolic expression, the truth of the propositional content, the truthfulness of the intentional expression and the rightness of the speech act with respect to existing norms and values. . . . In these validity claims communication theory can locate a gentle, but obstinate, a never silent although seldom redeemed claim to reason."[13] Habermas faulted modernity for failing, despite this claim to reason, to achieve "consensual interaction," with the resultant splitting of knowledge, justice, authenticity, and taste into separate realms. In the arts, Habermas attacked surrealism in particular, but the critique applies to the work of Max Jacob, who was never a seeker of reason or consensual truth.

Postmodernism

The transition between modernism and postmodernism can be described in several ways, one of which might be via Benjamin's theme of the phantasmagoria of modern life, specifically, the consumer products of late nineteenth-century France. These phantasmagoria's are forerunners of the "simulacra" of Baudrillard. In present-day hyperreality the delirium of early capitalism has become institutionalized. The break between object, meaning, and image is accepted as normal in the postmodern world. Images, printed products, phantasms, sound bites, codes, the rhetoric of the sales pitch, telemarketing are the substance of everyday life. But how can we attribute the simulacra of postmodernism to a poet who wrote with a pen and never drove a car or saw a television commercial? To understand Jacob's second postulation, his postmodernism, it will be useful to look at several themes of postmodern theory.

On July 9, 1923, André Gide commented in his *Journal* on Max Jacob's novel of family life and intrigue in Brittany: "Badly disappointed by *The Terrain Bouchaballe*, that I so much wanted

13. In Richard Bernstein, *Habermas and Modernity* (Cambridge: MIT Press, 1985), 20.

to like. At the two extremes, Suarès and Max Jacob: the first is only interested in himself and is only interesting when he speaks of others; the second is only interested in others and only interesting when he speaks of himself."[14] Gide's points to what has often been seen as a fundamental flaw in Jacob's work: its dryness, its lack of affect and of personal reference. Yet from the beginning, this man of histrionic personality had been working toward an impersonal poetics. Gide has identified for us one of the main features that makes Jacob's work postmodern: its lack of an aura. Benjamin defined the aura as a special radiance, originally associated with the work's cultic value, then, in modernism, with the author's personality and the sense of beauty. The aura surrounds the work and causes it to transcend space and time. The aura's demise, according to Benjamin, is announced by Atget's photographs of empty streets, devoid of any human presence.[15] The work's monumentality, another modernist feature, is associated with the myth of the artist as creator. Just as we can assert that Jacob created no work of monumental proportions, we can assert also that he never gives us the sense of subjective radiance that we find in works by Apollinaire, Joyce, Picasso, or Proust. The "externalization" mentioned earlier is always interrupted or blocked by one of numerous disruptive devices that are constantly at work in the poems. Lévy has analyzed the ways in which the poems of *Cornet* constitute dice throws, each of which is designed to "become a mirror of the poet's astrological and physiological identity. Self-revelation is ultimately the name of the game" (*PT*, 39). But in fact nothing is revealed except for the mask, worn and discarded, in each poem. The poet is disguised as a beggar, a rag-picker, a sultan, an evangelist, Dostoevsky, Dante,

---

14. André Gide, *Journal 1889–1939* (Paris: Gallimard, 1948).

15. Benjamin's view of the aura is one of those suggestive but problematic notions that catch on because of their very vagueness. (A comparable example is Barthes' notion of "the zero degree of writing.") The aura was invented to distinguish between machine-made art, such as the camera, and the work of the painter or sculptor. But even here there are difficulties, since film may be considered the most auratic of all the arts. See Benjamin's "The Work of Art in the Age of Mechanical Reproduction," in *Illuminations*, ed. Hannah Arendt (New York: Schocken Books, 1969).

or Vergil—the list is endless. But there is no resolution, no closure. The poem ends with a blackout or a blur, transparency gives way to opacity. Jacob's concept of the subject reflects that passivity discussed in the previous chapter. He conveys this in one of his best-known epigrams: "The first result of the inner life is to make oneself permeable."[16] That is, the goal is to receive, to undergo, to be acted upon rather than to act. Permeability is associated with the transformation of thoughts into feelings: "They [ideas] cease being ideas if you . . . hold them with passion, with experience, if you transform them into feelings."[17] This brings us back to the dichotomy between Jacob's affective theory of poetry and the affective deficit of the actual poems. Affect has always appeared as the primary sign of the subject, the mark of personal identity; but it is lacking in Jacob, dispersed among the masks. In Jacob, textuality replaces subjectivity. Jacob was a secular exemplar of the *chachem*, the scholarly interpreter of sacred books. His *œuvre* shares the interminability of the talmudist who knows his commentary can have no end. One thinks of the work of Jacques Derrida, a veritable *talmid chachem*, who, with the esoteric versatility of a cabalist, has turned his vast learning to the reinterpretation of western literature. The *chachem* is a scholar with a lifelong passion for the written text, one who prizes *écriture* (writing) above *parole* (speech) and considers any text an inexhaustible labyrinth of meanings. Though he may have dazzling verbal gifts, as in the case of Derrida, he may not possess the ability to sing. He may not, in other words, be a poet in the lyrical tradition of Baudelaire or Apollinaire. Jacob could spin a seemingly endless linguistic combinatory, a kind of lexical prayer wheel, producing texts whose principal aim was the play of language itself. He expressed doubts about the validity of this kind of exercise in the *Conseils à un jeune poète*, written a few years before his death: "One might ask whether all poetry is nothing else but superficiality. My answer is 'Yes.' Too bad. But one can call on oneself to try something else. In any case, the only works that will survive are those that are not superficial, I mean those which,

16. Max Jacob, *Conseils à un jeune poète* (Paris: Gallimard, 1945), 16.
17. Ibid., 17.

having the appearance of superficiality, have passed through the abyss of the serious."[18] He seems to contradict himself, but in that contradiction lies his struggle to use his dazzling but narrow poetic gifts to achieve permeability, that is, to be the passive site where textuality is continually renewed. Lévy emphasizes this passive and definitionless subjectivity: "the poet is playing a passive role which negatives revelation. . . . It could therefore be stated that even if Max Jacob managed to play the game, to throw the dice successfully, the result would invariably be negative because they were not intentionally thrown; instead, they fall by chance, and are thus unable to reveal anything to him concerning his search" (*PT*, 35–36). Mallarmé is one of the great precursors of modernism and there is an interesting contrast between his *Un Coup de dés* and Jacob's *Le Cornet à dés*. Jacob wrote Jacques Doucet that he chose the title for his collection of prose poems "because of the diversity of their appearances and the random aspect [*côté hasardeux*] of the collection."[19] The modernist metaphysic of chance that underlies Mallarmé's masterpiece is absent. Jacob offers minimal resistance to chance, while Mallarmé thematizes it and incorporates it into the texture of his work. Mallarmé defines himself against chance. Jacob risks himself with each role of the dice. There can be no monumentality in such a practice; instead, Jacob explores the detail—exotic, linguistic, phonetic.

Emphasis on details rather than the whole is another feature of postmodernism. The work is no longer organic but becomes encyclopedic. Instead of development in an analogy with the living organism, we have the accumulation of details. This is reinforced by the fragmented narratives that traverse the work. Although the Christian narrative dominates in Jacob's *œuvre*, it is continually inverted and subverted by stories from other narrative sources—cabalistic, oriental, mythological, and so on.

18. Ibid., 16.
19. Max had this to say about Mallarmé in a letter to Jacques Doucet: "I profoundly admire Mallarmé, not for his lyricism, but for the 'divinely geographic situation' of his work. I understand by the situation of a work that species of magic which separates a work (whether pictorial or musical) from the amateur, that species of transplantation which allows the work to put you into another universe" (*VMJ*, 108).

Underlying them is the hidden subtext of Jacob's own personal story, with its accumulation of grievances, its flight into abjection and loss of self. But, as might be expected, that story of loss involves a paradoxical fulfillment. This will be discussed in Chapter 9 in terms of the transformation of eros and the true attainment of permeability.

I want to conclude this discussion of Jacob's postmodernism with a further study of the modernist theme of truth and its postmodern counterpart, delusion. Lévy has made the issue of "efficient communication" a crux of his study of Jacob. He examines in detail how that communication is disrupted, overturned, and undermined in *Le Cornet à dés*. Concluding an analysis of the prose poem "Conte de Noël" ("Christmas Story"), he asks why the character who figures in this poem, an architect (or maybe a horse), cannot construct the cathedral of Cologne in Philadelphia. Lévy writes: "The reason for this failure, as I shall attempt to demonstrate, is also a matter of repetition—not the repetition of meaning in different forms, as in translation; but, because we are dealing with artistic *forms* (a cathedral), the repetition of forms, of signifiers" (*PT*, 102). The architect is also a horse (*cheval*) for two reasons, the first being the repetition of the "ch" sound in both words. The second reason is that he is supposed to be able to transport a form from one place to another—the cathedral of Cologne to Philadelphia. If the architect were able to function as a horse, that is, to transport the form of the cathedral from one city to another, it would constitute a case of logical predication. "This cathedral is the exact copy of the one in Cologne" is equivalent to the proposition "A is B" that underlies all truth statements. Predication is necessary both for truth statements (Lévy's "efficient communication") and for personal identity. Lévy finds both types of predicative disruption in the Fantomas poem, where the transformations of Fantomas as doorknocker, Buddha, gorilla, sailor, and so on, match the transformations of the subject/predicate relation. Lévy writes: "Max Jacob's Fantomas is a modern hero: a pure, self-generating form, undetermined by any content whatsoever" (*PT*, 111).

Fantomas is thus part of a line of empty "heroes" that in-

cludes the impotent *architecte / cheval*. Fantomas evaporates and
the architect fails in his mental effort of translation. Translation,
defined by Lévy as "the simple, efficacious, and satisfying
passage between two points," is the process on which communication is based (*PT*, 121). The poem "fails" as efficient communication not only because the architect fails in his grandiose
(i.e., delusional) project, but also formally and phonetically,
because it disrupts its own discursive structure. Its "failure," of
course, is intended. There is a continual and systematic introduction of elements that Lévy identifies as "'subjective' interference," elements that seem to come from sources extraneous
to the poem's immediate context. Lévy calls these elements
"subjective" because they refer to the poet's self-masking and
"the predicament of the poet trapped by his inability to com-
municate" (*PT*, 41). The signifying chain does not compress in a
rush to resolution but, rather, stretches out, marked by what
Lévy calls an "in-between," precisely that "*entre deux*" that I
spoke of in respect to Camus, who was, like Jacob, a transitional
figure and a forerunner of postmodernism. Lévy writes:

> This "in-between" was identified by different names, each suited
> to the discussion at hand: in speaking of his life, I referred to
> "marginality"; I spoke of "front" when attempting to situate his
> texts; "obstacles," "windows," and mirrors were used in a dis-
> cussion of the relations between that poetry and the world;
> "mask," "riddle," "parody," "diversion" were the terms adopted
> to discuss the poet's relation to his text and to the reader; and,
> finally, "channel of communication" was used in the context of
> translation. (*PT*, 121)

Lévy then insists on the blocking or interference that occurs
each time a transition is attempted across the in-between,
through the channel of communication. Predication, the basis of
logical discourse, cannot occur; instead, there is static, a seeming breakdown in communication, which is itself a different
kind of communication. One that calls attention to the marginal
rather than the central, the contingent rather than the necessary,
the detail rather than the whole.

It is possible to look at these figments (details, margins,
accidents, masks) as phantomatic or delusive. Each dice throw

of words calls them up within the process of logical predication, causing it to swerve unpredictably from the generation of truth statements to a different order of expression akin to dreams, apparitions, hallucinations, or delusions. They are empty visions of hyperreality, densely refracted simulacra pulled from the cultural stream. This is pastiche precisely in the manner defined by Fredric Jameson as typifying postmodernism, pastiche of styles, pastiche of all the artifacts of culture. Max Jacob sampled many categories of simulacra, but in the end it was Roman Catholic ritual and mythology that served best to mobilize his imagination.

Catholic iconography appears everywhere in his work, deployed in a way that is absolutely distinctive. Although he used François de Sales and Ignatius of Loyola as the basis for the meditations he worked on daily in the last years of his life, the poetry itself differs from any other known devotional poetry. It is a postmodern devotional poetry, where the content seems almost irrelevant to stylistic pastiche and the play of language. We can distinguish several distinct genres here. There are the classical devotional meditations, addressed directly to God or one of his surrogates. There are confessional and penitential works. And there is a third class of prose poems that, while combining elements of devotion and confession, are essentially philosophical reflections. *Derniers Poèmes en vers et en prose* includes fifteen such works, which are among the best the poet ever wrote. The presence of pastiche is a constant, as in the Sandian title of "Confession à la mare ou la mare au diable et l'autre" ("Confession to the Pond or the Devil's Pond and the other") or, more subtly, in the echo of Verlaine in "La Terre" ("The Earth"). Verlaine's "Colloque sentimental" ends with the famous line "Et la nuit seule entendit leurs paroles" (And only the night heard their words). In Jacob's poem this becomes: "Et l'arbre et l'église et la Loire n'entendirent dans l'ouate que ces paroles ce jour-là" (And the tree and the church and the Loire heard in the padding that day only those words).[20]

---

20. *Derniers Poèmes en vers et en prose*, 94. All further references are given in the text as *DP*.

These texts can be seen as dealing, in one way or another, with the struggle against delusion. In each poem the struggle is articulated thematically, sometimes explicitly, as in "Mystique" which begins with these lines:

> Un, homme perdu au milieu des arbres.
> Avait-il l'esprit dérangé? (*DP*, 73)
>
> [A man lost among the trees
> Was his mind deranged?]

The mystic may appear crazy to others, but his craziness is the search for truth. The truth/delusion dialectic then develops within the tensions and play of language.

"Taie Divine" ("Divine Leucoma") is based on a conceit. The corneal cloudiness, known medically as leucoma, would normally be a threat to vision, but here physical blindness is invoked as antidote to the blindness of sin:

> Tache blanche sur l'univers
> tache qui descend en la poitrine
> et qui descend tous les matins
> jusqu'à la croix des intestins!
> Dans la grande horreur de ma vie
> fais reculer la myrrhe noir
> toute l'ancienne comédie
> le jargon des monts
> des démons
> et leur lugubre fantaisie. (*DP*, 71–72)
>
> [White spot on the universe
> spot which descends into the chest
> and which descends every morning
> into the cross of the intestines!
> In the great horror of my life
> make the black myrrh recede
> all the oldtime comedy
> the mountain jargon
> of the demons
> and their lugubrious fantasy.]

"Taie" (the "white spot") means pillow-case as well as leucoma and its association with morning evokes the poet's awakening to early-morning depression (the great horror of my life). This pillow-case, cloud, leucoma moves into the poet's body, which is crucified by constipation and / or self-loathing. It becomes the divine cloud, preceding Moses, as he calls on it to roll back the Red Sea, which is equated with the myrrh offered to the infant Jesus but also used to anoint the dead. No doubt the latter meaning prevails, since it is "la myrrhe noire." Generally in Jacob "the old comedy" means his Montmartre years and the turbulent period of the School of Paris. The word "monts" suggests Montmartre but also supports a pun, "le jargon des monts" (the demonic / demented jargon); this too the divine pillow-case must dispel.

The theme of "noirceurs" (blacknesses) expelled by the white spot continues with various transforms: the spot become the milky interior of an oyster-shell, a window, and then, antithetically, a brine or marinade perhaps associated with embalming fluid:

> voilà le miracle où j'en suis
> depuis Vous-moi et depuis
> moi-Vous, ma grande ambition célestique
> depuis moi mort que l'on exhume
> un horizontal présenté, reçu? mal reçu? expulsé?
> Il entrera dans la nacrure?
> il restera dans la Saumure
> où le crocodile s'alimente . . .

> [there's the miracle where I am
> since Your-self and since
> me-You, my great celestial ambition
> since me death that they exhume
> self horizontally presented, received? badly received? expelled?
> will he enter the pearly gates?
> he'll rest in the Brine
> where the crocodile feeds . . .]

For all its apparent seriality, the poem neatly recapitulates Jacob's conversion, the automobile accident that sent him to the hospital, and the fear of death that haunted him from that time on. His fear translates into anguish about God's judgment on his life and his exhumation / translation into the afterlife. When the "horizontal" cadaver is presented, how will he be received? Will he enter into pearly paradise or be sent instead to a swampy brine to feed the crocodile "in the sulphur and its vapors"? The poem concludes with these lines:

> Ce que tu fais, ce que tu dis
> te fais masquer le Paradis.
>
> [What you do, what you say
> makes you mask over Paradise.]

The white spot is evoked to blot over his life, past and present, which is delusively masking him from spiritual truth. The luminescent spot functions as a matricial image that is transformed by various interferences as the poem develops. It can be argued that these interferences are heterogeneous and unrelated—bodily discomfort, Montmartre, crocodiles, and the Styx. But thematic unity can be reclaimed in the interplay between vision and blindness or, to return to our central issue, delusion and awakening. This is an early-morning poem, a poem about waking up and the various forms of obscurantism that impede true moral or spiritual awakening. Jacob recognizes the karmic impediments to vision, notably the burden of his bodily ills and his past life that impede the effort to see clearly. Hence it is better to see "through a glass darkly," through a milky cloud, until he can, as St. Paul puts it, know (God) even as he is known.

Over the years I came to view Max Jacob as a mentor and spiritual guide even though we had never met. Friendship was the dominant theme of his life, and I reasoned that I deserved a place among all those who had tried to promote his work, commiserate with his hardships, or learn the secrets of poetry from him. That friendship was cemented at UCLA on the very day that I taught my first graduate course on the poet. The goal of the course was to present Max Jacob as a pre-postmodern poet. After the first session, I checked my mailbox and found a letter from—Max! There was no accompanying note, but the envelope was postmarked Lausanne. The letter had originally been sent to Roger Lannes on October 4, 1938. In it Max thanked Lannes for a poem, adding, "*tu est le premier d'une nouvelle lignée de poètes, inventeur de miroirs multipliés, signes purs d'absence, comme je suis fier d'avoir eu le privilege de te diviner. . . ."* (you are the first of a new lineage of poets, inventor of multiplied mirrors, pure signs of absence, how proud I am to have had the privilege of divining you. . . .). This was the new school he dreamed of founding, which has become that no longer arcane thing called "postmodernism." It has proliferated into every corner of contemporary culture so that (like the diaphanous Max himself) we no longer even know it is there!

CHAPTER 9

Eros and Devotion

The solution of Plotinus is transparency. . . . "Like those diamonds filled with the same water, whose every gleam is nourished by fires which reflect against other facets, so that the same infinitely repeated light is only defined by those fires but yet can never be explained. . . ."

Camus, *Christian Metaphysic and Neoplatonism*

I glimpsed something, for an instant, of the reality behind sex. Something which we reach out toward, as we take the human body in our arms. It is what we really want, and it eludes us in the very act of possession.

Christopher Isherwood

TWICE during 1949 I read *L'Homme de cristal*, the book that Jean Denoël had given me. Published in 1946, it brought together fifty-two poems that Max had been working on at the end of his life. Written over a period of about ten years, the poems form a combinatory in which themes are adumbrated, disappear, and return. At the time of my first reading, I was still powerfully influenced by Camus and not attuned to Max's phantasmagoric imagination. But I was able to identity the theme of eroticism and its apparent counter-theme of religious devotion. As I've said, I had an instinct for devotion, which is more than the passivity-abjection discussed in Chapter 6; it is also and more importantly the path of love that the mystics talk about and which most of us experience in bits and pieces during the course of our lives. Love for a parent or children; for husband, wife, lover; even the sublimity of desert, cliffs, and sea to which Camus was so sensitive. This impulse, so the mystics say, can be directed toward the person of God. Their incredible message is that earthly love is only the shadow of something immense, locked in our unconscious and our dreams. Because the erotic side of life is so easily available we need guidance to learn that it can be a path to the divine. This was the message of Plato and many spiritual teachers before and since. I perceived this in a confused way on reading *L'Homme de cristal*. In this chapter, I want to focus on that book, using it as a kind of mandala or meditative device for exploring my own effort to move from eros to devotion.

Numerous color lithographs enrich the text of *L'Homme de cristal*. They are related, whether directly or implicitly, to the book's thematic combinatory. There is a portrait of Verlaine (that emblem of pious debauchery) in monk's habit on which it is noted "Often he fell asleep." There is a naked man surrounded by animals in a prehistoric forest. There is a Pegasus, and there is the high-priest, Caiaphas, ripping his clothes in rage.

My second close reading left me confused as to how the book fused its two antithetical themes—spiritual aspiration and erotic love. The one organizing principle I detected was a hidden narrative beneath the dense intricacies of the text. I remembered Denoël's allusion to Jacob's last unhappy love affair, with a young poet named René, who ridiculed the older man and hastened his final return to Saint-Benoît. At that point I began to see the illustrations as more than simple instances of Jacobean themes. They present images of the hidden narrative: the sylvan aspiration to naked innocence; Verlaine, with his failed efforts to rise from degradation; Pegasus, symbol of flight; Caiaphas, the ugly face of worldly self-interest.

The fact that the book is about unrequited love becomes

apparent in the second poem. Titled "Phèdre," it consists of a long monologue spoken by the unhappy princess:

> Ton sourire, Hippolyte, est une guillotine . . .
> Tu presses le bouton avec des joies câlines.
> Suis-je morte ou vivante? J'accueillerai la mort
> entre les mains d'un dieu que je désire encore. (11)

> [Your smile, Hippolyte, is a guillotine. . . .
> You press the button with tender joys.
> Am I dead or alive? I will welcome death
> between the hands of a god whom I still desire.]

Phèdre's suffering becomes delirious and, in a lascivious torrent of images, she imagines herself shot, crucified, assaulted by the desires of many men:

> Sur cette joie opiniâtrement belle
> des hommes affamés ont posé leur bouche;
> de nouveaux hommes ont vu rouge
> d'autres hommes encore ont vu rouge sur elle . . . (12)

> [On that stubbornly beautiful joy
> hungry men have fixed their mouth;
> newcomers saw lipstick where
> still other angry men saw blood. . . .]

She laments that Christ can do nothing to appease her pain. This appears anachronistic, till we realize that Phèdre is a feminized Jacob, screaming his jealousy and loss. This is the hysterical side of Max, both deluded princess and abused child. The classical allusions disguise the anguish of unresolved desire. In Max Jacob as in Proust, sex is the matrix of identity. This theme, which will be reinvented by Michel Foucault, moves sexuality out of the realm of pleasure. The sexual becomes the ground of our struggle to go into a forbidden zone, what Foucault (following Heidegger) called "being beyond being." How that zone is defined sharply differentiates Jacob from the Heideggerean, Foucault.

The central motive of Max's book—erotic transformation—

is initiated in the Phèdre poem. It will take many forms as
L'Homme de cristal unfolds. In the poem's ending, jealousy leads
to a Proustian equation of love with delusion:

> Oui, je souffre en dormant car je me transfigure
> en un nouvel amour qu'à l'aube j'inaugure. (15)

> [Yes, I suffer asleep for I transfigure myself
> into a new love that I inaugurate at dawn.

This could be a threat: I'll get even by taking a new lover. Or,
more in keeping with the orientation of the book, it could be the
promise of a new spiritual love to be attained by inventing a
new poetic language.

This new love and its language involve a duality, defined by
the book's oxymoronic title "the man of crystal." The dictionary
tells us that crystal is: "a solidified form of a substance in which
the atoms or molecules are arranged in a definite repeating
pattern so that the external shape of a particle or mass of the
substance is made up of plane faces in a symmetrical arrangement."[1] But a man is protoplasm, which, again according to
Webster's, is "a semifluid, viscous, translucent colloid, the essential matter of all animal and plant cells: it consists largely of
water, proteins, lipoids, carbohydrates, and inorganic salts."
This paradox of a "crystalline man" defines the book's problematic.[2] Sexuality is a matter of protoplasm. Spirituality, as Max
first envisages it in the title poem, seems to involve the grotesque transformation of a cellular, watery human being into

1. *Webster's New Twentieth Century Dictionary Unabridged* (Collins World,
1975).
2. According to Carl G. Jung, the self is often represented in dreams as a
stone. He writes: "In many dreams the nuclear center, the Self, also appears as
a crystal. The mathematically precise arrangement of a crystal evokes in us the
intuitive feeling that even in so-called 'dead' matter there is a spiritual order-
ing principle at work. Thus the crystal often symbolically stands for the union
of extreme opposites—of matter and spirit." *Man and His Symbols* (Garden
City, N.Y.: Doubleday, 1964), 209. I am arguing here that Jacob attempted to
create a crystalline self and failed, because it could not accommodate his
sexual reality.

one who physically incorporates the "plane" surfaces of Catholic doctrine into his own body:

> Au pilori le Christ est dans mes hanches
> La Vierge enfant métope de mon front
> Onze disciples veillent en mes côtes blanches. (9)

> [On the pillory Christ is in my loins
> The Virgin child is the metope of my forehead
> Eleven disciples keep vigil in my white ribs.]

This assertion of literal incorporation restates the doctrine of the Corpus Mysticum: all communicants are "members" of the Mystical Body of Christ. It may also be viewed as a poetic conceit, "an intricate or far-fetched metaphor, which functions, through arousing feelings of surprise, shock, or amusement. . . . The term 'conceit' is derived from the It. *concetto* (concept), and all types of conceit share an origin which is specifically intellectual rather than sensuous."[3] Max's use of conceit involves other typical features associated with the figure, notably shock, the yoking of opposites, wit, and paradox. The conceit is thematically justified by the fact that incorporation into the Mystical Body is a phantasm, a wish, not a reality. (Even in Catholic theology there are grounds for seeing it as a construct rather than a statement about reality.) This wished incorporation draws strength from the poet's physical suffering. But it also foreshadows the books deeper theme, which is the poet's impulse to fuse his personal story with the Christian metanarrative. All this conceded, we are still left with the image of a man who wants to annihilate his sexual, protoplasmic reality through the assimilation of Christian doctrine. This is self-mutilation, not a new language of love; but, at least for me, it reveals how an authentic spiritual life can begin in neurosis, perhaps must begin that way. This coincided with my devious path toward greater insight, a path that involved my own

---

3. *Princeton Encyclopedia of Poetry and Poetics* (Princeton: Princeton University Press, 1974), 148.

misery and, alas, suffering inflicted on others, notably my then wife and companion, Jean.

The year was 1953, my Fulbright year in Italy, Perugia first at the Scuola per Stranieri, then Florence to study Italian poetry with Dante scholar Maria Sampoli and poet Vieri Nannetti. At the same time I was finishing my Ph.D. thesis on Jean Cocteau. The fatal meeting took place in Perugia. While pushing my daughter in her stroller over the cobblestones of the Corso Vannucci, I met a group of Smith College girls in Italy for a year of culture and fine art. It was 1948 all over again. Her name was Caroline, a charming undergraduate who hadn't planned to get involved with a married man, but it happened. After our second meeting, I was head over heels in love with my beautiful blonde imago. This was mortal sin country, but I put my embryonic conscience on hold, using St. Augustine's impeccable dodge, "God, make me pure but not yet!" As luck would have it, Caroline was also going to Florence after her month at the Scuola per Stranieri. I knew she was living near the English cemetery where Keats is buried and spent many hours there, reading the tombstones and memorizing the poems of Eugenio Montale as I waited in vain for her to show up. We finally met one Sunday morning in the American Church and begin an on-again-off-again affair, clutching each other in the parks of Florence till the cold drove us into carriages and doorways. It was all romantic, uncomfortable, and doomed. She would break things off; then I would pursue her, and we would start all over again.

In April I traveled to the French Riviera to interview Jean Cocteau. I was writing my Ph.D. thesis on his theater and wanted to test out my ideas in a discussion with the great man himself. Cocteau was president of the Cannes Film Festival and invited me to meet him at the Hotel Carlton where the bigshots congregated and made their deals. As I walked along the Croisette, phosphorescent whitecaps licked at the gravel below, and a steady wind rattled and snapped the palm fronds overhead. I felt well prepared for the interview. Not only did I have a list of questions, but I had read every word Cocteau had written. I entered the hotel where great filmmakers, beautiful women, bankers, and industry pimps sat around the lobby. Cocteau met me in the bar. He was charming, especially when lit up with a couple of martinis. I will never forget entering the dining-room alongside him, a platoon of waiters and maître d's in frontal assault, a hundred heads turning to focus on the favorite of the evening. We were given an alcove table and Cocteau ordered for both of us, *"Un petit loup de mer? Des pommes rissolées? Pour dessert un soufflé au chocolat?"* I got down to business, firing off questions about his work; then we went to a screening; and the next evening, met again. This time, as dinner was ending, I asked him about his friendship with Max Jacob. Especially, the little-known aspect of Max's love life. It seems to have been very secretive, I suggested, concealing the fact that I knew about Cocteau's own involvement with the poet.

"The secret is that there is no secret. Max was unlucky in his love affairs, always getting involved with people who didn't give a damn about him. The exception was Henri Sauguet, a wonderful composer. They lived together in the Hôtel Nollet, but how they fought! They had a famous fistfight on the Place Clichy, not exactly secret. Sauguet was the best of the lot, but there were others who came and went.

"With all that, he was the most secretive of men. Almost too modest for somebody with his desires. Max dreamed of chastity, and he was always punishing himself because he could never attain it. Even at the end, in St. Benoît, there was some trouble, a grocer boy with whom he had a flirtation. . . . *Et toi?"* he asked with a half-smile, "are you one of us?"

When I said that I wasn't, Cocteau lost interest. We went to see a bucolic Russian film about tractors and overblown peasants that put Cocteau to sleep, while I went out to catch the night train for Marseilles where I would spend several days with Jacques and Colette Hallez.

Not long after I returned to Florence from the Riviera, Jean found out about Caroline. There were scenes, I told her I wanted to separate. Her response was an attempted suicide. Half a bottle of cognac, superficial cuts on the wrists; her despair was as real as it was theatrical. Suddenly acts had consequences. My wonderful romance was somebody else's nightmare. The fact that I wasn't emotionally ready for marriage or that Jean and I weren't right for each other was irrelevant. I had assumed responsibility for a wife and child and had to give them the support they needed. To hurt people you care for is the worst muddle you can get into; you get lost in a maze of recriminations against them, the innocent victims, and yourself; and it is not long before you start to spiral down into hell, the real one, where the fake images of self that you have invented start to come unglued. The mind churns, night dreads and sweats grip you, but you can't let go of the very delusions that have put you in hell—who you are, what you need, what you want from others. Pascal saw it in his own dark night of the soul, "*Le moi est haïssable.*"

During my Fulbright year to some extent and, much more intensely, during the three years of psychoanalysis that began when I returned to New Haven, Max Jacob was a companion, his work a mirror of my efforts to transform disordered sexuality into something finer—a happy and uncomplicated relationship would have been nice. I began to realize that it is next to impossible to skip the intermediary steps, *brûler les étapes* as the French say, between normal loving and devotion. If you try to, you are kidding yourself. You'll remain in a frozen molecular state, a man of crystal. If love for God is possible, you have to begin by unfreezing your psyche, loving whatever life puts in your path: easy to say, hard to do.

L'Homme de Cristal

First Stage

The initial poem, "L'Homme de cristal," deals with the transformation of the "vieil homme," that is, natural or sinful man, into "the man of crystal" who would be Christ. The pillory where the poet hangs is both figurative and literal: the deep, almost paranoid sense of being the butt of public humiliation and the harsh reality of the life he had led and continued to lead—

impoverished, depressed, physically fragile since the 1920 accident and a second accident in Brittany some years later, until in old age, his stigmatization as an object of hate and derision by the Jew's yellow star. The concentrationary experience was not far off; indeed, it is foreseen with hallucinatory precision in one of the final poems appropriately titled "Death":

> Je sens tout le froid de la Terre,
> Où sont mes pères et grand'mères
> Et cet homme étendu: c'est moi. (161)

> [I feel the intense cold of the Earth,
> Where are my fathers and grandmothers
> And that man stretched rigid: it's me.]

The book progresses via a double thematic: physical suffering in all its forms, identification with the Mystical Body of Christ. But in the beginning Christ is viewed through the distorting image of crystal: not a Man of Sorrows but a man of symmetrical planes. Obviously, this is not the necessary reconciliation.

Second or Middle Stage: Part One

There is a spiraling inward movement by which the book / mandala charts the progress of inner change.[4] It is both a symbolic map and a representation of the poet's body. At the start of the journey through the mandala maze, the protoplasmic body appears hideous and disgusting. His nude flesh is a "gangrene" (33), his life "a slow agony" (50), his face a "death mask" (53), his life a living purgatory of hunger, fatigue, nausea, and depression (70). The awareness of the self as biologically broken is the starting point of the mandala. Through it he must follow the erotic principle's ever-changing forms, until he reaches the center and a promised awakening. Jacob's mandala, though

---

4. "A Mandala consists of a series of concentric forms, suggestive of a passage between different dimensions. In its essence, it pertains not only to

expressed in words rather than visual form, contains many of the classical biological and mineral forms found in traditional ideograms.[5]

Progress through the maze first involves the attempt to change bodily images into mineral forms, to become a "man of crystal." He writes: "Mes émerveillements me changent en comète!" (My wonderments change me into a comet!) (11). There is constant tension between mineral and organic imagery, usually with a return to the falsely imagined crystalline body of Christ.

Second or Middle Stage: Part Two

The transformative impulse may take the form of explicit statement:

> Ce qui s'est brisé
> à travers les luths, ce qui s'est fané
> mon front lauré, c'est Aphrodité. (24)

> [What is broken
> among the lutes, what is faded
> my laureled brow, is Aphrodite.]

---

the earth but to the macrocosm and microcosm, the largest structural processes as well as the smallest. It is the gatepost between the two. . . . To Westerners, the popular reintroduction of the Mandala concept can be specifically traced to the work of Carl G. Jung, who rediscovered the Mandala as a basic structural device in the alchemical tradition of the West, and as a therapeutic, integrative art form created by patients in their own search for individuation." José and Miriam Argüelles, *Mandala* (Berkeley, Calif.: Shambhala, 1972), 12–13. Note also this observation: "In the Tibetan yogic rite of Non-Ego, the change of attitude is symbolized by an offering of the Mandala conceived as the yogin's own body" (126).

5. Jacob had an eclectic knowledge of esoterica, and there are scattered references to Asian thought in his work. Although he probably knew little of yoga and the mandalic tradition, there is something universal here that he grasped intuitively. Again from Argüelles: "The primitive Mandala was doubtless a circle drawn upon the ground. Stepping forth from that circle, the initiate moved through a world of magic in which he was but a tongue of the earth chanting her song to the stars." Ibid., 127.

Here, poetry and Eros are equated. Max abandons both, with (as the refrain suggests) only the faint hope that there may be an alternative:

> Au fond du miroir reluisant
> y eut-il une fleur plus douce?
>
> [Deep in the glittering mirror
> was there a sweeter flower?]

The earlier poems in the volume (e.g., "Phèdre") suggest that the obstacle to transformation is "sin," a heavily weighted word in Max's vocabulary. Its principle connotation was sexual; yet he knew this was a misreading of his moral condition. His real sin wasn't anything he did or didn't do but his sense of unworthiness, the abjection discussed in Chapter 6. This was his biggest flaw, the ultimate self-indulgence. Authentic religion teaches that you must love the god in yourself before you can love any other version of godhead. If you can't love yourself, how can you love others, how can you love God? The aspiration to be a "man of crystal" amounted to the desire to be something other than what he was. To become crystalline would mean to abandon humanity. But Christ was not crystal, he was human. The crystalline man of the title (summed up by Camus' reading of the diamondlike Plotinus) is a transitional figure. He represents the midpoint of the ascetic process, not the end.

Third and Final Stage

The end is not to be a man of crystal. Rather, it is what Max called solubility: "tant est soluble ma pauvre âme / tant soluble et friable . . ." (so soluble then is my poor soul / so soluble and crumbly. . . .) (*DP*, 78). To be soluble or permeable to Christ, through the incorporation of the Eucharist (the body of Christ), is Max's ultimate aspiration.

This then is the process that the book narrates, though with many detours: from organic (i.e. protoplasmic) materiality to crystallinity and then to a deepened humanity, via the Cross,

until the dissolution of the body in the permeability of death/
salvation.

I was crystalline, full of hard unresolved edges that spring in
Italy, caught between guilt and high romance. I stopped seeing
Caroline and tried to make life bearable again for Jean. Much of
my Ph.D. thesis was written. In June we packed up our ménage
and took the train to Paris where we moved into a small apartment on the Rue Blanche lent by my psychiatrist friend, Alain
Giabicani. It was a small cramped place in a high walk-up. We
were kept awake much of the night by music from the Casino de
Paris, half a block away, which opened its roof for ventilation on
summer evenings. All the sensuality and lust of *Paris canaille*
poured out of that roof. The squalling brasses, the drums, the
tempestuous applause for the girls strutting naked on the *piste*
trumpeted the easy sex that would never be mine, puritanical
dreamer of orgies, whose brief Italian romance had driven a
young wife to despair. I had no perspective on myself or on
Jean, whose embittered moodiness reached a crescendo during
those final weeks. I loved this Pigalle neighborhood with its
prostitutes and *boîtes de nuit*, but it terrified Jean, already traumatized by what she had gone through in Florence. I seemed a
monster in her eyes, instead of a twenty-seven-year-old Jewish
romantic with a few problems. After we returned to the States,
we separated. Jean took Noelle and moved to New York for a
year. Jean took up her work as a painter and I drove down from
New Haven every two weeks to visit them. There was a reconciliation and some good years ahead in Los Angeles. Our son
Daniel was born there. He and Noelle (and later Alicia) would
give Jean and me all the joys of parenting, even if we had little
joy left in our marriage.

The years just before and during our L.A. sojourn and for
some time afterward were professionally productive but also
deeply troubled. From 1953 onward, I ate, drank, and slept
delusion, loving and being loved badly. Yet always I knew there
had to be something better than this, some way to love that was
not fraught with anxiety. I read the mystics, recalling the line
from Dante, "of your loves guard for God the highest"; and
toward the end of this period, I went back to *L'Homme de cristal*.

Toward Devotion

In the poem "Eternel Gazon de nos têtes" ("Eternal Lawn of Our
Heads") there is an identification with the natural cosmos that
indicates Max knew he was an innocent, that he was as lovable
as the God to whom he speaks in the first line:

> "Je suis l'ordre immobile, le miracle c'est vous!"
> Calice! dans mes côtes et poussons le verrou!
> Le monde est humecté, Dieu valétudinaire,
> de votre exhalaison que votre mort libère.
> En descendant la chair et le sang de l'Espirt
> dans la sphère cerclée par les dix infinis
> vous avez métamorphosé la créature
> la pâte du cosmos, ce bouillon de culture. (47)

> ["I am the immobile order, you are the miracle!"
> Calyx! in my ribs and shut the bolt!
> The world is moistened, valetudinary God,
> by your breath that your death set free.
> By sending down the flesh and the blood of the Spirit
> into the sphere circled by the ten infinities
> you have metamorphosed creation
> this dough of the cosmos, this culture medium.]

The astrological overtones here ("the ten infinities") emphasize
his sense of oneness, his incorporation into the cosmos redeemed by "the flesh and blood of the Spirit." He is made up of
cosmic dough, destined for redemption; the green grass that
will grow over his head (another premonition of death) is a sign
of eternity. The sense of innocence and the realization that his
sexuality is only a part of nature come slowly, with many
countermovements in the pulsating dynamic of the book. One
of these is the witches' sabbath, brilliantly captured in a poem
that recalls Victor Hugo's famous "Les Djinns":

> Pardon la nuit en Bretagne
> Et de noir! et de noir! et de rose
> ce qui s'échappe: les chevaux
> et de gris: un Dieu gris.
> A la fête nocturne, l'échevau
> des gens noirs des glacis . . . (40)

[Night Pardon in Brittany
And black! and black! and rose
Which unrolls: the horses
and gray: a gray God.
At the nighttime fest the spindle
Of folks glazed with black. . . .]

Like "Les Djinns," Max's poem ends with emptiness, everything wiped out. The sea destroys the land, just as history
erodes Breton folk rituals. Max had emphasized the importance
of Breton ritual and superstition in his early religious development. It both attracted and repelled him. In its negative aspect it
represented the shadowy part of his psyche, the part that he
wanted to make crystalline. It becomes clear that Max's un-
reconciled sexuality was emblematic of cultural and familial
influences, parts of himself that are continually mourned and
celebrated even as he tries to work out his impossible destiny.

In the poem "Mort d'une chimère," he develops the paradox
of the man who loves his sin and regrets its passing. His sin, his
chimera, is Pegasus, killed by the weapon of a friend ("un
cheval mort avant hier / et de la lance d'un ami" (a horse dead
day before yesterday / and by a friend's lance). In the first
stanza, the poet, virtually a dead man, searches for what he has
lost:

Il est sorti d'une voiture
un monsieur porteur d'un trésor
ce trésor qu'est une blessure.
Qui penserait que c'est un mort?
Mort! que cherches-tu vers la terre?
Le cadavre de ma chimère. (29)

[There came out of a carriage
a gentleman carrying a treasure
this treasure that is a wound.
Who would think that he is dead?
Dead man! what are you looking for on the ground?
The corpse of my chimera.]

The depressive initial stanza sounds a note often heard during
Max's last years. It is where he begins, with the sense of sinful-

ness. Sin has a solidified quality—a dead horse! The poet is bewildered, interrogated by an offstage voice, cop or angel: "What are you looking for on the ground?"[6]

Slowly, painfully the poet rises out of his depression by building a rhetorical energy as language itself energizes the process of transformation. The intricate pattern of assonances (ure, eur, or, avre, ère) provides a bass line. The "trésor/blessure" (treasure/wound) assonance-antithesis initiates the redemptive theme: You carry this treasure like a burden, it weighs you down. But it is also the salvific wound. In the second stanza he temporizes, indulging his nostalgia:

> O mes chimères, votre endurance
> fut mon trapèze et mon tremplin
> vous m'aviez montré l'espérance
> d'être plus fort que mon destin.
>
> (O my chimeras, your endurance
> was my trapeze and my trampoline
> you had shown me the hope
> of being stronger than my destiny.]

Then he mourns the loss of Pegasus, dead from the (phallic) thrust of a friend's lance. But the mourning is undercut by a series of seemingly frivolous puns:

> Oui Pégase était mon enseigne
> cheval de course et favori
> ou bien pélican ou bien cygne
> fanion pour bersaglieri.
>
> [Yes Pegasus was my emblem
> racehorse and favorite
> or either pelican or swan
> pennant for the bersaglieri.]

He mocks his chimera, Pegasus but also pelican and swan, a flag

---

6. An echo of words spoken to the disciples, looking in astonishment at Christ's empty tomb. So in Luke (23, 24): "and as they were frightened and bowed their faces to the ground, the men [angels] said to them: 'Why do you seek the living among the dead?'"

for Italian sharpshooters. Then, in a sustained development of
twelve lines, he evokes his long cohabitation with Pegasus:

> Nous avions survolé des côtes
> des châteaux, des bois, des villages
> des océans et des pinacles . . . (30)

> [We overflew the coasts
> the chateaux, the woods, the villages
> the oceans and the peaks . . .]

But death has overtaken the disconsolate chimera. No more will
the poet/Bellerophon soar on the wings of sexual excitement
and release. His sex life is a cadaver. Every older man mourns
his youthful sexuality, though he may also concede, as Socrates
remarked, that it was a burden from which he was glad to be
relieved. In the poem's conclusion comes just such a hint of
absolution and release:

> Rien ne m'est plus. Ma guerre est close.
> Sur mes erreurs passe le vent.
> En deuil mes parterres de roses.
> Mon aube est devenue couchant.

> [Nothing counts for me anymore. My war is done.
> The wind passes over my errors.
> My beds of roses are in mourning.
> My dawn has become sunset.]

Sin then equals solidity, materiality, the compulsion to repeat.
Anchored in the body, it partakes both of the innocence and the
immutability of the material order. But materiality can be transformed. This "cushion of painful love" can burst like a pus-
filled blister (101). Change occurs through language, here the
language of Christian mysticism. Max's poetic language is dynamic and unstable. Its unpredictability makes it a powerful
instrument of change. Eros (with its connotation of materiality
and sinfulness) is transformed through a linguistic dynamic
focused on the crucifixion and the poet's incarnation in the
body of Christ. Returning constantly to this theme, the man of
crystal becomes soluble man, the man who bleeds.

There are several crucifixions and Ways of the Cross in
L'Homme de cristal. There are trees that weep, there is the Holy
Face, and numerous other icons of the suffering Christ. There is a
poem on the Holy Sepulcher, there are angelic congregations. All
are examples of poetic work by which the language and doc-
trines of Catholicism are re-energized through the play of language. This process of revitalization was undertaken, at least in
part, in view of Max's tireless mission to convert his friends. But
its principle goal is self-transformation. I want to illustrate this by
comparing two poems, the first of which, though entitled "L'Amour
enterré" ("Buried Love"), contains a long erotic passage:

> Moi patient sous le fouet de solitude amère
> je me dévêts de l'eau de ton amour, puits caché!
> De ta petite oreille, j'oublie les longs secrets,
> ton sourire d'enfantelet, l'éphèmere
> qu'on n'ose pas baiser, les paupières
> aveuglées par mes lèvres, sources claires du destin
> froides chaudes comme la lune en juin:
> imperturbable oubli! Vers un autre penchée
> de la même douceur pour le trouble d'un autre
> tu naîtras le matin pour un nouveau péché
> altérée des lèvres salées d'un homme.
> Ton miroir est signé par moi et tu le donnes
> tu me quittes avant que ne me quitte la vie. (76)

> [I patient under the whip of bitter solitude
> Divest myself of the water of your love, hidden well!
> I forget the long secrets of your little ear,
> your childish smile, ephemeral
> that I daren't kiss, your eyelids
> blinded by my lips, clear springs of destiny
> cold hot like the moon in June:
> imperturbable forgetfulness! Toward another bent
> with the same sweetness for the arousal of another
> you'll be born again tomorrow for a new sin
> slaked by the salty lips of a man.
> Your mirror is signed by me and you give it away
> you abandon me before life leaves me.]

Crystal or soluble, Max remained a sexual being, as jealously
devoted to the ear or the eyelids of his faithless lover as any

Renaissance writer of blazons. The poem is admirably modu-
lated, suggesting the classic alexandrine rhythm, though its
lines are of uneven length. It recalls Ronsard's "Quand vous
serez bien vieille" and many poems by Petrarch or Scève. In this
volume, it serves to anchor the sexual theme. It documents the
poet's humanity, the ordinariness of his suffering. And it contrasts with the powerfully transformative rhetoric of "Nouveau
Baptême" ("New Baptism"):

> Ton nom est "A Jamais!" ton oreille
> du bruit de l'univers entendra la coquille.
> Vont mourir à Tes pieds, ô Seigneur Jésus-Christ,
> l'écume des prières, l'écume de l'esprit.
> Pôle des longtitudes dont le rail est la foi
> ai-je aperçu Ta sphère et l'oeuf triple du toit?
> Foudre esperée bien loin des horizons du monde,
> à peine si je crois ta grâce correspondre
> à ma chaleur d'enfer, bâton sec et coupé!
> Dans l'ennui de mes nuits et la nuit de mes jours
> tu remettrais à flot mon antique chaloupe.
> Sous le clair embellé de ta lune d'amour
> je me celais moi-même à l'immense aquarium
> où vivent les démons les anges et les hommes.
> Ma barque était à l'ombre et sous les nélombos
> dans les sommeils antiques, et pareille au tombeau,
> mais lorsque tu descends plafonnier des prophètes
> le sang coule de notre tendre chair en muette.
> Ton arc en ciel radium aux 100.000 couleurs
> charge la croix de terre sur de nouvelles têtes
> et change en volupté la passive douleur. (45–46)

> [Your name is "Forever!" your ear
> will hear in a shell the noise of the universe.
> At your feet come to die, O Lord Jesus-Christ,
> the foam of prayers, the foam of the spirit.
> Pole of longitudes whose rail is faith
> have I perceived Your sphere and the triple dome of its roof?
> Thunder wished faraway from the world's horizons,
> scarcely can I believe that your grace corresponds
> to my hellish heat, branch cut and dried!
> In the boredom of my nights and the night of my days
> you will refloat my antique sloop.

Under the brilliant clarity of your moon of love
I hid myself from the immense aquarium
where live demons and angels and men.
My boat was in shadow and under the nelombos
in ancient sleeps, and like a tomb,
but when you descend light of the prophets
blood from our tender flesh mutely flows.
Your radium rainbow of 100,000 colors
burdens new heads with the earthly cross
and changes passive suffering in sensual joy.]

Here we have the cosmic Christ about whom Teilhard de Chardin was meditating and writing at this same time. Christ, who listens to the world in a sea-shell, at whose feet mankind's prayers come to die like the endless repetition of the waves. The maritime motif, familiar to the Breton poet, swells into a kind of spiritual "Bateau ivre," as in the long anguish of his nights Christ sets him afloat upon the immense aquarium of existence. Embarked on this voyage through the sleep of history, he is awakened (in another Rimbaldian image) by the radioactive light of Christ that projects the cross of suffering on mankind. The last line is capital for any consideration of self-transformation in Max Jacob. Passive suffering, abjection, self-hatred, become positive, even voluptuous. Sexual eros becomes spiritualized, Agapé, to use the conventional term.[7] In the dark night of the body, abjection and passivity can be transformed. They may lead to an awakening.[8]

7. "Agape. (Gr. 'love'). The characteristic term used in the NT, especially in John's gospel, the letters of John and Paul, to designate the love of God (or Christ) for us and, derivatively, our love for God and one another." Gerald O'Collins, S.J., and Edward G. Farrugia, S.J., *A Concise Dictionary of Theology* (New York: Paulist Press, 1991), 7.

8. The intense effort to transform passivity appears in the dignity of André Schwartz-Bart's Ernie Lévy in *The Last of the Just* (New York: Atheneum, 1960). This hidden saint, whose moral rectitude keeps God's wrath at bay, stands outside the ovens, waiting his turn (372): " 'O God,' the Just man Ernie Lévy said to himself as bloody tears of pity streamed from his eyes again, 'O Lord, we went forth like this thousands of years ago. We walked across arid deserts and the blood-red Red Sea in a flood of salt, bitter tears. We are very old. We are still walking. Oh, let us arrive, finally!' " Awakening/arrival are always in the future.

Max was my traveling companion through that period of trouble. I saw how hard he worked at prayer. I saw how, as the dark night of history swept over France, he had used his own experience of suffering to assume that of his people. It was the only thing that released him from his self-absorption. Identification with the suffering of the Jews gave him a way to use his sense of sinfulness, his sense of failure. I would learn from him eventually that failure is the royal road to devotion.

Broken Narratives

CHAPTER 10

My Sister Simone

I see you, you know, even though it's dark, no way I can be wrong about it, you've really got the family mug, with that frizzy hair, growing every which way, and your poor nearsighted eyes and your glasses. All you lack is the beret, the family uniform.

Sylvie Weil

I LIVED at International House in a room overlooking the Hudson River while working on my Master's degree at Columbia. During the winter of 1951 I often walked past 549 Riverside Drive, the apartment building where Simone Weil had lived from July to November 1942. It was from Jacques Cabaud that I learned about Weil. Cabaud was collecting materials for his Ph.D. thesis which would become the first major biographical study of Weil, and he used me to test out his interpretations. The fact that I was a Jew with Catholic leanings made me a useful informant, although at first glance we appeared as very different people.

Weil was one of that special breed of French intellectuals who are trained at the Ecole Normale Supérieure, the most prestigious school in all of France. Yet in spite of her world-class training in mathematics, classics, and philosophy, she defined herself by direct involvement in the syndicalist movement, giving workers classes on Marxism, helping them organize their campaigns, becoming their spokesperson in confrontations with government and management. Known as "the Red virgin," she fought for the workers with such vehemence that her teaching career was threatened. She had a famous argument with Trotsky, when he was a guest in her family's home; he was amazed at her brilliance and ferocity. She behaved with a reckless courage that took her to the war in Spain, then later to the United States and London, where she joined the French government in exile. She struggled with all her might to convince the Free French authorities to let her parachute with a corps of nurses back into German occupied territory. She wrote only one complete book, is known mainly by her essays on disparate subjects, yet she became a luminous presence after her death in a France that was torn with dissension and had no sense of direction. Even Camus, that great moral figure, found inspiration in her life and work; and he was responsible for publishing everything she wrote from his editorial position at Gallimard. Weil was a wholly unique creature with a tragic destiny, but I found surprising affinities with her, as if we had come out of the same gene pool.

As his book demonstrates, Cabaud had grasped the fundamental truth of Weil's *œuvre*: that it was outside of all genres and represented an effort to reconcile conflicting narratives by an act of experiential synthesis. His position is stated in the Preface: "The thought of Simone Weil is nothing less than a drama of conscience of eminent quality and one which displays a striking continuity."[1] As we walked and talked on the streets around Columbia, Cabaud unfolded for me the dramatic quality of Weil's search for truth amid the conflicting narratives into which she was born and raised. Cabaud, who had once been a seminarian in France, would go on to teach philosophy at Fordham. But he did not fall into the trap of evaluating Weil's orthodoxy or attempting to resolve the ambiguities of her relationship to the Catholic Church. Rather, he wanted to place her in the context of French spiritual thought while exploring the

---

1. Jacques Cabaud, *L'Experience Vécue de Simone Weil* (Paris: Plon, 1957), 9.

marginality that gave unique value to her *expérience vécue*, her "lived experience."

I was flattered to be Cabaud's sounding-board and, with his help, began to grasp the complexities of Weil's thought. In the process, I was able to rethink some of the issues that had first drawn me to Camus and Jacob. She displayed the same intense aspiration toward morality—and the same deep confusion about what the moral good ought to be in her time, which she saw as one of "disarray, anxiety, expectation of who knows what, and where men imagine they have the painful privilege of being a generation with an exceptional destiny."[2] Both Camus and Weil tried to achieve their aims by working through the political order; then both withdrew, Camus into the art of memory and Weil, closer to Jacob, into a search for the god within.[3] As I was in the delirium of conversion, I was happy to encounter this Jewish woman who had loved Christ, though not the church that claimed to represent him. Along with her Christianity came her rejection of Judaism. There was a pathology here that I shared and that I knew one day I would have to explore. Weil was seen by her Jewish critics as a betrayer, which would have astonished her, yet there is a deep question here, which resonates in my own history. Ethnic loyalty is not an unmitigated good. There are no clear criteria, in this pluralist age, which fetishizes diversity, for judging how much loyalty is owed to race, tradition, and family. Maybe only one thing is clear, what Henri Bergson saw, when he reined in his leanings toward Christianity: the right to choose an affiliation gives way before the obligation to stand up with the victims. Weil stood up for many groups but not for the victims of Hitler's extermination machine. At some point, I would have to think through my complicity with Weil on this score.

Weil attracted me in another way. I was fascinated by her relationship to her body. Having begun to use psychoanalysis as a vehicle for literary theory, I saw Weil as an obvious subject.

---

2. Simone Weil, "Désarroi de notre temps," in *Œuvres completes, ecrits historiques et politiques*, vol. 3 (Paris: Gallimard, 1989), 93.

3. Camus' *Le premier homme* shows how even a childhood of deprivation may be rich in affective experience.

Her migraine headaches—like my own—had to be of genetic and psychosomatic origin. If I could understand her migraines, maybe it would help to relieve mine. I can remember my first migraine, which occurred when I was well into puberty. From the start I knew that this intense pain was somehow connected with sexuality turned away from the object of desire and back against the self.

As I will show in Chapter 11, Weil never really understood the mechanism that drove her migraines; but she knew everything about the pain. A central statement on migraine appears in her letter to war-invalid and poet Joë Bousquet:

> You say that I pay for my moral qualities by distrust of myself. But my attitude toward myself, which is not distrust but a mixture of contempt and hatred and repulsion, is to be explained on a lower level—on the level of biological mechanisms. For twelve years I have suffered from pain around the central point of the nervous system, the meeting-place of soul and body; this pain persists during sleep and has never stopped for a second.[4] For a period of ten years it was so great, and was accompanied by such exhaustion, that the effort of attention and intellectual work was usually almost as despairing as that of a condemned man the day before his execution; and often more so, for my efforts seemed completely sterile and without even any temporary result.[5]

I admired Weil's ability to work through pain but wanted to know more about that pain itself. Clearly it was not "biological" in character, since her father was a medical doctor and had often taken her to be examined by specialists to learn if her headaches were the result of a physical abnormality. Medical tests were negative, making it apparent that her headaches were psychosomatic in origin, but the point of origin was so deep, so early in

4. Given Weil's Cartesianism it can be assumed that she is refering here to the pineal gland or, more broadly, the head; the pain involved is migraine headache. It should be noted, however, that true vascular migraine seldom occurs on a daily basis. So-called "status migraine" is tension headache with other components, vascular, sinus, and so on. These and other views on migraine are drawn in part from Oliver Sacks, *Migraine: Evolution of a Common Disorder* (Berkeley: University of California Press, 1970).

5.Quoted in George A. In Panichas, ed., *The Siimone Weil Reader* (New York: David McKey, 1977), trans. Richard Reese, 90–91.

her development, that she was never able to work her way through it.[6] Here again was something that I shared with Weil, a profound physical *malaise*; and strangely, for both of us, this was connected to the religious turn. Weil offers a unique test case for the hypothesis that neurosis and sickness are a primary source of spiritual insight. It was the very quixotic and inexplicable character of Simone Weil—her migraines, her self-exile, her contradictions—that drew me to her in 1951 and continued as a bond between us later on when I went into analysis and began to explore my own complex corporeality.

The views put forward here represent the summary of a reflection that has gone on since February 3, 1951, when Jacques Cabaud first gave me *Waiting for God* and pointed out that Weil and I had the same birthday. Simone Weil is like my twin sister. I know her in certain way that I don't know my blood sister, Nancy. I know Weil's face, her body type, her anxieties, her changes of mood, her gaiety and depression. I understand her jokes, her passions, her likes and dislikes. I know all this because, in ways that took me years to unravel, we are mirror images of each other. As much affinity as I feel with Camus and Jacob, it is in Weil that I most see my own delusions, notably the humiliating, distracting, and confusing power of physical pain. She suggested this connection between pain and delusion in her letter to Bousquet:

> I believe that the root of evil, in everybody perhaps, but certainly in those whom affliction has touched and above all if the affliction is biological, is day-dreaming. It is the sole consolation, the unique resource of the afflicted; the one solace to help them bear the burden of time; and a very innocent one, besides being indispensable. So how could it be possible to renounce it? It has only one disadvantage, which is that it is unreal. To renounce it for the love of truth is really to abandon all one's possessions in a mad excess of love and to follow him who is the personification of Truth. And it is really to bear the cross; because time is the cross.[7]

---

6. The predisposition to migraine is genetic, but the migraine mechanism, once established, becomes a disease in its own right.

7. Quoted in Panichas, *Simone Weil Reader*, trans. Richard Rees, 90.

One way in which I imitated Weil was by working with the
poor. This led me to Friendship House in Harlem where I
worked off my missionary zeal. Following the trail of Thomas
Merton I made the trek to 135th Street and Lenox Avenue.
Along with the apartment on 135th Street there were several
storefronts which served as library, kitchen, and rec room.
Friendship House was a kind of soteriological zoo, peopled
by ex-seminarians, ex-nuns, ex-Catholic Workers, cut-ups and
would-be saints of all ages and descriptions. Most of them were
risk takers, people who lived against the grain of their time.
They did it not so much for ideological reasons but because they
were outsiders bearing social or psychological wounds. Black
people came and went, some shy young ones, some burnt-out
cases, some militants who made a game of provoking the biblical nutcases who had wandered into the fiery furnace of Harlem. As the crow flies, Harlem was only a short distance from
Columbia, but Morningside Park was a no-man's-land where it
was unsafe to go. I had to take the IRT subway south from
Columbia to 96th Street, change trains, and go north again to
125th. Every time I walked from the subway to 135th Street
I remembered a smoking city we'd scouted in Germany—
splendor changed into a battlefield. Harlem was full of ruins,
ghosts in the radio and traffic noise, eyes looking at you and
alien smells. What I liked best was the craziness of Friendship
House, always in an uproar with one crisis or another. We were
chronically broke and always running out of the food that was
distributed twice a day; but the place kept functioning, energized by a dynamic permanent staff and volunteers like myself,
who kept turning up out of the blue. This was my first taste of a
Catholic community, and I threw myself into it, singing Latin
hymns, jubilating in Weaver-style African or Israeli folksongs,
talking and jiving with the clients—the homeless, the mentally
ill, the outcast, the sick, the same kinds of people Simone Weil
had interacted with in the industrial slums where she usually
lived. There was a lot of spiritual energy swirling around,
coming from the few deep contemplatives whose mere presence could pull you up on to a cloud of prayer, but there were
also the god-clowns and some of us for whom devotion was a
turn-on. I was half in love with a pretty Irish-American girl,

who went on to become a nun; from her and others I heard stories of convents, seminaries, and monasteries, those nurseries of Catholic identity, places that fascinated and pulled me with a deep attraction. I started visiting monasteries myself that year, quiet places with intense undercurrents where you found, along with the stark beauty of plainchant, mania, paranoia, and love in every imaginable form. I brushed up against unknown saints, with the realization that there are a few people whose meditative power brings God down into human society and keeps us from self-destruction. I met a Jewish psychiatrist, known as Father Raphael, who was a member of a Trappist monastery in Rhode Island; for weeks after that, I was gripped by the desire to throw everything away and become like this puckish intellectual consumed with the love of God. It was his very reticence, his deprecating humor, his flashes of insight that showed the steel inside him, the utter drivenness that had made him what he was. I began to wonder if excessiveness didn't define the truly spiritual person, this sense of always going too far, always being beyond the pale. As a kid I had read a book called *The Way of the Transgressor*, and the word stuck with me even though the transgressions in question seemed mainly to involve getting some reluctant women into the sack. My Friendship House coworkers, at least the authentic ones, were risk takers for the most part, but some were authentic transgressors in the manner of Father Raphael. They were living against the dominant culture, doing things that other people considered futile or crazy, sometimes even dangerous. This could be catching. I remember one night when I decided to walk home through Morningside Park. It was no worse than some of the battlefields I had crossed. I put on the shield of faith, the armour of righteousness, and climbed through small groups of hostile kids, more interested in their drug deals than the crazy honky going past. After that I would often go out into the tenements, looking for people who had begun studying French with me, then dropped out after a few weeks. I wanted to give them self-esteem through French, my way of trying to save them. But sometimes in dark kitchens populated by roaches and babies I would look into the oppressiveness of their lives and feel dismay. Any tendency to patronize them dropped away and I felt the admiration mixed with anger Merton expresses: "No, there is not a Negro in the whole place who can fail to know, in the marrow of his own bones, that the white man's culture is not worth the jetsam in the Harlem River."[8] This was the same anger I recognized later in the writing of Simone Weil and Michel Foucault. It is what motivates the transgressor, the person who risks his life to change the social order. I didn't have it, although I recognized it; and I admired it in Simone Weil. It was during my Columbia year that I formed a bond with her, though it would take much longer before I could grasp the meaning of her work.

We had something else in common, love of that region of France called Languedoc. It was some twenty-two years later, as director of a Dartmouth foreign study program in Toulouse, that I read Weil on the Cathar civilization. These essays, which develop a myth of purity, were a revelation of the hidden meaning of Weil's life and of her vocation of pain. It was the spring of 1973 and I was in Toulouse, the rose-brick city that Weil herself had explored when she fled Nazi-occupied Paris. My first apartment here was on a street of small Arab-owned shops not far from the train station. Across the way a transvestite bar lit up and boomed far into the night. Returning late, I was accosted by drag queens wearing spangled blouses, high leather boots and beehive hair. Halfway across the city, in another proletarian quarter, was a church basement where every Tuesday night I joined a group of charismatic Catholics who spoke in tongues. Rushing through the rain along the glistening streets, I always had a book by Weil in my briefcase along with my class notes and texts.

It was in Toulouse that I discovered Weil's curious writings on the Cathars, a cult that, for her, embodied the impossible purity she dreamed of. My apartment on Rue Arnaud Bernard was a ten-minute walk from the Rue du Taur, where our classes met on the old university campus. At the end of that street was the great barrel-shaped church of Saint-Sernin, dating back to the early middle ages and the time of the Albigensian massa-

8. Thomas Merton, *The Seven-Storey Mountain* (New York: Harcourt, Brace, & World, 1948), 346.

cre.[9] In 1209 the Northern Barons, led by Simon de Montfort, set out for Languedoc, where they killed thousands of Cathars in the region around Toulouse. For a century the massacre went on, ending in the virtual extinction of the heresy and, not incidentally, the confiscation of vast amounts of land by the invaders. The Inquisition, aided by the brilliant preaching of the Dominican friars, also played its part. There is controversy over how many died. Some historians say the number is greatly exaggerated. But the believers, who frequent the esoteric bookstores on Rue du Taur today, insist that it was a true holocaust.

By mid-March I had became absorbed in the two articles on Catharism that Simone Weil had written for the *Cahiers du sud*, published in a special number on "Le Génie d'oc" in 1943. These were given to me by Bruno Tollon, our Art History Professor and a specialist on the Romanesque art of the region.

Weil's interest in the twelfth-century Cathar sect was an attempt to escape from the terrible realities of wartime France into what she most reproved, a dream. Weil judged daydreaming evil because it deflected from the pursuit of truth. For her revery was allied with her principal sin, laziness. This in turn was allied with the temptation to introspection. All three "sins" coalesced in her tendency to passivity and devotion. Against these, she brought to bear a formidable power of will in the pursuit of total wakefulness. Whenever she undertook a project, she worked incessantly, depriving herself of sleep as well as food for days at a time. Her biography is full of accounts of the continuing struggle to function, whether sitting with a migraine in front of a classroom or standing all day at a factory stamping-press with burnt hands and aching bones. She fought the tendency to revery yet was human enough to daydream in spite of herself. I find her reflections on Catharism to represent the most poignant example of this. Catharism was a world of delusion that offered escape from the realities of life—persecution, illness, and intellectual confusion. It appeared to offer her a way of recuperating justice in a world driven mad by the obsession with power. Twelfth-century Toulouse also pro-

9. The Cathars of southern France were known as "les Albigeois," because they were most numerous in and around the city of Albi.

vided her with a compelling image of *"l'enracinement,"* that deep involvement in a communal life which is both intellectually and spiritually fulfilling. This was something she had tasted at Solesmes during a weekend visit or during her work at harvest time in the vinyards of Provence. Since she could never recover it intact, she invented it in her revery on a lost civilization.

Weil's visit to Carcassonne during Easter 1942 was preceded in 1940 by her reading of Déodat Roché, an exponent of Catharism, to whom she wrote shortly thereafter, expressing her sympathy for a lost civilization: "Your studies have confirmed a thought of mine which I already had before reading them. It is that Catharism was in Europe the last living expression of pre-Roman antiquity."[10] Her interest in Catharism was motivated in part by negative factors, most notably her hatred for the Great Beast—institutional power as represented by ancient Israel, ancient Rome, and their continuator, the Catholic Church. She wrote to Roché: "The influence of the Old Testament and that of the Roman Empire, a tradition continued by the papacy, are in my opinion the two essential sources of the corruption of Christianity."[11] Though Weil's thought eventually took an anarchistic turn against all established order, she continued to view ancient Greece and its reincarnation in twelfth-century Languedoc as successful societies. Her evocation of Toulouse, through the epic fragment "Song of the Crusade against the Albigensians," has a joyous recognition about it, as if she were seeing her homeland from afar:

> The poet of Toulouse feels intensely the spiritual value of the threatened civilization; he dwells on it continually; but he seems impotent to express it and he always uses the same words: *Prix et Parage*, sometimes *Parage et Merci*. These words, which have no equivalents today, refer to chivalric virtues. Yet it is a city, it is Toulouse, that lives in the poem; it quivers with life, as a whole, and with no distinction of classes. The count does nothing without consulting the whole city, *'li cavalier el borgez e la cuminaltaz'*;

10. Letter to Déodat Roché in *The Simone Weil Reader*, ed. George A. Panichas, trans. Richard Rees, 83.
11. Ibid.

he gives no orders, he asks for its support; and this support is given by all—artisans, merchants, knights—with the same joyful and complete devotion. The army resisting the Crusaders is harangued before Muret by a member of the Capitol of Toulouse; and what these artisans and merchants, these town citizens—the word *bourgeois* is not applicable—were willing to save at the cost of their lives was Joy and *Parage*, was a chivalric civilization.[12]

This is Weil's gentle evocation of a lost Atlantis. Yet her idyllic essay on the Cathars never loses sight of their forced submission to the power of the King, a reality that traverses the dream: "Everything that is subjected to the contact of force is defiled, whatever the contact. To strike or to be struck is one and the same defilement. The chill of steel is equally mortal at the hilt and at the point. Whatever is exposed to the contact of force is liable to degradation. Everything in the world is exposed to the contact of force, with only one single exception, which is love" (*SE*, 49). This dream of purity coexists in the mind with its opposite, defilement by force, momentarily held in check. In what had been Languedoc, Weil discovered her own Golden Age, the Romanesque civilization that produced the troubadours and the poetry of courtly love. From the early twelfth century, the Cathars were an organized church with a hierarchy, a liturgy, and a system of doctrine. Catharism existed throughout Europe but assumed its most radical form in Italy and southern France, where it was an article of faith that Satan was not merely one of God's fallen angels but an independent deity who had created the material world. Hence, this world was evil, and the "perfect," who were separated from the ordinary "believers," pursued a life of extreme self-discipline and renunciation in order to attain communion with God.

Weil celebrated Catharism for what she saw, rightly or wrongly, as its spiritual freedom, its spirit of tolerance, and its purity, that is, its doctrine of sexual abstention. In an apparent reference to celibacy, a central theme of neo-Manicheism, she writes: "This country which embraced a doctrine so often stigmatized as anti-social was an incomparable example of order,

---

12. "A Medieval Epic Poem," in *Selected Essays by Simone Weil, 1934–1943*, trans. Richard Rees (London: Oxford University Press, 1962), 39. Hereafter *SE*.

freedom, and social harmony" (*SE*, 39). Sex had to be excluded from Weil's myth of happiness. Her obsession with purity, negatively grounded in an obscure childhood terror, was given a positive formulation in her philosophical work.[13] She wrote in an early essay for Alain: "The only force in this world is purity; anything that is unadulterated is a morsel of truth. No rich fabrics were ever equal in value to a beautiful diamond. . . . The only force and the only virtue is to refrain from acting."[14] Weil's Toulouse was a dream of community and order, untroubled by desire; so real was this dream that she never recognized it as delusive. For her it played a prelapsarian role, representing humanity before its long fall into Romanitas and, eventually, modernity with its attendant evils. Weil's dream is less sensual than Coleridge's Kubla Khan but more human than Plato's Republic, its immediate model: "The essence of the Languedocian inspiration is identical with that of the Greek inspiration." She interprets this to mean an understanding of "supernatural courage" and contempt for the use of force: "To understand force is to recognize that it is almost absolutely supreme in this world, and yet to reject it with loathing and contempt. This contempt is the other face of the compassion which goes out to everything that is exposed to the ravages of force" (*SE*, 48–49). "Compassion" provides a bridge to the theme of chivalrous love, which she identifies curiously with Platonic same-sex love. Her discussion here is blurred, pointing to a failure of experience. Weil's writing lacks any erotic edge. The circularity of her argument indicates a libidinal void in her thought and life:

> In Languedoc, chivalrous love was the same thing as Greek love, although this identity is masked by the very different role played by women. But it was not contempt for women that led the Greeks to honour love between men, which today is something base and vile. They equally honoured love between women, as is

13. André Weil told Simone Pétrement that his sister had been accosted by an exhibitionist in the Luxembourg Gardens, though he minimized the psychological repercussions.

14. Simone Pétrement, *Vie de Simone Weil*, I (1909–1934); II (1934–1943) (Paris: Arthème Fayard, 1973), I 81. Hereafter *VSWI, II*.

seen in Plato's *Banquet* and in the example of Sappho. What they were thus honouring was nothing other than impossible love. Consequently, it was nothing other than chastity. Owing to the too great license of manners, there was practically no obstacle to sexual indulgence between men and women, whereas every well-ordered soul was inhibited from contemplating an indulgence which the Greeks themselves qualified as unnatural. . . . The sacred tie of marriage was an obstacle equivalent to that provided by the identity of sex. The authentic troubadours had no more taste for adultery than Sappho and Socrates for vice; what they aspired to was impossible love. Today, we can only think of Platonic love in the form of chivalrous love; but indeed it is the same love. (*SE*, 49)

The passage is incoherent, moving between philosophy and sexual mores as if they were continuous. She claims that platonic homoeroticism (in the *Dialogues* or in Greek daily life?) is pure because it is sublimated to a transcendent goal, that is, the knowledge of being itself.[15] To this abstract and desexualized eros she analogizes the purity of "chivalrous love." Weil writes about sexuality as if it were some kind of pure essence, unconnected with real-life experience.

Weil's love affair with the Cathar civilization had to do equally with the beauty of its churches and its poetry and its doctrine of asexuality, which nourished her dream of a life free from desire—her own and that of others. With desire and the will to control the bodies of others comes the use of force, her ultimate evil. This was a theme of her teaching during her last job at the lycée of Saint-Quentin seventy miles north of Paris: "If it is true that society is founded only upon relations of force and if it is true that the soul is subjected to outside pressures,

---

15. Weil's attack on certain forms of homosexual behavior finds an echo in Foucault. He writes: "It would be completely inexact to see here [in the *Thesmophories* of Aristophanes] a condemnation of the love of boys or what we call in general homosexual relationships; but we must recognize here the effect of extremely negative judgments in respect to certain possible aspects of the relations between men, as well as a lively repugnance for anything which could mark a voluntary renunciation of the prestige and the symbols of the virile role." Michel Foucault, *L'Usage des plasisivs* (Paris: Gallimard, 1984), 26.

nothing is more injurious to man than society."[16] Desire seems
fatally linked with the rise of the Great Beast—Israel, Rome, the
Vatican. Catharism stood for the way things had been before the
advent of the Great Beast, the juggernaut, the power of the state,
and, ultimately, that French monarchy which allied with the
Vatican to crush the Cathars in 1209. Their annihilation was for
Weil an unconscious symbol of her own inner repressiveness,
the violence she did to her own body.

I was beginning to understand this twin sister. While I did
not have her obsession with purity, I shared the deep, organic
discomfort with which she inhabited her body. As I began to
work out why we had both experienced this strange destiny, I
saw that, quite unexpectedly, it had a bearing on something else
that we shared—alienation from our Jewish heritage.

16. Cabaud, *Simone Weil: A Fellowship in Love* (New York: Channel Press,
1964), 166.

CHAPTER 11

Living in a Jewish Body

You tremble, old carcass!

Attributed to General Turenne and to Simone
in her bath at age five

I am one of those *marranes* who no longer say they are
Jews even in the secret of their own hearts.

Jacques Derrida

I N this chapter I want to explore Jewish alienation, that loss of
group identity that occurs in all religions but is viewed
especially seriously in Judaism, where *shiva* is said for the
apostate and he is treated as one dead. There is a long tradition
of Jewish renegades, dissenters, and outlaws. I would like to
believe that I belong with the *talushim* (the dangling men)
described by David G. Roskies: "This leaves us with the characters who agonize so long and hard about their place in the world
that their confrontation with society, when such occurs, leads
nowhere. They are alienated urban intellectuals, perennial students who recently returned from some place in Switzerland, or
self-taught philosophers who mercilessly expose their own mo-
tives and those of others."[1] The *talushim* were tortured souls,

1. David G. Roskies, *Against the Apocalypse: Response to Catastrophe in Modern Jewish Culture,* (Cambridge: Harvard University Press, 1984), 143.

secular illuminati. Our family friend, Isaac Rabinowitz, who later became a famous scholar of Semitic languages, would tell me stories about them, desperately scribbling their incoherent griefs as their candles guttered and died in the night. Isaac was a magical storyteller, and I hung on his tales of tormented geniuses, searching for incandescent truths. Perhaps these stories helped motivate my career; but I was not sufficiently Jewish even to be a *talush*. My father and mother were embarrassed by my conversion, but there was no *shiva*. My favorite uncle called me "that little son of a bitch!" and left it at that. Later a flamboyant rabbi used my novel of conversion, *A Change of Gods*, as the proof text of his sermon at Shaar Emmeth temple, calling me a Nazi in the presence of many relatives and friends. A few walked out. My cousin, Nancy Shapiro, wrote a strong letter in defense of my novel, if not of what I had done.

What is this breaking off of the roots? Is it just lack of education, the fact that we had no appreciation of the Jewish heritage, which had never been presented to us as a thing of value? Given this omission, does our lack of Jewish commitment amount to a betrayal? To people such as Simone Weil or myself, self-alienation appears first as a liberation and then, only if we live long enough, a serious affliction. Even if you have found a substitute, as I did in the Catholic Church, you are left with a kind of phantom limb pain, the regret for lost possibilities of emotion and expression, shared Sabbaths, rituals of remembrance, rites of passage; as bad as anything there is a loss of connectedness with a powerful and resonant history, so that you can never be a whole person, having lost the organic connection with your racial past. You become a kind of ghost, like the man without a country in that story we all read in junior high school, the man who is never allowed to come home.

There are ways to explain self-alienation in the case of Simone Weil. There was that cosmopolitanism, so typical of assimilated European Jews; there was the disdain of those same successful Jews toward the masses coming in from eastern Europe, uneducated and unkempt, bringing their ancient and embarrassing superstitions. These assimilated Jews, of whom I was one, saw the beliefs of their correligionists as akin to the beliefs of those Christian masses who had persecuted them and driven them from one country to another in hideous pogroms. Thinking back now, I realize that the thing my father hated most about my conversion was that it appeared stupid, aligning me with the very superstitions that brought persecution on the Jewish people. It wasn't, so far as he was concerned, the disloyalty that mattered; it was aligning myself with the forces of darkness.

Judy has been my wife since December 12, 1979, when we were married by a probate judge in Lebanon, New Hampshire. She is beautiful, with a dancer's turned-out walk, and what I call the light touch. Although she is loving and devoted, she can cut through pretension and affectation (mine or anybody else's) with a word or simply a change in the color of her green eyes. There is a surgical quality about her wit. She uses it to pinpoint my delusions and get me back on course. Judy is my moral compass, giving me the depth of emotional insight and strength of purpose that I have searched for ever since those early years, when I encountered Camus and brooded over what it meant to take responsibility for one's life. Judy spent much of her childhood watching old films on television; so, despite the difference in our ages, we share the same iconography—the same comedy routines, songs, and narratives. Our life together is based on a shared popular culture; but, far more significantly, it depends on a communality of temperament and values. The affinities are passionate and go deeply into the texture of our daily lives— opinions, habits, entertainment, even food.

Judy knows my likes and dislikes. Recently, she brought home a chicken pot pie, a dish I despise, bringing back memories of dreary school cafeterias, food fights and mindless hubbub, always followed by boring afternoons courses that lasted till the best of the day was gone.

"Well, I love it, because it's the ultimate Christian food. I mean it's the essence of bland." Curious reasoning for the granddaughter of a rabbi. She explains, "Chicken pot pie has made me more tolerant, accepting, broadminded, and culturally diverse."

"You're just being a contrarian."

"Am I? What about you?" She gives me her tender, crooked smile. "You always wanted to be gentile—yet you love Jewish cooking! You would have made a good Jew, but you were never bar-mitzvahed, that was the fatal omission."

I shrug. "So instead of being a good Jew, I became a mediocre Catholic."

"You found a sense of belonging to a community when you joined the French Church. It must have been very seductive for a Jewish boy with no religious background to discover one of the great cultures of Europe. And it worked for you. Ultimately, you did find where you belonged."

"You think it was all just as simple as that? That I wanted to be gentile and so I became a Catholic?"

"Of course not! If you were going to make it simple, you wouldn't have become a Catholic. That remains your biggest unresolved dilemma."

I think back, trying to get at the core of a disaffection that seems rooted in me more strongly than the Jewishness that, Judy insists, is a basic fact about me, no matter what I call myself.

I never saw the power and beauty of Judaism, only the disadvantages. I would (I like to think) have loved G-D with all my being but found no percentage in being an ethnic Jew. It kept me on the outside, chasing the inaccessible blondes, fighting whenever I was called a kike. For my first junior high school year, in San Antonio, Texas, it meant being tormented by a gang of bullies, boys who liked me well enough but felt it their duty to beat up on the only resident Jew. In the morning, if I got to class early, they would hold me down on a hot radiator. In the afternoon's tackle football game they would say, "Let blue eyes carry the ball," because I was the best runner on the team. Like Simone Weil, I had no allegiance to Judaism, no sense of connection; instead, I had a longing to join the gentile world of art and culture, whose Jewish component I did not recognize. My father kept *Rememberance of Things Past* on his bookshelf. I asked who Proust was. "A Jewish writer," he said, which was enough to make me lose interest. This is the simple explanation, the obvious one. The other is more arcane, and it goes by the relay of Simone Weil.

She was born prematurely on February 3, 1909. When she was six months old, her mother developed appendicitis. Simone Pétrement writes: "From that time on [i.e., the start of her mother's illness], Simone did poorly and became difficult to raise. She used to joke later on about this early impairment, caused apparently by a change in her mother's milk due to illness. She complained with a smile of having been poisoned in her early infancy. 'It's because of that, she said, that I'm such a failure' " (VSW, I, 21). Simone was weaned at six months while gravely ill. There was no attempt made to find a wet-nurse, although the infant refused solid food. Feeble, receiving inadequate nourishment from her bottle, the infant's life was at risk. As Pétrement recorded: "Thus Simone was sick from the age of eleven months till twenty-two months, and there was little hope that she would become a normal child." At the age of two, she suffered from infected adenoids and, at three, had a life-threatening attack of appendicitis. It is worth noting that her first words, on waking after a night of fever, were: "Bad Mamam, bad." When her fever abated, she was operated on, but stayed in hospital for three weeks making a difficult recovery. From that time on, she feared doctors, had an exaggerated horror of germs, and conveyed a sense of physical awkwardness and malaise that are noted in the many descriptions of her by friends and acquaintances.

Commentators have noted another critical factor in Weil's development, rivalry with her brother. From the start, André was an outstanding student always at the head of his class. As a small girl Simone imitated her brother in everything, but, by age thirteen, despair at following his achievements set in. She writes of her feelings at that time: "I did not regret external successes, but rather that I would never be able to gain access to the transcendent realm where authentically great men alone may enter and where truth abides. I preferred to die rather than live without that" (VSW, I, 54). There is more than a trace of the grandiosity and melodrama (she speaks of suicide) that are not uncommon in teenagers; but Simone doubted profoundly her own abilities, especially when compared to those of her brother. Her physical ineptitude was reinforced by the competency of her brother.[2] Both as a clever boy and a mathematician, André

2. Pétrement comments on her lack of manual dexterity, especially obvious (and dangerous) during her year of factory work. Friends who tried to dance with her, even those worker comrades with whom she was most at ease,

easily attained mastery over things and dealt easily with concepts. He seemed destined to enter Plato's realm of pure ideas, which she, the true Platonist, could never enter. Though ironically, she may have secretly reaffirmed her Platonism through the relay of an eating disorder, representing an overwhelming desire to escape from her body.[3]

Weil's mother (née Salomea Reinherz, she changed her name to Selma but was often known by the nickname "Mime") was an admirable woman, doing everything possible to protect her reckless accident-prone child. Mime always did so discreetly, showing great sensitivity and respect for her daughter's fierce independence of spirit. The numerous letters that the two exchanged over the years are proof of their mutual devotion. There is much negotiating in these letters: Simone asking to be authorized to miss a vacation, to take a trip; Mime offering to bring food, to find lodgings in a new town. When Simone went to the Spanish War in 1936, her parents followed and provided medical attention for her injuries. These were admirable parents, a close and nurturing family, but Simone suffered from a psychic wound that was nobody's fault. Like the wound of the Greek archer, Philoktetes, it was the price of her intellectual and moral achievement.[4]

Pétrement has documented the playful side of Simone Weil, the child who giggled and played practical jokes, the normal young girl who became a dedicated student, striving to maintain her place in the cohort at Henri IV and the Ecole Normale. But this was also the girl who disguised her beauty and felt a horror of physical contact, even though she longed for tender-

---

commented on her clumsiness and her despairing complaint, "I don't know how, I don't know how" (*VSW*, I, 377).

3. Susan Bordo writes: "Anorexia is not a philosophical attitude; it is a debilitating affliction. Yet quite often a highly conscious and articulate scheme of images and associations—one could go so far as to call it a metaphysics—is presented by these women. The scheme is strikingly Augustinian, with evocations of Plato." "Anorexia Nervosa: Psychopathology as the Crystallization of Culture," in *Feminism and Foucault*, eds. Irene Diamond and Lee Quincy (Boston: Northwestern University Press, 1988), 94.

4. Pétrement quotes Mme Weil: "How much I would have preferred for her to be happy!" (*VSW*, I, 20)

ness and affection.[5] She found femininity a handicap and gave it up, preferring the flat shoes and mannish suits typical of the "revolutionary intelligensia."[6] Around 1934, after a failed attempt to console a jilted friend, she wrote in her notebook: "Definitely give up the idea that X can be anything more than a shallow friend for you; he belongs, he condemns himself to belong, to the realm of shadows. You have no power to bring him out of the cave—even though you may try, but using what words? In any case, you must forbid yourself to wish it. And further, you must avoid if possible such whole-hearted attachment as you felt for S.G., and without real and fully reciprocal friendship. Those things belong to adolescence. Learn to be alone, if only to be worthy of true friendship." (*VSW*, II, 16). The internal obstacles to any kind of sexual experience appear to have been insurmountable.[7] In her emotional solitude, Weil was impelled to pursue that "purity" that she increasingly saw as her moral and spiritual calling. She had always been a cryptic Cathar. That imaginary kingdom of Albi was the only place she felt comfortable, the place where body and soul could cohabit with a kind of peace.

It is not uncommon for an extraordinary vocation to begin in neurosis. Proust shows how emotional illness can be transformed into art. Weil transformed the horror of her own sexuality into a mystical vocation based on purity. But as her sexual

5. "Simone did not like to be touched; she preferred not to be kissed." This "dégoutation" even included her mother. One of her friends wrote of her: "She had a desperate desire for tenderness, for communion, for friendship, and what she desired so deeply she did not always find" (*VSW*, I, 50, 58).

6. Other explanations for the assexual appearance come to mind, notably the association with eating disorders. One reference among many: "The identification, however, is not exaggeratedly masculine; it would be better to say that a narcissistic, sexless existence is seen as providing a refuge from feminine, genital sexuality." Thoma quoted in Angelyn Spignesi, *Starving Women: A Psychology of Anorexia Nervosa* (Dallas: Spring Publication, 1983), 15.

7. Bordo shows that anorexia and fear of sex are connected. After referring to several cases she concludes: "the desire to appear unattractive to men is connected to anxiety and guilt over earlier sexual abuse. Whether or not such episodes are common to many cases of anorexia, 'the avoidance of any sexual encounter, a shrinking from all bodily contact,' according to Bruch, is characteristic." "Anorexia Nervosa" (96).

feelings were repressed and transformed, Weil paid a heavy price in psychic suffering. One of the gaps in the literature of mysticism is precisely the cost of repression. We perceive this cost in the anxieties, the headaches, the doubts, and rages of Simone Weil. Due to the early illnesses that affected both mother and daughter, irreparable damage was done to Simone's psychic organization. This damage involved the infant's self-image and the perception of herself as a functioning being in the world. Here it is worth quoting William Willeford:

> The mother–infant relationship gives the infant experiences of receptivity and mutuality that remain important in the later development of the individual and in cultural life, partly because the mutuality of that relationship reflects the self-balancing tendencies of the self, thus making them incarnate and giving them specific character, in personal lived experience. Within the mother–infant dyad, both mother and infant mediate experience of both ego and self for one another. The receptivity developed through such early experiences may assume a more active form in feeling and imagination as interrelated processes of the ego, processes that are also unconscious and ego-transcending. Such felt and imaginative active receptivity may figure valuably in the relations of the ego to the world of community and to the deeper regions of the psyche, as these relations reflect the workings of the self, often in ways that have emotional concomitants needing to be read.[8]

The give and take of release and control, of mastery and surrender that characterize all interactions between self and world are learned in the intimacy of the mother–child relationship. When one looks at Simone Weil it is precisely this self-balancing performed by the ego that seems lacking, while there is a

8. William Willeford, *Feeling, Imagination, and the Self: Transformations of the Mother–Infant Relationship* (Evanston, Ill.: Northwestern University Press, 1987), 16. Further support of this view is found in a recent article by Elaine Showalter. She writes: French feminist theorists maintained that hysteria was a female language with a 'privileged relation to the maternal body.' . . . "'Hysterical' discourse is thus connected to the pre-Oedipal phase of feminine development in which the baby daughter takes the mother as her primary object of desire. . . ." Elaine Showalter, "On Hysterical Narrative," *Narratives*, I(1) (Jan. 1993): 28.

fundamental distortion in the relation of her ego to the world. Significantly, she attached importance to the search for balance, as if aware that she had not found it: "The secret of the human condition is that there is no equilibrium between man and the surrounding forces of nature, which infinitely exceed him when in inaction; there is only equilibrium in action by which man recreates his own life through work."[9] She idealized the Greeks who possessed the sense of balance that she lacked: "This is the idea expressed in their notion of harmony, of proportion, which is the centre of all their thought, all their art, all their science, and of their whole conception of life."[10] There was a fundamental imbalance in Weil that can be related to the nutritive trauma of her early years. Her avidity for nourishment, that is, for equilibrium with the outside world, was frustrated in infancy and became transposed from the physical to the mental domain. She was driven by cravings that took first an intellectual, then a political, and, eventually, a mystical form. Her object-relations narrative turns on her damaged relation to her mother and, inevitably, her own body.

Pétrement quotes a letter, written by Simone to her mother in spring of 1934: "I had a strange dream this morning. I dreamed that you told me: 'I love you too much, I can't love anybody else.' And it was terribly painful" (*VSW*, I, 409). In the daughter's dream, she is the object of her mother's exclusive love, that love she was deprived of at the age of six months by Mime's illness. The "Bad Maman" of her infancy survives in her unconscious, barring the way to a plenitude that she herself has rejected. The archaic wish for a nurturing mother becomes an intolerable burden in the present. The impulse to appease and console her mother is "terribly painful."[11] Simone as adult cannot accept the mothering that the infant in her still desires,

9. "The Mysticism of Work," Quoted in Siân Miles, ed., *Simone Weil: An Anthology*, trans. Emma Craufurd (New York: Weidenfield & Nicholson, 1986), 158.

10. Quoted in Richard Rees, ed., *Selected Essays, 1934–1943, by Simone Weil*, trans. Richard Reese (London: Oxford University Press, 1962), 46. All further references in the text are given as *SE*.

11. It is common for women who suffer from eating disorders to feel responsible for their mothers' physical and emotional well-being. See Spignesi, *Starving Women*, 41.

because she has had in place for many years an infantile strategy to cope with her mother's "rejection." Under certain circumstances, the child appropriates what she perceives as "mistreatment" in order to negate the worst feature of this treatment,
namely, the fact that she suffers it passively.[12] The child then
goes on actively to seek out that suffering which, in the beginning, had been imposed on her as an infant.

Weil's "joke" about being poisoned by her mother's milk
recalls a similar topos in Proust that has been analyzed by Serge
Doubrovsky. We recall that the Narrator, after a miserable
winter's day, returns home and, "contrary to his habit," accepts
his mother's offer of a cup of tea. We know from other passages
that he despises tea, which makes him ill and which he views as
a veritable poison, yet, on this occasion, he accepts the tea
together with a madeleine. The rest, of course, is literary history:
the dipping of the madeleine, the momentary euphoria that is
lost, recaptured, lost again, and then by an effort of will transformed into the lengthy second evocation of childhood in Com-
bray. The Narrator misperceives his mother's concern as an
attempt to poison him with food but consumes the food nonetheless. Doubrovsky analyses this as a cannibalistic act, in
which the Narrator eats his mother and excretes her as Com-
bray. The interpretation focuses attention on the way in which
the individual uses the nutritive act and his own body to
achieve mastery over the mother, his beloved enemy.

Doubrovksy's adventurous analysis of Proust has the merit
of being based on several exemplary texts, while there is no
single textual basis for a comparable analysis of Simone Weil.
Yet an overall view of her work does reveal features that sub-
stantiate this approach. There is, as Robert Coles has noted, a
recurrent thematics of hunger, feeding, and drinking throughout all her writings. There is also a long speculation throughout
these writings on the topics of will, mastery, and effective
action. The theme of mastery is in a condition of binary opposition with contrasting themes of renunciation, abjection, suffering, and "decreation." This opposition symbolically reinstates

12. Edmund Bergler coined the term "psychic masochism" to describe this
strategy that was originally identified by Freud.

the mother–infant struggle for balance that, as we have seen, was tilted to Simone's detriment in the direction of abjection and revolt. An analysis of the emotional tone of her work also supports this hypothesis: that it involves a tension between opposing impulses toward mastery and abjection. Here, abjection takes the form of a disbelief in her own reality, accounting for her indifference to death. If she was not really alive, she couldn't die.

It is risky to put diagnostic labels on a genius such as Weil, but the label helps to identify a symptomatic matrix, which in this case is hysteria. Weil was probably suffering from hysteria with headaches as the conversion feature.[13] Hysteria is considered an "old-fashioned" condition today, but Weil was in many ways an old-fashioned girl. Her prototype is no doubt Freud's Jewish princess, Dora, but also Mallarmé's fictional princess, Hérodiade. Both were fiercely virginal mental warriors. Both Hérodiade and Simone Weil (together with Proust's narrator) demonstrate the principal features of hysteria. Hysteria is based in infantile trauma, it involves gender confusion, fantasy, and sexual panic, and it is accompanied by some type of physical or conversion feature. As the hysteric's anxiety becomes engraved in the body, the body becomes a relay for responding to external threat, for example, threat of sexual contact with others. Eventually, the hysteric uses her body to negotiate with or symbolically control the external world. This is relatively easy in childhood when, for example, the child's threat of tears (Proust) or refusal to eat (Weil) can compel its parents to change their behavior; but in adulthood, the strategy no longer works.

Infantile Traumas Real and Imaginary

Judy shakes her head. "You've got to be joking! I just went to Isaac's *bris*. He cried for a minute, then he was fine. I don't even think there was any real discomfort."

I assume a pained look. "Easy for you to say."

---

13. Freud considered the so-called "hysterogenic zones" to be libidinally cathected.

"Now, after all these years, you're still traumatized by your circumcision? Look, it was the price you paid to be one of us, the chosen people."

I rush into my study, come back with a handful of papers. "A 'small price to pay'?" Listen to one of our greatest scholars, Maimonedes. He admits that circumcision was instituted:

> to bring about a decrease in sexual intercourse and a weakening of the organ in question, so that the activity be diminished and the organ be in as quiet a state as possible. . . . The bodily pain caused to that member is the real purpose of circumcision. None of the activities necessary for the preservation of the individual is harmed thereby, nor is procreation rendered impossible, but violent concupiscence and lust that goes beyond what is needed are diminished. . . . For if at birth this member has been made to bleed and has had its covering taken away from it, it must indubitably be weakened.[14]

I look up to see what kind of effect this reading has produced. Judy is pragmatic. She lives in the real world and is not given to argument on theoretical questions. "Well, if you want to obsess over something you can't do anything about. . . ."

"It's a crime, Judy!" I shuffle more papers, come up with a quotation from Derrida. "'the presumed crime I am calling circumcision and the role of the mother in circumcision. . . .'"

"So now you want to blame your mother because you're a neurotic Jew?" Judy grins, "Give me a break!"

"I'm not blaming her, but I think that circumcision can be devastating to an infant. If a mother is nurturing, the harm can be overcome, but my mother was too overpowering, too intrusive."

I used to watch her with my kids, leaning over the bed kissing and tickling them, stimulating and pouring emotion into them; and I understood why, at the age of seven or eight, I withdrew from her.

As explanatory myth, this bizarre hypothesis fits the circumstances and gives me a sense of closure on an old puzzle. One

14. Quoted in David Biale, *Eros and the Jews* (New York: Basic Books, 1992), 91.

last piece of evidence: my mother tells me that, after the *bris*, which took place in the hospital, she heard a baby crying. "That's my baby," she told the nurse, "he's hurting! Bring him to me or I'll go get him!" When they unwrapped me, I was still bleeding.

Our psychic narratives, mine and Simone's, are similar and then diverge, since circumcision was not her problem. But the narratives converge again on a second theme, racial exile. Alienation from mother, from our bodies, from our birth people, the Jews. There are many reasons for Simone's failure (like my own) to feel a connection with the Jewish people, not just the peasants of eastern Europe but the assimilated Jews of Paris and Amsterdam and Prague as the Nazi machine closed in on them, as the Final Solution was put into effect, the roundups, the death trains, the ovens. Thomas R. Nevin, who has given a complete and balanced account of this issue, identifies Weil with those middle-class nonobservant Jews who had heeded the calls to assimilation, thinking falsely it would put an end to anti-Semitism.[15] As the Dreyfus Affair, the success of Drumont's book *La France juive,* and the Action Française movement all show, anti-Semitism remained a permanent and virulent strain in French culture. But none of this adequately explains the unheeding, inconsiderate, and reckless character of Weil's denial of her Jewish heritage; and that is why we have to go back to the theme of the body, this frail, wounded, vulnerable body with which she was always out of touch. One has only to think of her needless death. As is well known, she died from tuberculosis in a sanitarium in Ashford, Kent, in 1943 after being forcibly

15. Nevin surveys postwar Jewish critiques of Weil, including those by Buber, Rabi, Mandel, Lévinas, and Améry, who censure her ignorance of Judaism and her Judeophobia. He summarizes, "In a profound and lasting sense Weil's story is part of the family tragedy of European Jewry. The issue goes far deeper than her outlandish and rebarbative words on the Torah. Her ignorance of Judaism, partly circumstantial, partly willful, reflects the horror many Jews have had to face and internalize when assimilation into a 'Christian' culture becomes limited and complete integration is made impossible." Thomas R. Nevin, *Simone Weil: Portrait of a Self-Exciled Jew* (Chapel Hill: University of North Carolina Press, 1991), 258–59. Hereafter *SW*.

removed from a London hospital where she insisted on restricting her food intake to the ration allotted to people in occupied France. There was no available antibiotic at that time and her condition was aggravated by her refusal to take nourishment. In Kent she became even more intransigent. Cabaud writes: "The painful struggle about her food began all over again. This time, she refused all nourishment. The English doctor tried to compel her to eat. Revolted and exhausted, she murmured, in a state of semi-consciousness, that she wanted to share the suffering of the French, that she could not eat.[16] Finally the doctor gave in, and the order to feed her by force was rescinded. Her meals were brought to her as usual, but the food was untouched when the nurse came to remove the tray. . . ." On her death certificate the physician wrote: "Cardiac failure due to myocardial degeneration of the heart muscles due to starvation and pulmonary tuberculosis. The deceased did kill and slay herself by refusing to eat whilst the balance of her mind was disturbed."[17] A variation on the classical "anorexie hystérique" is the eating disorder that has been called pseudo-anorexia: "The pseudo anorexia nervosa patients . . . are chiefly concerned 'with the eating function', which they use 'in various symbolic ways'; that is, by their eating behaviour they seek to manipulate others and gain their ends."[18] Weil's repeated statements about her "powerlessness" are, precisely, a means to opt out of this

16. "France" was merely a pretext for some obscure psychological process. The following may have relevance: "Thoma holds this symbiotic bond [between mother and child] responsible for the anorexic's autarchy and freedom from anxiety in the phase of the deathly starvation, since it can be seen as an 'unconscious union with the imaginary picture of the beloved person. The patients live as though they were still unconsciously united to a nursing mother.' This union with the mother's presence, he sees, leads to the patients' claims with 'delusional insistence that they were *their own providers*, and thus were not dependent on actual food supplies.'" Spignesi, *Starving Women*, 40. It can be argued that Weil was victim of an unconscious double bind, remaining linked to and separated from the nurturing / poisoning mother of her infancy.

17. Cabaud, *Simone Weil: A Fellowship in Love* (New York: Channel Press, 1964), 348.

18. Peter Dally, Joan Gomez, and A. J. Isaacs, *Anorexia Nervosa* (London: Heineman, 1979), 7. Rather than classifying Weil as suffering from anorexia nervosa, Robert Coles prefers to state simply that she suffered from an eating disorder. *Simone Weil: A Modern Pilgrimage* (Reading, Mass.: Addison-Wesley, 1987).

vicious circle of hysterical behavior. They are related to Jung's observation that the hysteric repeats endlessly, "I don't know why, I don't know!" If she has no power over the world, then she has no need to respond to it by the manipulation of her body or emotions.

At the end she chose a frightening form of quietism, yet one that is not unknown in certain countries such as India where voluntary and involuntary starvation are common. (Weil read various Hindu texts and was especially attached to the Gita.) The starvation narrative is another fragment in that collection of broken fables to which her life gives a semblance of unity.

It was after I had spoken to Juliet Mitchell and read an extract from her work in progress that I gained a new insight into Weil's hysteria, one that also applies to Michel Foucualt, who is considered in Chapter 13. The hysterical symptom has a cognitive as well as a somatic dimension. The cognitive dimension (in reality a refusal of cognition) lies in the hysteric's refusal or inability to acknowledge the reality of death.[19] In the course of her mission to the Partisans during the Spanish Civil War, Weil observed that she was never afraid. When bombs were first dropped on her patrol and she fired up at the planes, she comments: "Wasn't at all scared" (*VSW*, II, 99). She offered herself for a suicide mission, to locate a friend who had disappeared behind the Franquist lines. The unreality of this proposal struck her commander who replied scathingly: "Simone, you don't know what you are asking for. Your dedication is extraordinary, but you don't speak Spanish and your physical type is different from the women of the region. You'll be caught immediately. You're going to sacrifice yourself, and not only destroy yourself, but also compromise Maurin [the individual in question]" (*VSW*, II, 97). Weil was repelled by the execution and torture that she witnessed, but never made the connection with her own death. Still, when she finally took herself out of the war, by stepping into a basin of boiling oil, the usual explanation, that she was near-sighted, is inadequate. Mitchell's hypothesis imposes itself: She wounded herself in order to stop

---

19. Juliet Mitchell said of Weil, "An anorexic doesn't know what death is" (private conversation).

thinking about the death and destruction all around her, making it possible for her to focus attention on the third-degree burn on her leg rather than the reality of death. This helps us understand Weil's "courage," especially in its more grandiose (i.e., hysterical) dimensions. She was fatally alienated from her body, from her tradition and people, as distant from Judaism as she was, in the end, from Catholicism, which also requires a material engagement, soul and body together.

Spanish Jews who converted under Inquisition pressure were called *marranos*, pigs, by their new coreligionists. The betrayal of Judaism by Jews takes many forms. So too is the intellectual betrayal of which Derrida accuses himself, the fascination with the philosophical tradition promoted by gentiles, which is a form of assimilationism. This was one of the forms taken by Weil's self-exile and betrayal; but, as I have argued here, there was a grounding in her corporeality, which was the crucial determinant of this turn away from her origins.

There is an irony here. As Holocaust testimony shows, the Jews in the camps were also alienated from their own bodies, so that in a sense they too became *marranes*, losing that very Jewishness for which they were being tortured and killed. This was the purpose of Hitler's regime, not simply to wipe out these people but to destroy what they represented, that ancient and powerful tradition that by some inexplicable miracle still survives. So that Weil, unknowingly, was involved in a travesty that mimicked the violence of the camps. She did to herself (and I did to myself) what was done by the S.S. guards and their lackeys in Auschwitz and those other infamous places where Jews were confined. Christ told Peter that the gates of hell would never prevail against the Church, but the Church has never known the violence to which Judaism has been subject, a violence that too often came from the Church, an unknowing act of self-mutilation and attempted suicide since all authentic Christians are also Jews. We have to understand that there are two covenants, two interrelated promises, linked by blood, yet historically and culturally distinct. One of the ways Christianity has tried to destroy Judaism is by muffling its uniqueness within something called "the judaeo-christian tradition," a conceptual hyphenation that drains the specificity and living presence of Judaism, making it a mere appendage to the dominant culture.

When I told Professor Marie-Jean Durry that I was not a Jew, when Simone Weil wrote to Jerome Carcopinio, Minister of Education, that she should not be a considered a Jew, we were trying to walk across that hyphen, to snatch an idealized identity based on rational free choice. We did this in the shadow of the camps, where identity was recognized as cellular, genetic, an imprint from which abdication was not possible. In this sense, the Nazis had it right. Once a Jew, always a Jew. So Sartre's view, that the Jew must assume his Jewishness at the risk of inauthenticity and bad faith, is fundamentally right, although it involves also a certain determinism that has to be contested. Change is possible, if first you assume your identity, recognize who you are before you become other. What this means is that I could not become a Christian until I had, once and for all, assumed the privileged burden of being a Jew. This came late in life, but it did come, thanks to my Jewish wife. For Simone Weil, it never came at all; and maybe that is why, in the last analysis, she could never ask for Christian baptism.

CHAPTER 12

Messages

If God sent us his messengers we would surely heed
them. Events are those messengers.

Pascal

THERE was something else I had in common with Simone
Weil and Max Jacob. We shared experiences of a type that
are usually dismissed as superstitious tomfoolery along
with UFOs, diabolical possession, and otherworldly voices. But
what if such experiences leave you with a deep and continuing
resonance? You know that no objective criteria exist for evaluating what may well be a hysterical symptom or a perceptual blip;
but what if these bizarre events are, as Simone Weil puts it,
"openings in the soul through which creation looks at God"?
Weil had such events in her life; we have a record of two of
them. The first is her discovery of the sonnet "Love" by Georges
Herbert, during her visit to the Benedictine Abbey of Solesmes
in 1938. The second is an allegorical narrative that reprises the
theme of divine visitation in the Herbert sonnet. Back in Paris
after the visit to Solesmes, she often recited the Herbert sonnet,
sometimes with her mother:

> Love bade me welcome; yet my soul drew back,
>   Guiltie of dust and sinne,
> But quick-ey'd Love, observing me grow slack

194

From my first entrance in,
Drew near to me, sweetly questioning
  If I lack'd any thing.

A guest, I answer'd, worthy to be here:
  Love said, You shall be he.
I the unkinde, ungratefull? Ah my deare,
  I cannot look on thee.
Love took my hand, and smiling did reply,
  Who made the eyes but I?

Truth Lord, but I have marr'd them; let my shame
  Go where it doth deserve.
And know you not, sayes Love, who bore the blame?
  My deare, then I will serve.
You must sit down, sayes Love, and taste my meat:
  So I did sit and eat.

Recitation became prayer, and, in the autumn of 1938, she had a mystical encounter: "And it happened that as I was saying this poem . . . Christ Himself came down, and He took me."[1]

Several things about Weil's mediative or "sacramental" use of the poem are striking. First, it was a poem in a foreign language. Not only did this serve to mediate the otherness of the mystical experience, it provided an escape from her native language, that is, herself. Second, the poem recapitulates the craving to be loved for herself, in all her imperfections: "I cannot look on thee," she says, but love replies, "Who made the eyes but I?" She feels that the mere exercise of sensory power is sinful. He overwhelms that argument: Love himself made the body. The poem concludes with the taking of food, emblematic for Weil of that nourishment she had always craved but denied herself.

The visitation allegory, written while she was in Marseilles waiting to leave for New York, recapitulates the poem in a narrative form while deepening and expanding the mystical encounter. Nevin says of this text: "Although it defies generic classification—it is neither memoir nor fiction nor allegory nor

---

1. Jacques Cabaud, *Simone Weil: A Fellowship in Love* (New York: Channel Press, 1964), 170.

reverie—it might be called Weil's version of a gospel episode, with herself cast at the center, with Christ as 'He'" (*SW*, 276). This is a central text in Weil's *œuvre*,[2] generically similar to other modernist allegories by Kafka, Camus, Borges, and so on. Nevin goes on to see it in precisely this way, emphasizing its ambivalence and noting its contradictory mix of submissive love and resentment. This Kafakesque narrative approaches meaning asymptotically, without ever achieving full clarity. It reenforces the view that Weil's life was marked by unfulfilled sexual desire, which turned out to be her path to transcendence.[3]

> He entered my room and said: "Poor creature, you who understand nothing, who know nothing. Come with me and I will teach you things which you do not suspect." I followed him.
>
> He took me into a church. It was new and ugly. He led me up to the altar and said: "Kneel down." I said "I have not been baptized." He said: "Fall on your knees before this place, in love, as before the place where lies the truth." I obeyed.
>
> He brought me out and made me climb up to a garret. Through the open window one could see the whole city spread out, some wooden scaffoldings, and the river on which boats were being unloaded. The garret was empty, except for a table and two chairs. He bade me to be seated.
>
> We were alone. He spoke. From time to time someone would enter, mingle in the conversation, then leave again.
>
> Winter had gone; spring had not yet come. The branches of trees lay bare, without buds, in the cold air full of sunshine.
>
> The light of day would arise, shine forth in splendor, and fade away; then the moon and the stars would enter through the window. And then once more the dawn would come up.
>
> At times he would fall silent, take some bread from a cupboard, and we would share it. This bread really had the taste of bread. I have never found that taste again.
>
> He would pour out some wine for me, and some for himself—

2. David McLellan begins his book on Weil by quoting this text as "Prologue." *Simone Weil: Utopian Pessimist* (London: Macmillan, 1989).

3. It is important to note that Weil feared and despised sexual desire when it was directed at her, though she was not hostile to the idea of sexuality for others.

wine which tasted of the sun and of the soil upon which this city was built.

At other times we would stretch ourselves out on the floor of the garret, and sweet sleep would enfold me. Then I would wake and drink in the light of the sun.

He had promised to teach me, but he did not teach me anything. We talked about all kinds of things, in a desultory way, as do old friends.

One day he said to me: "Now go." I fell down before him, I clasped his knees, I implored him not to drive me away. But he threw me out on the stairs. I went down unconscious of anything, my heart as it were in shreds. I wandered along the streets. Then I realized that I had no idea where this house lay.

I have never tried to find it again. I understood that he had come for me by mistake. My place is not in that garret. It can be anywhere—in a prison cell, in one of those middle-class drawing-rooms full of knick-knacks and red plush, in the waiting-room of a station—anywhere, except in that garret.

Sometimes I cannot help trying, fearfully and remorsefully, to repeat to myself a part of what he said to me. How am I to know if I remember rightly? He is not there to tell me.

I know well that that he does not love me. How could he love me. And yet deep down within me something, a particle of myself, cannot help thinking, with fear and trembling, that perhaps, in spite of all, he loves me.[4]

Nevin observes: "If 'He' is Christ (who else could give her the bread and wine?), he is also a cad and a bully. Not even the eucharistic sharing, the old friends' talk, the stretching out on the floor (a tableau of adolescent sexuality) can overcome his peremptory tone and violence. Why should she want this creature to love her? This curious story is ammunition for those who presume Weil was masochistic" (SW, 277). The text might also

4. Published as Prologue to *La Connaissance surnaturelle* (Paris: Gallimard, 1942). The translation from Richard Rees is slightly modified (*Selected Essays, 1934–1943, by Simone Weil* [London: Oxford University Press, 1962]). As to the date of composition: "the text describing this event was not written until late 1940 or 1941. It is difficult to decide between those close to Simone Weil who place this occurrence in Paris in February or March 1940, and those, equally close, for whom it took place in Marseilles, in the following year." Cabaud, *Simone Weil*, 195.

be interpreted in terms of the Freudian linking of fantasy and hysteria. Fantasy, which has been called "the specific object of psychoanalysis," represents an effort to reach back and down through repression, to the bedrock of experience, which may lead in turn to differing symbolic orders, including the spiritual.[5] Nevin interprets the fantasy as follows:

> It seems obvious that this composition interprets her experience of Christ after the visitation in 1938. The entry into her room is the mystical rapture; the altar and the garret are settings for an initiation to which she feels inadequate. They might respectively symbolize the church she finally could not enter and the intimacy within it which she feared might leave her complacent and compromised. Her expulsion, a casting out into the wilderness, is an involuntary *imitatio Christi*, an indication of how emulously she looked upon Christ, the suffering servant. The loves-me, loves-me-not conclusion marks a furtive confidence in her own position beyond the church, that she had been divinely appointed to an itinerary away from the deceptively comforting garret. She has a mission "in spite of everything"—a phrase that says much about her sense of inadequacy and failure and also about her being a Jew. Unlike the transcendent realm of genius, to which she had not won admission in childhood, the garret was accessible but turned out to be a mere way-station, and she leaves it, although precipitously, as an initiate. The very exclusion adumbrates acceptance: it is the Christian paradox of being chosen an outcast. Weil had discovered that Christianity does not evade suffering but uses it. (*SW*, 277)

Nevin's excellent analysis falls short in that it does not deal with the literary character of the text as a Kafkaesque parable. The fact that Weil's "He" is a cad and a bully recalls many instances in literature where a protagonist behaves in a way that is arbitrary and inexplicable. One thinks of Kafka's Land Surveyor, Camus' Meursault, Beckett's Molloy. In these modernist allegories, psychological coherence is not to be expected or even desired. Arbitrary behavior disconnects action from psychology,

---

5. J. Laplanche and J.-B. Pontalis, "Fantasy and the Origins of Sexuality," in *The Language of Psychoanalysis*, trans. Donald Nicholson-Judith (New York: Norton, 1973). 7

pointing to the absurd character of life and the contingent nature of experience. Weil's text deals with her lifelong desires for meaning and for love and the frustration of those desires in a meaningless world. Also implicit is her inability to give love: the rejection she submits to (since she is its inventor) is also her rejection of lived desire. The inscribing of unfulfilled desire becomes an end in itself, since it maintains the subject in that condition of endless vulnerability which Weil struggled to achieve: "A rock in our path. To hurl ourselves upon this rock as though after a certain intensity of desire has been reach it could not exist any more. Or else to retreat as though we ourselves did not exist. Desire contains something of the absolute and if it fails (once its energy has been used up) the absolute is transferred to the obstacle. This produces the state of mind of the defeated, the oppressed."[6] Desire—obstacle—hurling oneself against it—defeat—oppression. These are also the themes of the allegory, but there desire takes the shape of a personified encounter with an Other being who, though arbitrary, leaves her with the hope that He might return. The allegory ends: "I know well that he does not love me. How could he love me? And yet deep down within me something, a particle of myself, cannot help thinking, with fear and trembling, that perhaps, in spite of all, he loves me." Weil's conflicting drives are mirrored in the paradoxical behavior of her absent-present visitor, an angel or the Crucified One himself. Doubt, fear, remorse, those familiar emotional states, blot out the momentary experience of happiness. She writes it down feverishly, an inadequate record that conveys a factualness that can't be argued away.

Max Jacob also had his mystical encounter, his apparitions, his overwhelming sense of being loved. In Chapter 6 I gave an account of the Christ who appears in one of the poet's own drawings: "He is in a landscape, a landscape that I drew some time ago, it is He! what beauty! elegance and sweetness! His shoulders, his manner! He wears a robe of yellow silk with blue trimmings. He turns and I see that peaceful and shining face."[7]

6. Quoted in Siâm Miles, ed., *Simone Weil: An Anthology* (New York: Weidenfeld & Nicholson, 1986), 199.
7. Max Jacob, *La Défense de Tartufe* (Paris: Gallimard, 1964), 101.

In a later text, entitled *The Story of my Conversion*, Jacob adds
further details on the apparition: voices speaking around him,
as if he has already joined the heavenly host, ecstacy, and "an
uninterrupted series of forms, colors, scenes that I didn't understand at the time but were later revealed as prophetic."[8] This
event, which the poet undercuts by pastiche and self-mockery,
gains credibility when we see how it changed Jacob's life. The
vision on September 22, 1909, marked a decisive turning point,
causing him to give up his career as art critic and break with
many of his friends. Some months later there was another
apparition, this time on a movie screen: "At the movies, just
now! I'm sure of it, it was he in a white robe, hair long and black,
somewhat curly, curving in at the neck; I think he had a poor
child with him."[9] Both apparitions warn Jacob against his licen-
tious behavior, telling him he cannot expect to be saved if he
does not reform: " 'How dare you present yourself before your
guardian angel soiled and stinking of yesterday's drunkenness,
for you're incapable of depriving yourself for love of me. . . .
Cleanse yourself of your dirtiness, your vanity. You're nothing
but a popinjay. . . . God will regret the gifts he has given you
and from which you draw no profit.' "[10] It sounds so literary, so
contrived! But I didn't dismiss it, because I had my own para-
normal experiences to puzzle over, one of them actually a
warning similiar to those given to Jacob. Prior to that, four
months after my baptism, there had been a different kind of
message altogether.

The first message came during Holy Week, 1951. I was in full
euphoria, buoyed up by my missionary work at Friendship
House and my visits to the Trappist monastery in Rhode Island.
Thinking I might have a vocation to one of the contemplative
orders, I began to pray seriously for guidance. Why not? In that
period of jubilation anything seemed possible. But I needed
some sign of the path I should follow.

I was in the Church of the Annunciation on Convent Avenue
in New York, praying the Stations of the Cross. As I stopped at

8. Max Jacob, *Récit de ma conversion* (Paris: Rouperie, 1959), 6.
9. Jacob, *La Défense de Tartufe*, 124.
10. Ibid., 123.

the ninth Station, where Jesus falls for the second time, I asked to be shown the path. What should I do with my life? At that point I heard a voice inside my head: "Neal, follow me."

There was nothing obviously delusive or hallucinatory about it. I was in a perfectly sober and rational state. Not only did I hear it, I recognized the speaker. Those words were the call that Jesus spoke to his disciples. Not just the twelve, but many others who followed him. It was intoxicating but also frightening. I thought of the rich young man to whom he said, "Give all you have to the poor and follow me." Was I prepared to give up everything? Was I capable of following him? If you hear the call and don't respond, then what happens?

Later, I put the words in a broader context. There were many ways to follow, many versions of the *imitatio Christi*. My life of following him was to be a continual falling down and getting up again, a crucifixion of the body by pain and anxiety, digression into false turns, by-paths, mazes, and labyrinths; but the message told me to continue forging ahead, whatever the cost, because he had spoken my name. Many times since I have asked myself if this really happened, if I have really been called; but, whatever my spiritual condition at the time, I have never been able to explain it away.

The second incident took place shortly after my first marriage. Jean and I were in Chicago, visiting her aunt and uncle, who was a professor at the University. The summer was almost over and a heat wave descended on the neighborhood of brick houses and old trees that surrounded the campus. I was restless, driven by demons like those that tormented Max. At the de Sales Center chapel a few months earlier I had vowed fidelity, but my imagination wouldn't comply. One Saturday night I left the house on Blackstone Avenue and took the train into downtown Chicago where I prowled around, ending up in a dance hall where I met a pretty girl who was suffering the same kind of anxiety. She was going to be married in a week, this was her last fling. We close-danced under the spotlights, drank beer, exchanged our stories, becoming almost-lovers for an hour or so till her friends pulled her away. I wandered back out onto the street, full of self-pity and anger at myself, at Jean, wondering if

I would ever emerge from the labyrinth of sex. I went down the steps of the Randolph Street IC Station, pushed through the heavy glass doors. I looked up at the board to catch the time of the next southbound train, then wandered over to the big circular newsstand. The morning newspapers were stacked on the floor in knee-high piles. I glanced down to read the headlines and saw in black letters three inches tall: THIS IS MY BODY. I stared till everything around the headline disappeared. The words of the consecration. The operative words that change bread into the body of Christ; in the present context, an added meaning struck home. Your body is the body of Christ, don't abuse it, treat it with reverence, it's a thing divine. The focus is transubstantiation but there is also a secular message here about respect for the human body—mine and those I interact with. And, for the long term, guidance about how this problematical long-suffering body is to be treated. I blinked, turned, and walked away, the message vibrating through my nerves. This was a warning about the consequences of misusing the body, a wake-up call to realize that the body is all we have in this life, that it is the median point connecting us to the rest of the universe, and that it is subject to some sensible rules, one of them being a rule against promiscuity, even a largely mental or fantasized promiscuity.

When I first read Jacob and Weil, I was inclined to believe that they were both victims of delusion. Later, certain experiences such as the one in the Randolph Street IC Station, left me convinced that we live at the juncture point of different orders of reality that may sometimes intersect. These are delusions to the sceptic, subjective truth-effects to the agnostic, God's messengers to the believer that I have been intermittently, that I now am once and for all.

CHAPTER 13

Transgressive Acts

All those who, from point to point in our history, have tried to evade that will to truth and to place it in question against truth, just there where truth tries to justify the prohibition and to define madness, all those who, from Nietzsche, to Artaud and Bataille, must now serve as signs, noble without a doubt, for our work day by day.

Michel Foucault

How much fuss over the death of a woman!

Camus, *Caligula*

Toulouse. Autumn 1975.

The city was smoky with truck traffic and the whirling particulate of leaves. Dust-devils spun through the streets and in the *allées* of Le Grand Rond, a park in concentric circles like Dante's inferno. This park with its cohort of infants, checker players, young lovers, and unemployed was only a block from my apartment on Rue Ninau, a quiet street of antique shops and galleries close to the Cathedral of St. Etienne. I spent many hours walking through the sculpted box hedges and gardens of Le Grand Rond, often meeting my students for conferences there or comandeering a bench where I could spread out my books or weigh the merits of student papers. Until the cold weather began in late October, I avoided the apartment, which was dark and windowless, hung with stiff draperies over papier-mâché alcoves and mantels. The fake opulence of it depressed me. The only redeeming thing about the building was Hélène, the retired prostitute who lived upstairs with her poodle and entertained her lover in most respectable style, although sometimes the fake crystal chandelier in my ceiling would shake. Hélène and the students kept my spirits up as I went through a difficult period. My marriage had turned into an emotional black hole, and I had to make a decision about the future.

The students were an exuberant lot. It was the first post–Vietnam year, and a weight had been lifted from their shoulders. In the year just past Nixon had resigned in the aftermath of Watergate, Saigon had fallen to the army of Ho Chi Mihn, the new order had arrived in Vietnam. In October I took some of them to see a revival of Camus' *Caligula*, commemorating the play's thirtieth anniversary. It had first been put on in 1945, with Gérard Philippe in the lead role. When we discussed it afterward, one or two wanted to see Nixon as Caligula, that angel turned monster, and I felt that they had a point. The play dealt with the mysterious impulse that sometimes grips the most ordinary man, impelling him to incredible acts of violence— such as the bombing of Cambodia or the Watergate break-in. Or, conversely, acts of heroism and self-sacrifice. Not long after that, in a momentary episode of what the Surrealists call *hasard objectif*, I found an old copy of Bataille's journal *Critique* in a secondhand book store. It contained Michel Foucault's article entitled "Preface to Transgression." Transgression struck me as a wonderful explanatory concept, one that cut across the work of many writers I was interested in, including Camus, Max Jacob, and Simone Weil. Each one, though in a different way, had gone against the grain of social conformity and conventional truth, each had risked reputation and finally life itself in pursuit of something transcendent—something other, invisible, and totally absurd.

Foucault's essay led me to Bataille's 1957 volume *L'Erotisme*, in particular the chapters on transgression. Sexuality is, for Bataille (who knew and despised the asexual Weil), the willful violation of taboo. This interplay between taboo and transgression, between the rational order and its explosion, between the institution and the outsider's challenge to it, between its discursive practices and the rhetorical rupture of conventions is taken up by Foucault where it constitutes the field of his investigations. The field is based on a tension that grows out of Foucault's perception of his own sexual activity as transgressive and as offering a challenge to norms of every possible kind—moral, social, epistemological. Foucault used his own inner violence as the motive for his research, giving to that research the transgressive character that he drew from his private life.[1] In his "Preface to Transgression," Foucault employs a strategy that was invented by Rousseau and used by other transgressive writers, notably Jean Genet. This involves taking a fundamental principle and turning it upside down. Rousseau argued that civilization was not beneficial but, rather, the cause of all evils. Genet (whom Foucault parallels in many respects) argued that the murderer is the hero of a moral order that inverts the value system of bourgeois society and attains a deeper poetic / mystical insight. Foucault argues that sexuality kills God, although He might have once been thought to invent it. The underlying argument seems to be that, since men use the name of God to interdict sex, sex must be turned back to destroy Him. Not only that, sexuality must take His place. What Foucault wants to do is fill the blank left by the death of God with the energy of sexuality, especially that sexuality which is threatened or interdicted, i.e. transgressive. This substitution drives the dynamic of Foucault's rhetoric, not only in this essay but in all his works.

---

1. James E. Miller gives a range of incidents, including many suicide attempts and an attempt at crucifixion. The hysterical symptomatology seems apparent. *The Passion of Michel Foucault* (New York: Simon & Schuster, 1993).

It is obviously a social rather than an ontological argument. Foucault views the God concept as an instrument of repression and sets aside as irrelevant any question of God's existence.

The link between Weil and Foucault was Georges Bataille, the Dionysian writer who spent his days as a librarian at the Bibliothèque Nationale. They had known each other and repeatedly clashed when both were members of the anti-Stalinist Cercle Communiste Démocratique (CCD).[2] Bataille hated Weil instinctively, just as she was repelled by him. Yet he recognized some deep kinship, as he acknowledges in his essay on her: "It is a good method to draw from an author a truth which escaped him. . . . Looking for my own way, I can interest myself in the seduction felt by someone who followed a contrary way. The coincidence of minds entirely opposed can have a decisive value."[3]

Bataille sensed that this driven, sexless woman was moved by the transgressive impulse, the need to hurl her body against social barriers. Her approach was to challenge the norms, but this challenge included what was for Bataille and Foucault the dominant thematic, sexuality. Their supercharged eros becomes, in Weil's construction of transgression, the asexuality of the Cathars. She invented the Cathars in her own image, as a delusional vessel for her transgressive rejection of sexual de-

---

2. Weil and Bataille were both members of the CCD. But Bataille, a one-time Catholic convert who lost his faith in 1920, was hostile to Weil, whom he called a "cadaver" and parodied as "Lazarus" in his novel *Le Bleu du ciel*, written after the dissolution of the CCD. In his 1949 article in *Critique* he avowed that "few human beings had interested him as much" as Weil. Despite her "incontestable ugliness," which "horrified," him, he claimed that she had also "a true beauty." He adds that "she was certainly an admirable being, asexual, with something deadly about her." He finds this deadliness not only in her appearance but also in her "marvellous will to futility." Bataille goes on to attack her "blind passion for lucidity" and the *outrance autoritaire* of her moral position in *L'Enracinement*. This recalls Foucault's attack on the "terrorism" of Sartrean "authenticity" and, indeed, any positive moral position. When Weil learned that Pétrement was working at the Bibliothèque Nationale, she warned her friend against any contact with Bataille. "La Victoire militaire et la banqueroute de la morale qui maudit," Review of *L'Enracinement*, *Critique* 5 (Sept. 1949): 795.

3. Ibid.

sire. The word *Cathar* comes from the Greek *Katharoi*, meaning "pure," a concept diametrically opposed to the deliberate transgression of behavioral norms celebrated by Bataille. The obsession with purity, with self-dispossession, or "decreation" as she called it, runs throughout her work and is summed up in this manichean line: "Concupiscence is life itself."[4] Still, if she refused concupiscence, desire, sexuality, materialism, and sensual pleasure in her own life, she never denied the legitimacy of the desires of others. She tried to serve the needs of ordinary people with respect, although she never appeared to share them.

Often that fall, while brooding over Weil and Foucault, I discussed them with the pastor of the Cathedral Saint-Etienne, a young aristocratic priest named Monsieur François Remaury. The church was unfinished, looking like a split meteor that had fallen out of the sky. Once you ran the gauntlet of beggars and found your way inside this ominous pile you would be lost, since there was no clear orientation of nave or transept, only a collection of half-decorated halls peopled by second-rate statues and paintings of second-rate saints. I would seek out Monsieur le curé in his rectory ice-box, where he shuffled weakly through the records of his aging and diminishing parish and, as the weekend neared, composed eloquent sermons of quiet desperation.

"Foucault et Weil? Mais encore?" He thought it was quixotic to want to bring these two writers together. Surely they would have hated each other, just as Weil and Bataille had done; yet, as I pointed out, they had a lot in common, beginning with their attendance, some twenty years apart, at two of France's greatest schools, the Lycée Henri IV and the Ecole Normale Supérieure. Both had a kind of wild recklesness that I admired, both knew how to draw all the disparate forces of personality into the clenched fist of a single defining action. Their aims were transcendent and they put their lives on the line to attain them, true heroes of our time. I began to wonder if I could talk to him about

---

4. Simone Weil, *La Connaissance surnaturelle* (Paris: Gallimard, 1950), 43. All further references are given in the text as *CS*.

the transgressive act that I myself was contemplating, divorce.
For a time I held off, knowing in advance what he would tell me.

Transgressors are people who change the world, but they
often destroy themselves or others in the process. They are different from the fanatics and the ideologues, people with dead-
ening absorption in a single issue; they are akin to visionaries
and mystics, who see what is on the other side of the last
horizon. Weil and Foucault were all of this, and both also had a
compulsive drive for self-destruction. Weil's goal was to change
the world, and she would not stop until she had killed herself.
When Cabaud first told me about Weil's death I was left with an
awful sense of waste. (Years later I felt the same emotion on
learning that Foucault had participated in unprotected sex in
the bathhouses of San Francisco while he was teaching at Berkeley, leading to his death from AIDS in 1984.) When I thought
about these deaths I realized that transgression involved more
than going against social norms; its deepest sense was going
against yourself. This could be productive, it could be sanctify-
ing; or it could be destructive. It took all three forms for Weil
and Foucault. With these insights, I edged closer to my own
transgressive decision.

Foucault describes transgression as "an action which involves
the limit, that narrow zone of a line where it displays the flash of
its passage, but perhaps also its entire trajectory, even its origin;
it is likely that transgression has its entire space in the line it
crosses." When did Weil go over a line? There were several
periods of transgressive activity in her life, notably between
December 1934 and July 1935 when she did manual labor in
three different industrial plants. Chronicled in her *Journal
d'usine*, these months brought to her the conviction that "man is
a slave and that servitude is his natural condition." In spite of
headache, injury, and crushing fatigue, she chronicled the miseries of piecework along with the interpersonal frictions of factory life. Pettiness, competition, physical danger, and the threat
of being laid off accompanied the grinding work. One day's
account is typical:

> Friday 5 July. Next day, time off: what happiness! Slept poor-
> ly (teeth). . . . Headache, fatigue [also worries, which don't

help. . . .] Only three more weeks! Yes, but three weeks, it's one week times three! So only enough courage for one day, only one. Even that, in gritting my teeth with the courage of despair. The week before the little Italian told me: "You're getting thin. . . ."

Exhausted, seeing my co-workers (head-splitting noise of the machine . . .) getting ready to wash their machine, at their suggestion I ask Lerclerc if I can leave at 7 o'clock. He says dryly: "You didn't come in just to work two hours did you!" That evening Philippe makes me wait forever, just to annoy me. And I, gripped by disgust. . . .[5]

As she saw it, factory life involved a negative transgression, the driving of body and mind into a living hell. She was convinced this applied not only to herself but equally to her coworkers who were physically stronger and inured to suffering. They too were dehumanized, brutalized, enslaved by this meaningless and interminable work.

This was the first time that Weil crossed the line; but several years later, she would cross it in another direction in an affirmative or upward transgression. We see that flash of mind and spirit as they break through the barrier of ordinary experience between July and November 1942 in New York City. During five months of intense reflection and introspection, she turned away from the topics that had previously occupied her into feverish and sometimes incoherent speculation. The seven notebooks she kept in 1942 were published by Albert Camus in 1950 under the title *Cahiers d'Amérique* as part of a larger volume, *La Connaissance surnaturelle*. These texts, never intended for publication, are the most fragmentary of all her writings, yet they have a central focus that makes them unique. Their focus is on thinking about God and thinking oneself in relationship to God. They accompany her efforts to find the lost companion of her allegory, to enter into a mystical dependency with the unknown, to will herself into the abjection of a love slave. Focused on a hypothetical Christ, they explore forms of nonsexual transgression. Repeatedly here, I find what Foucault speaks of: "transgression incessantly crosses and recrosses a line which

---

5. Simone Weil, *Journal d'usine*, in *La Condition ouvrière* (Paris: Gallimard, 1951), 125.

closes up behind it in a wave of extremely short duration, and thus it is made to return once more right to the horizon of the uncrossable."[6] It is significant that, during these months, Weil was obsessed with the idea of a crossing. She wanted to go back across the Atlantic to England, hoping to put into effect her proposal for a corps of nurses on the front lines (*VSW*, II, 428–29). When she did finally return in December, "the horizon of the uncrossable," death itself, was not far off. As she wrote these feverish notes in her continuing exploration of world religion and philosophy as well as the neighborhoods, the people, and the churches of New York, she moved mentally and emotionally toward a final transgression, that crossing that lay less than a year in the future. Close as death was to her, it was still unthinkable. Yet her own unconscious death drive was reaching a crescendo.

These texts have a special resonance for me. When Weil wrote her notebooks she was walking the streets around Columbia University that I crisscrossed eight years later with Jacques Cabaud. She attended Mass daily at the small brick church of Corpus Christi where Thomas Merton was baptized in November 1938 and where I was baptized in October 1950. I went back to these same broken fragments of mystical revery and spiritual hunger in 1975, letting them resonate with my own episodic spirituality. I had spent years reading arcane, obscure, sometimes indecipherable texts; now I found that I could assimilate if not explain these fusional pages where all boundaries blur, pages written as Weil entered a condition described by Beckett's words "all things run together in the world's long madness."

During this period in 1942 Weil entered that madness that for Foucault places the transgressor outside the social context and makes him or her a pariah—Sade and Artaud in the asylum, Nietzsche the insane Anti-Christ, Mandela in prison. Madness or delusion is not, for Foucault, a question of truth content or congruence with "reality." Madness is thought that trans-

---

6. Michel Foucault, "Preface to Transgression," in *Language, Counter-Memory & Practice: Selected Essays and Interviews by Michel Foucault*, Donald F. Bouchard and Sherry Simon, eds. (Ithaca: Cornell University Press, 1977), 34.

gresses the limits set on discourse by the social order. Madness represents, along with sex and criminality, the triple crown of transgression. Simulated madness was one of the paths Foucault followed in his own self-exploration. The common feature in all of this may be the hysterical use of fantasy as a performative path to experiences that remain beyond the boundaries of what can be cognitively known and accepted. Both Weil and Foucault used themselves as laboratories for the study of society. Both undertook what Foucault called "experimentation on ourselves . . . the sacrifice of the subject of knowledge."[7] For both, this was the only possible response to the failure of liberal humanism, the dead-end of reform and revolution. You had to put your own body on the line, use it as an instrument of change. It is irrelevant that this may be self-destructive, since there is no other response to the irredeemableness of the human condition. Although Weil does not subscribe to anything comparable to Foucault's Nietzschean call for "the death of man," there is throughout her work a powerful sense of humanity as flawed, distorted, deluded by the weight of its institutions and the lunacy of institutional thinking. Her response was not the humanist's one of improving institutions but, rather, the mystic's impulse to self-sacrifice. While still a student she spoke of "reducing our bodies to the role of a tool, our emotions to the role of signs" (*VSW*, I, 147). This impulse was materially expressed by her year of factory work during which she was transformed. Her emotions took on a new intensity; they were not simply responses to intolerable working conditions but became signs of a mystical process driving beyond the fundamental limits of human existence.

Weil was a deeply transgressive thinker in ways that are both similar to and different from Foucault's. Like Foucault, she attacks "the taboos thrown up around the will to truth."[8] In his essay on transgression, Foucault sets the "will to truth" against

7. Foucault wrote that "to put into question the signifying subject" was a practice "that ends in the veritable destruction of the subject, in its dissociation, in its upheaval into something radically other." Quoted in Miller, *Passion*, 93.

8. Quoted in Charles C. Lemert and Garth Gillan, *Michel Foucault: Social Theory and Transgression* (New York: Columbia University Press, 1982), 64.

"truth," that is, the inner dynamic of the mind against the simulacra of the social order. And just as Weil spoke of becoming a "sign," so Foucault names certain transgressive individuals "who must serve as signs . . . for our work day by day." This work, where both Foucault and Weil expressed their will to truth, was directed toward the analysis of power and its underlying structures in the human sciences. Her early writings, when she was active in the syndicalist movement, consist almost wholly of analyses in which the subterfuges and disguises of power in the language of political writers are ruthlessly unveiled.[9] She attacked head-on the conventional limits of truth seeking, first in syndicalism, then in religion and philosophy as she continued her search for spiritual meaning.

Weil had in common with the great transgressors invoked by Foucault (Nietzsche, Artaud, Bataille) her insistence that the social order must be challenged materially, by the way she lived her life. She was often enough called a saint, even by her own mother, but this misses the point. The Christian saint is impelled to extravagant behavior by love of God. Weil was impelled by her desire for justice and her love for people. One has only to read the anecdotes of her relationships with her fellow syndicalists or factory workers or comrades in the military units in Spain to realize that, in her, libido had become truly fraternal, truly compassionate. If there is such a thing as sublimation, then we can argue that Weil's gift for friendship was eros transformed. Here she is on a meeting with two fellow-workers, during a period of unemployment: "Total camaraderie. For the first time in my life, in fact. No barrier, no class differences (since it's suppressed), nor in the difference of sex. Miraculous" (*VSW*, I,

---

9. David McLellan, author of many studies on Marxism, writes: "Weil was the very opposite of any abstract, ethereal thinker. This firm anchorage in economic and social reality rather than political ideology enabled her to produce analyses of state socialism of the Soviet model and of Nazism that were to be the keystone of Arendt's *Origins of Totalitarianism*, as well as of the more contemporary reflections of such writers as Castoriadis. Her searching exposures of the psychological and material bases of power are akin to those of Foucault. And the relevance of her critique increases with the power of technocracy and the centralization of the modern state." *Simone Weil, Utopian Pessimist* (London: Macmillan, 1989), 269.

38). Her commitment to others was a fundamental principle of her nature:

> I have the essential need, and I think I can say the vocation, to move among men of every class and complexion, mixing with them and sharing their life and outlook, so far that is to say as conscience allows, merging into the crowd and disappearing among them, so that they show themselves as they are, putting off all disguises with me. It is because I long to know them so as to love them just as they are. For if I do not love them as they are, it will not be they whom I love, and my love will be unreal. I do not speak of helping them, because as far as that goes I am unfortunately quite incapable of doing anything as yet.[10]

Repeatedly her need to express this love for others came up against those "ritual forms" of discourse that are the barriers against which the transgressor hurls herself, needing to break through to some domain beyond the discourse of oppression. This takes us back to Foucault. He writes:

> I suppose that in any society the production of discourse is at once controlled, selected, organized and redistributed by a certain number of procedures whose role is to conjure away the powers and the dangers, to master the unexpected even, to set aside the heavy, the redoubtable force of materiality.
>
> In a society like ours, one knows, of course, the procedures of exclusion. The most evident, the most familiar, is the *interdiction*. One knows well enough that one doesn't have the right to say everything, that one cannot speak of whatever one likes in every circumstance, that nobody, finally, can speak of whatever he pleases. Taboo of the object, ritual of circumstance, privileged or exclusive right of the speaking subject.[11]

Interdiction weighed on Weil, this inability to say whatever she liked, to speak from the heart. It was internalized, largely self-imposed; in her *Journals* we find it constantly coming into play. The transgressor's strength comes from the fact that she has internalized the taboo yet overcomes it anyway. Foucault the-

10. Simone Weil, *Waiting for God*, trans. Emma Craufurd (New York: Putnam, 1951), 48.

11. Michel Foucault, *L'Ordre du discours* (Paris: Gallimard, 1971), 10–11.

matized his sexuality. Weil repressed hers, yet the repressed returned continually in transposed forms that energized her thought more than diminishing it. All such forms involved, in one way or another, her need to put her ego, her security, her comfort, her health, and, ultimately, her life on the line. These correspondances or crossovers between the Christian and the Nietzschean are less startling than they may at first appear, if seen as reverse images appearing in the same cultural mirror.

Weil's transgressive spirituality erupts throughout the *Journal d'Amérique*. Here, in yet another crossover, she anticipated Foucault's idea of the sacrificial life as limit-experience. The following passage echoes themes from Chapter 11, in which I explored Weil's relation to her own body. It is one of a few texts in which she recalls her distress as a newborn infant:

> To supplicate is to wait for life or death from outside of ourselves. Kneeling, head bent, in the most convenient position for the victor, by a sword's blow, to sever our neck. . . . Thus in silence several minutes of waiting go by. The heart empties of all its attachments, frozen by the imminent contact with death. A new life is received, made entirely of mercy.
>
> > We must pray God in this way.
> > Waiting is the foundation of the spiritual life.
> > Filial piety is only an image of the attitude toward God.
>
> If the soul cried toward God its hunger for the bread of life, with no interruption, indefatigably, as a newborn that its mother forgets to nurse cries. . . .
> May those cries that I uttered when I was one or two weeks old resound in me without interruption for the milk which is the seed of the Father. (*CS*, 44)

This represents one of the rare moments in Weil's work when she cognizes and confronts death. When, in other words, she stands outside the hysteric's position and brings all her conflicting elements into a unity. The desolation of the newborn, the deprivation of the body, the love of God. The limit is the beginning of life, a kind of non-being scarcely differentiated from life's end: "God created me as a non-being who seems to exist, so that in renouncing for love what I take as my being, I may emerge from nothingness. Then there is no more I. The I is nothing. But I have no right to know this. If I knew it, where would the renunciation be? I will never know it" (*CS*, 42). In this frenzy of negatives, there are several strands. There is, first, her overwhelming sense of worthlessness, grounded in the experience of early childhood. But upon that she affirms a classical insight of ascetic theology: the ego, the self must become porous and dissolve in order for the higher self, the Atman, the soul to emerge from nothingness. She concludes with the epistemological paradox common to all mystical thought: Faith is knowing without demonstration. *Credo quia absurdum*. Faith is the measure of commitment not only to God but to other men:

> To feel compassion for an unfortunate, the soul must be divided in two. One part must be absolutely preserved from all contagion, from all danger of contagion. The other part contaminated unto identification. That tension is passion, com-passion. The Passion of Christ is this phenomenon in God.
>
> So long as one does not have in the soul a point of eternity preserved from any contagion by suffering, one cannot have compassion for the unfortunate. . . .
>
> Any movement of pure compassion in a soul is a new descent of Christ on earth to be crucified. (*CS*, 42)

Christ himself is the most radical transgressor. Breaking the unity of the Godhead, he enters the human order where his death becomes the ultimate limit-experience. She writes:

> Theological use of the notion of the limit.
>
> The instant where Christ expires on the cross is the intersection of the created and the creating. Until then the unity of the divine and the human must have been in a certain way virtual, tending toward the plenitude of a reality touched only in that instant (a plenitude impossible to touch—a limit at the same time possible and impossible, like the paradoxes of Zeno or the infinite series that give a finite sum). (*CS*, 136)

The visitation allegory, written a year before her departure for New York, begins with an insistence on her ignorance, her unknowing: "Poor creature, you who understand nothing, who know nothing." This coincides with the negative epistemology sketched above. The allegory records moments of communion with nature and comradeship—viewing the city, eating bread, and drinking wine. The created and uncreated intersect. Then this brief communion is shattered. Plenitude is impossible to touch, she falls back into the world of paradox. Yet like Zeno's arrow that both reaches and does not reach its target, there is closure and release. The allegory ends: "I know well that he does not love me. How could he love me? And yet deep down within me something, a particle of myself, cannot help thinking, with fear and trembling, that perhaps, in spite of all, he loves me." Weil's transgressive drives are mirrored in the paradoxical behavior of her absent-present visitor, an angel or the Crucified One himself. Doubt, fear, remorse, those familiar emotional states, blot out the momentary experience of happiness. She writes it down feverishly, an inadequate record.

Weil's life was built on unsatisfied cravings. There was her infantile craving for nourishment that became its rejection. There was the desire to emulate her brother and enter the world of genius. While a student, she aspired to a condition of pure contemplation akin to prayer. Later, there was the desire to achieve solidarity with the poor and oppressed. The last years of her life were consumed by a desire for sacrificial action in the war. When starvation set in at the end, she reverted to a longing she had expressed as a student, when she wrote, "The only force in this world is purity; everything unmixed is a fragment of truth. . . . The only force and the only truth is to keep from acting" (*VSW*, I, 81).

The *Cahiers d'Amérique* are the record of Weil's last paroxysmal surge toward truth that shimmers momentarily out of doubt and delusion. Words that Foucault wrote in 1963 could well apply to her: "It is in death that the individual becomes at one with himself, escaping from monotonous lives and their leveling effect; in the slow, half-subterranean, but already visible approach of death, the dull, common life at last becomes an individuality; a black border isolates it, and gives it the style of its truth."[12] The common narrative of Weil and Foucault was

12. Quoted in Miller, *Passion*, 20.

truth seeking, which is the narrative of all great philosophical lives. Yet they are different from most, since they pursued awakening at the cost of life. Such truth seeking changes the conditions under which truth is possible. Foucault speaks of the materiality of truth, of truth as experience, involvement, and ultimate risk. This was how Weil also saw the truth. She put her material existence on the line in the way of the authentic transgressor.[13] Weil's true radicality may appear to be clouded by her interest in Christianity, often seen as the enemy of radical awareness. But this notion fades when we read her. Her Christianity was tough-minded, sceptical, put to every test she could invent.

I can't say that reading Weil and Foucault that autumn in Toulouse "caused" me to make the decision I made, but it played a substantial part. Their work energized and encouraged me to face the fact that my marriage hadn't worked for a long time. There was no communication between Jean and me, only a deep hostility on her part and indifference on mine. I have in front of me some notes I took during a therapy session shortly before this time. Commenting on my marriage the therapist says that we both invent rigid schemata for controlling each other, and when these fail to work, we drift into anger and depression. "You both have a kind of tunnel vision so that there is no freedom, no spontaneity, only a continual grinding down, which is a major cause of your headaches."

It was true that I had no further headaches while I was alone in Toulouse that fall; instead there was a healing process at work, which began after the decision to break with Jean. For me this was a truly transgressive act, because it involved going against deeply held convictions. When I told the curé of Saint-Etienne what I was planning he became agitated, seeing me on the verge of an irreparable move fraught with both human and spiritual consequences. He used all his power of persuasion, telling me I would be violating a sacred commandment and that I could no longer be a communicant in the Church. At that point

13. This does not, however, eliminate the possibility of a delusive (i.e., hysterical) element in this trangressive behavior.

I knew I was entering the zone of transgression. If you believe that marriage should be permanent, indissoluble even; if you have made a commitment, if there are children, and by then we had three; then to break a marriage is to cross the flashing line of transgression.

Transgression is also when you take up arms against your own internal enemy, your superego, that monster inside who wrecks your nights with memories of everybody you have hurt or betrayed along the way. It is a very big deal, you know this as you do it. Even if 60 percent of all married Americans have done the same thing. It is your big deal, your idealized marriage, all your carefully cultivated fantasies about what a great parent you've been that are going up in smoke. What makes it worse is that you can't reckon up any possible benefit, you can't guess the outcome.

I sat down and wrote Jean a letter explaining that I wanted to end it. On a Sunday night at eight o'clock I walked from Rue Ninau toward the main post office. Through the sparse traffic on Rue Alsace-Lorraine, past the elegant jewelery shops and the Monoprix, past the ornate Renaissance bulk of the Capitole where the town offices are located. I thought of the brass plaque, in the vestibule, which marks the spot where the young Duc de Guise was assassinated. Blood on the sidewalk. Then took a left turn and stopped in front of the mail slot, which was set in the mouth of a huge brass lion's head. I held my letter, looked at it once, thinking that if it were lost in transit that would be a sign, then dropped it into the lion's maw. I crossed a shimmering invisible line, joining, according to the statistics, more than half the married population of the United States. It was a relief to acknowledge my fallibility, my mistakes. There was no sudden illumination, no flashing lights or warning trumpets. Only a feeling of release and, for the first time in years, I began to think about the future.

The Ghosts of Paris

What right do I have to insist upon remembering?

Simone de Beauvoir

Tuesday. October 25, 1994.

It's raining. A sinister day. Jacques Hallez, Judy, and I have taken the RER out to Drancy, a working-class suburb northeast of the city. The train doesn't stop there, so we overshoot and work our way back. Coming out of the station I ask a man and his wife for directions, receive a cautious answer that grows voluble. "I grew up close to the camp," the woman says, "we knew terrible things were going on there." They walk us part way, tell us to continue to the Gendarmerie, the camp is next door.

Résidence la Muette, once known as Drancy la Juive, is a large rectangular apartment block, five stories high. Originally, in an architectural flourish, several fourteen storey towers had embellished this place appropriately called "Residence of Silence," but the towers never functioned properly and were later demolished. It is silent today. A few delivery men, a mother pushing her baby carriage, clerks in a Social Security office. Silence and a crushing banality. Life going on in its mindless way where so many had their lives interrupted. The real Drancy, the concentration camp, is an iceberg, its tip barely visible above the casual ebb and flow of daily existence.

There is a monument near the entry, heavily symbolic and aesthetically crude. It was paid for by private subscription. The death wagon, a 40 & 8 freight car next to the monument, was vandalized by a drunk just two days before our visit. He had been drinking in Le Vouvray, across the street from the camp, where once German guards used to drink their schnapps and show the locals pictures of the wife and kids back in the *vaterland*. The owner of Le Vouvray did a nice business smuggling packages in to the detainees, enough to retire on after the war.

I learn this from the pharmacist, an expansive North African Jew, who with a few others has organized an information center at La Muette, with pictures, publications, and relics of the camp. A small whitewashed room with high windows. Random memorabilia, the wistful stares of dead men, women, children, rubbings of inscriptions, lists, official documents, a faded yellow patch in the shape of a five-pointed star embroidered with the word *Juif*. I stare for a long time at a photo of the old bus, quaint putt-putt from a children's book, which transported prisoners to the stations at Bobigny or Le Bourget where they boarded trains for the death camps.

We are joined by Gary and Lucy, British filmmakers, who are doing a documentary on French art during the war. There will be a segment on Max Jacob. With our pharmacist we go looking for the infirmary where the poet died. There is a plaque, but the door is locked. I peer through the window, see some kind of atelier. A man next door turns aside our questions. I ask Gary how he will present the camp in his film, how he sees it. "Lots of ghosts," he says, "sixty-seven thousand ghosts." The number of Jews who passed through Drancy on their way to Auschwitz.

The ghosts are here, but nobody sees them or hears them. The French government, which should have turned this consecrated ground into a memorial, has allowed its continued use as a housing complex. This really is the Residence of Silence. Standing there, apart from the others, I begin to hear the voices— accents from eastern Europe, *shtetl* voices, Russian Jews, Moroccan Jews, but above all, the accents of Paris, *parigot* from Belleville and Ménilmontant, Sorbonne voices, voices of bankers and lawyers and film stars, all standing in the debris, the filth, the garbage, assigned chores by the French police, doing what is expected of them or walking round and round, because it is forbidden to stay in the rooms by day, talking in a hundred dialects, making the best of it, wondering about their fate. At night women stand at the windows and scream for their children. A team of young men try to tunnel out of the camp and are caught three meters from their goal. Theodor Dannecker, a twenty-seven year old S.S. officer under the direct control of Adolf Eichmann, is in charge of the camp, organizes work schedules, surveillance, even makes arrangements for religious services, so there is an appearance of normalcy, giving people a false sense of security even while the little putt-putt makes its shuttle run two or three times a week to Bobigny and Le Bourget.

We leave finally, but I carry these voices in my head, these ghosts. For a few days they drown out the other voices. I have to fight this invasion before I can recapture my own personal memories of Paris; but they remain always in the background. The Holocaust has forever changed the way we understand memory. Since those events memory has been theorized, taking on a multilayered and tragic coloration. Less room is left for sheer random spontaneity, for the freedom of what the Surrealists called objective chance, for the romantic encounter that turns your life around. The Holocaust has become a final destination, where memory ends all its voyages.

Walking through the crowds, past familiar landmarks, ducking in and out of bookstores and cafés, I reacquaint myself with my chosen ghosts and with my mission as a literary critic, which is to propitiate and celebrate them. It seems that I do have what Simone de Beauvoir called "the right to remember." Because I came to France during the war and continued to return over a span of fifty years, my adult life coincides with the postwar period. I became involved with French studies just at the time it was beginning to develop in the United States and I lived through the period of its greatest expansion, doing my work as student and teacher during the heyday of French modernism, observing the turn around 1960 from an aesthetic to a theoretical orientation, continuing to be an involved observor of the current development of gender and ethnic studies. This gives me a role as witness to some of the great figures of the time and the movements in which they participated.

"Memory comes from somewhere else," writes Michel de Certeau, from another standpoint in the matrix of culture, a place that is not ourselves but that we make our own. He adds, "Memory is a sense of the other."[1] It is a recreated life world peopled by others whom we have made our own, from whom we draw our sense of identity as, through the shaping of a memorializing discourse, we create ourself from the texture and substance of their lives.

There has always been a danger for me in this process, especially the tendency to romanticize memory, to see myself as an actor in Verlaine's memory poem: "In the cold park solitary and vast, two specters evoked the distant past." The challenge remains to see things as they were, no more and no less, to be accurate in the details, not to change them to fit my aesthetic sense or the broader pattern of events. It is important to balance the sounds and colors of remembered events against their banality, to recognize that, often enough, I didn't understand their significance until months or years later. The soundtrack and the images were added, over the years, as I replayed them. This inner filmclip of memory is seen through a lens that is constantly refocused, never able to hold the image once and for all. When it comes to memory, we can never say, "Yes, that's it!" because there is always distortion, a polyphony of voices that modify or contradict, a fading in and out of the light that changes what I think I saw, what I think I see. Today, the cold banality of Drancy is a corrective to my tendency to embroider and reinvent the past.

A few days after the visit to Drancy, while we are having dinner in the Balzar with my Dartmouth colleague Faith Beasley, I think again about the ghosts of Paris and my relationship with them. They are the resource of our profession. A University teacher is a caretaker of ghosts. You bring the ghosts to life by reflecting on the meaning of their words. Through this reflection you transmit their strange ectoplasmic reality to the next generation, keeping them in some mysterious zone of half-life, the *entre-deux* which is that Elysian Field called literature. By doing this we reinvent culture that can be defined as the

1. Michel de Certeau, *The Practice of Everday Life*, trans. Steven Rendall (Berkeley: University of California Press, 1984), 87.

work of the dead modified by the living. Culture is not so much its artifacts as their meanings, a vast network of semiotic focii whose repair, extension, and interpretation must be undertaken by a priestly cult, the professionals. A while back we academics talked of "literary production" and "intertextuality," pretending that works engendered each other by a kind of virgin birth, without the intervention of human agency; but that fantasy of late Marxism has vanished. Now it is us and them again. Baudelaire wrote: *"Les morts, les pauvres morts ont de grandes douleurs"* [The dead, the poor dead have great sorrows]. As Sartre noted, libraries are like cemeteries, or, one might add, like those huge churches with their mausoleums and crypts that dot the landscape of Europe—houses where the living and dead mingle in the transmission of culture. Thinking about all this I remember my emotion when I first saw Les Alyscans, that vast necropolis of Provence and knew that, in some undefinable way, I had a connection with these dead. Only now am I beginning to understand what it is, this undertaking of the obligations and commitments of memory. In this year of 1994, memory has become the dominant theme of historians and critics. They ask what it means to forget Vichy, to forget the Holocaust—and also what it means to remember them. Along with the question of why we forget and what price we pay for that omission is Simone de Beauvoir's question: Who has the right to remember these things? Those who suffered them, of course, but also those of us who, though marginal to the events, feel that "consuming fever" for historical detail, a phrase from Nietzsche that Geoffrey H. Hartman borrows in the introduction to his collection of Holocaust essays.[2] A fever to possess the past is our ticket to memorialization. Time will sort out the witnesses, those who are worth hearing and those who aren't.

Our hotel is on Rue des Ecoles, a few blocks from the Sorbonne. Half a dozen times a day I pass the bronze statue of Montaigne, one of the great witnesses. He sits with a neck ruffle and doublet, legs crossed, right arm resting on his knee, the open book in his hand. This significant ghost has an amused smile on his blackened face as he watches the sorbonnards trek

---

2. Geoffrey H. Hartman, ed., *Holocaust Remembrance: The Shapes of Memory* (Cambridge, Mass.: Blackwell, 1994), 3.

past all day long. He offers his book, as if to say, "Passersby, read a little, then go on your way. Take something if you can. Argue with me. Love me or hate me. Stop and read. What's the rush?" You are sollicited everywhere in Paris to stop and read, to remember. It is a place of memory, everything heightened, intensifed to fever pitch, driven by fear that the memories will slip away.

In this city full of ghosts, I remember lovers and friends associated with certain streets, certain buildings, Reid Hall, the Montana Bar and Hotel, the Acropolis hotel where I first lived, now changed into apartments, the great Nabis painters who taught and painted at the Académie Ransom on 7 Rue Joseph Bara, now demolished to make way for an apartment block. I walk past 3 Rue Auguste Comte, where Simone Weil grew up, where later Camus came to vist Mime and Dr. Weil on many occasions. Their sixth floor apartment, facing the Luxembourg Garden, is only a short diagonal away from 7 Rue Joseph Bara. I make a swing past 1 *bis* Rue Vaneau, where Camus shared Gide's apartment during the war and where editorial work on clandestine *Combat* was carried on. Hallez and I look for Chez Rosalie, which has disappeared, along with most of our other Montparnasse hangouts. The Sélect is still there, but the Hôtel des Etats-Unis, where Garry Davis lived, has changed its name. Fifty years later the U.S.A. has lost much of its prestige, a process that began around 1947 as the French struggled with wounded pride and resentment of Coca Cola dollars. But, despite any shifts in French perception of us *Ricains*, it is infinitely stimulating to be here, with a kind of excitement I find nowhere else, an energy that heightens my appetite to walk another block, to go into another bookstore and pick up the latest novel or critical book, to turn the corner into other streets full of life, swarming with more ghosts from the past. Rue Monsieur le Prince, which I explored with Michel in 1948, looking for the flea-bag hotels where sixteen-year-old Arthur Rimbaud, writing his way into history, hung out during his fugue with Verlaine. Then there is the Hôtel Lauzun on the Ile St. Louis, where Baudelaire met to smoke and fabulate with the Club des Hashischins; Balzac's modest home, one of the world's great fiction factories; Proust's apartment house with its cork-lined bedroom on the elegant Boulevard Haussmann, now converted into a bank. Among these significant ghosts there are others for whom fame shows its usual ironic sense of timing. There is a painter I had met in the 1960s, a Russian exile of enormous energy, also a drunk. Success arrived only a few years back. I meet him on Boulevard Montparnasse, a girl on each arm. He opens a pouchful of ruined teeth and roars, "Too late! Too late!"

What am I looking for in this autumn of 1994? Dreams that have turned to dust, as in the old Kingston Trio song? No, none of this has the unsubstantiality of dreams. I have worked too hard to make it visible, give it reality through my forty plus years of teaching and writing. French culture, as I perceive it, has not been elaborated in the way of dreamwork, by displacement, condensation, and secondary elaboration; but rather by the pursuit of detail, the crafting of sentences, the production of a discourse. My dialogue with France, at its best, requires the waking mind, close listening, a crafted response that maintains a balanced exchange, teaching and taught, speaker and listener. I take memory as a privilege and a challenge, a condition that you have to merit and that it is hard to share. This dialogue, in those moments when true mutuality is achieved, is a process by which culture thickens and expands in a narrative stream that incorporates ideas and interpretation. Raised to a higher power by the introduction of a second language, English, this dialogue echoes and enlarges the primary culture. In an infinitesimal yet appreciable way, France needed me. As perceiver and interpreter, I am among the makers of French culture.

I am not looking for dreams because the present is too strong, too immediate, too rich compared to the smoky texture of the past. What I am looking for now in October 1994 is closure on the relationship with Camus, Jacob, and Weil, those three writers that, many years ago, my teacher, Henri Peyre called "my three angels." This trip to Paris is an opportunity to unpack the burden of a long cohabitation, to let them rest where I originally found them. Not to end this friendship that has gone on for fifty years, but to free myself to think about other writers with whom I have been intimately involved. Proust or Rimbaud are the first who come to mind.

There are consecrated ways to lay your ghosts to rest. Offerings and rites of remembrance, the building of a monument, this book undertaken in the spirit of a memorial. But even if it attains that status, with its blurb, its cover design, its photograph of the author, its pages covered with hieroglyphs that compress fifty years of life, even if it becomes a material object that can be read, reviewed, then put aside and forgotten, what place do these three "angels" retain in my mind and future existence? There has been a change, their status is already different. I'm suddenly aware of distance separating us, as if a boat carrying three friends with whom you have been involved in intense discussion has begun to move away from the dock. It happens very quickly. They have moved into my *entre-deux*, my zone of undecidability where I am in between France and the United States, in between Judaism and Catholicism, in between doubt and conviction, in between three writers who pulled me in different directions, each one showing me a different aspect of myself, in between the present moment and the never-to-be anticipated future.

What this means in respect to Camus, Jacob, and Weil is that I can let go of them, let them slip back into their twilight for other critics to take in hand, critics who will discover new and surprising aspects of their work. I have a sense of release as these old friends slip away. There will be new ones, new intellectual adventures, life is always richer than we can possibly imagine, there is still time for a new *folie amoureuse* in my long love affair with France.

Acknowledgments

I owe a special debt of gratitude to the memory of Henri M. Peyre, teacher and friend. From his retirement home in Connecticut Peyre urged me to write a personal memoir, and this book owes much to his inspiration and guidance. Heartfelt thanks go also to the friends and colleagues who encouraged me along the way, notably Lawrence D. Kritzman, Robert W. Greene, and Philip M. Pochoda. Mary Ann Caws, Jacques Hallez, Marianne Hirsch, Pierre Laborie, and Bruno Tollon helped at critical stages in the evolution of the manuscript. Others commented on the work in progress—Faith Beasley, Carla Freccero, Ronald M. Green, Sydney Lévy, Anne B. Macfarlane, and Walter Stephens. Thanks also to Robert Jaccaud of Baker Library.

A short version of Chapter 11 appeared in *L'Esprit créateur*, XXIV, 3 (Fall 1994). Permission to reprint is gratefully acknowledged.

Works Cited

Alexander, Jeffrey C., and Steven Seidman, eds. *Culture and Society.* Cambridge: Cambridge University Press, 1990.

Andreu, Pierre. *Vie et mort de Max Jacob.* Paris: La Table Ronde, 1982.

Antoine, Gérald. *Paul Claudel ou l'enfer du génie.* Paris: Robert Laffont, 1988.

Argüelles, José, and Miriam Argüelles. *Mandala.* Berkeley, Calif.: Shambhala, 1972.

Assouline, Pierre. *Gaston Gallimard: A Half-Century of French Publishing.* San Diego: Harcourt Brace Jovanovich, 1988.

Bataille, Georges. *L'Erotisme.* Paris: Editions de Minuit, 1957.

Benjamin, Walter. *The Paris of the Second Empire in Baudelaire.* London: Verso, 1983.

Bernstein, Richard J. *Habermas and Modernity.* Cambridge: MIT Press, 1985.

Biale, David. *Eros and the Jews: From Biblical Israel to Contemporary America.* New York: Basic Books, 1992.

Billy, André. *Max Jacob. Poètes d'aujourd'hui*, vol. 3. Paris: Seghers, 1949.

Birault, Henri. "Beatitude in Nietzche." In The *New Nietzsche*, ed. David B. Allison. Cambridge, Mass.: MIT Press, 1985.

Bordo, Susan. "Anorexia Nervosa: Psychopathology as the Crystallization of Culture." In *Feminism and Foucault*, ed. Irene Diamond and Lee Quinby. Boston: Northeastern University Press, 1988.

Brée, Germaine. *Camus.* New Brunswick: Rutgers University Press, 1961.

Cabaud, Jacques. *L'Expérience vécue de Simone Weil.* Paris: Plon, 1957.

Cabaud, Jacques. *Simone Weil: A Fellowship in Love.* New York: Channel Press, 1964.

Campbell, Joseph, with Bill Moyers. *The Power of Myth.* New York: Doubleday, 1988.

Camus, Albert. *Between Hell and Reason: Essays from the Resistance Newspaper "Combat," 1944–1947.* Ed. and trans. Alexandre de Gramont. Hanover, N.H.: University Press of New England, 1991.

Camus, Albert. *Carnets, mai 1935–février 1937*. Paris: Gallimard, 1962.

Camus, Albert. *Essais d'Albert Camus*. Ed. Roger Quilliot and L. Faucon. Bibliothèque de la Pléiade. Paris: Gallimard and Calmann-Lévy, 1965.

Camus, Albert. *The Plague*. Trans. Stuart Gilbert. New York: Random House, 1948.

Camus, Albert. *Le premier homme*. Paris: Gallimard, 1994.

Camus, Albert. *The Stranger*. Trans. Matthew Ward. New York: Knopf, 1988.

Camus, Albert. *Théâtre, récits, nouvelles*. Ed. Roger Quilliot. Bibliothèque de la Pléiade. Paris. Gallimard. 1962.

Camus, Albert, and Grenier, Jean. *Correspondance, 1932–1960*. Paris: Gallimard, 1981.

Claudel, Paul. *Correspondance de Paul Claudel, Francis Jammes, Gabriel Frizeau, Jacques Rivière*. Paris: Gallimard, 1952.

Claudel, Paul. *Journal I (1904–1932)*. Bibliothèque de la Pléiade. Paris: Gallimard, 1968.

Claudel, Paul. *Journal II (1933–1955)*. Bibliothèque de la Pléiade. Paris: Gallimard, 1969.

Claudel, Paul. *Œuvres en prose*. Paris: Gallimard, 1965.

Coles, Robert. *Simone Weil: A Modern Pilgrimage*. Reading, Mass.: Addison-Wesley, 1987.

Dally, Peter, Joan Gomez, and A. J. Isaacs, *Anorexia Nervosa*. London: Heinemann, 1979.

de Beauvoir, Simone, *Force of Circumstance*. Trans. Richard Howard. New York: G. P. Putnam's Sons, 1964.

Daniel, Jean, Czeslaw Milosz, Octavio Paz, et al. "La Revanche d'Albert Camus." *Le Nouvel Observateur*, 1544, 9–15 June, 1994, pp. 4–13.

de Certeau, Michel. *The Practice of Everyday Life*. Trans. Steven Rendall. Berkeley: University of California Press, 1984.

de Gaulle, Charles. *The War Memoirs of Charles de Gaulle. Vol. I. The Call to Honor, 1940–1942; Vol. II. Unity, 1942–1944; Vol. III. Salvation, 1944–1946*. Trans. Richard Howard. New York: Simon & Schuster, 1955, 1959, 1960.

Dostœvsky, Fyodor. *The Brothers Karamazov*. Trans. Richard Peaver and Larissa Volokhonsky. San Francisco: North Point Press, 1970.

Doubrovsky, Serge. *La Place de la madeleine: Écriture et fantasme chez Proust*. Paris: Mercure de France, 1974.

Duquesne, Jacques. *Les Catholiques français sous l'Occupation*. Paris: Grasset, 1966.

Encyclopedia of Psychoanalysis. New York: The Free Press, 1968.

Fabareau, Hubert. *Max Jacob*. Paris: Nouvelle Revue Critique, 1925.

Felman, Shoshana, and Dori Laub, M.D. *Testimony: Crises of Witnessing in Literature, Psychoanalysis, and History*. New York: Routledge, 1992.

Foster, Hal., ed. *The Anti-Aesthetic: Essays on Postmodern Culture*. Port Townsend, Wash.: Bay Press, 1985.

Foucault, Michel. *L'Ordre du discours*. Paris: Gallimard, 1971.

Foucault, Michel. "A Preface to Transgression," in *Language, Counter-Memory, Practice: Selected Essays and Interviews*. Ed. and trans. by Donald F. Bouchard and Sherry Simon. Ithaca: Cornell University Press, 1977.

Foucault, Michel. *L'Usage des Plaisirs*. Paris: Gallimard, 1984.

Gide, André. *Journal 1889–1939*. Paris: Gallimard, 1948.

Girard, René. "Camus's Stranger Retried." *PMLA*, 29 (1964): 519–33.

Glass, James M. *Delusion: Internal Dimensions of Political Life*. Chicago: University of Chicago Press, 1985.

Guiette, Robert. "Vie de Max Jacob." Paris: Nizet, 1976.

Hartman, Geoffrey H., ed. *Holocaust Rememberance: The Shapes of Memory*. Cambridge Mass: Blackwell, 1994.

Hoffmann, Stanley. *Decline or Renewal? France since the 1930s*. New York: Viking, 1974.

Hume, David. *Dialogues Concerning Natural Religion*. New York: Haffner Publ. Co., 1948.

Isherwood, Christopher. *My Guru and His Disciple*. New York: Farrar, Straus, & Giroux, 1980.

Jacob, Max. *Conseils à un jeune poète*. Paris: Gallimard, 1945.

Jacob, Max. *La Défense de Tartufe*. Paris: Gallimard, 1964.

Jacob, Max. *Derniers Poèmes en vers et en prose*. Paris: Gallimard, 1945.

Jacob, Max. *L'Homme de cristal*. Paris: La Table Ronde, 1946.

Jacob, Max. *Méditations religieuses*. Paris: Gallimard, 1947.

Jacob, Max. *Le Phanérogame*. Author, 1918.

Jacob, Max. *Récit de ma conversion*. Paris: Rougerie, 1959.

Jacob, Max. *Le Roi de Béotie, suivi de La Couronne de Vulcain et de L'Histoire du roi Kaboul Ier et du marmiton Gauwain* (éd. définitive). Paris: Gallimard, 1971.

Jameson, Fredric. *Postmodernism or the Cultural Logic of Late Capitalism*. Durham, N.C.: Duke University Press, 1991.

Jung, Carl G. *Man and His Symbols*. Garden City, N.Y.: Doubleday, 1964.

Kafka, Franz. *The Penal Colony: Stories and Short Pieces*. Trans. Willa and Edwin Muir. New York: Schocken, 1948.

Kamber, Gerald. *Max Jacob and the Poetics of Cubism*. Baltimore: Johns Hopkins University Press, 1971.

Kaplan, Alice Yaeger. *French Lessons*. Chicago: University of Chicago Press, 1993.

Lacouture, Jean. *de Gaulle the Ruler, 1945–1970.* Trans. Alan Sheridan. New York: Norton, 1991.

Laplanche, J., and J.-B. Pontalis, "Fantasy and the Origins of Sexuality." *The International Journal of Psychoanalysis,* 49 (1968): 1–18.

Laplanche, J., and J.-B. Pontalis, *The Language of Psychoanalysis.* Trans. Donald Nicholson-Smith. New York: Norton, 1973.

Lemert, Charles C., and Garth Gillan. *Michel Foucault: Social Theory and Transgression.* New York: Columbia University Press, 1982.

Lévy, Sydney. *The Play of the Text: Max Jacob's "Le Cornet à dés."* Madison: University of Wisconsin Press, 1981.

Lottman, Herbert R. *Albert Camus: A Biography.* Garden City, N.Y.: Doubleday, 1979.

Lottman, Herbert R. *The Purge: The Purification of French Collaborators after World War II.* New York: Morrow, 1986.

Malraux, André. *Anti-Memoirs.* Trans. T. Kilmartin. New York: Holt, 1967.

McBride, Joseph. *Albert Camus, Philosopher and Litterateur.* New York: St. Martin's Press, 1992.

McLellan, David. *Simone Weil: Utopian Pessimist.* London: Macmillan, 1989.

Merton, Thomas. *The Seven Storey Mountain.* New York: Harcourt, Brace, & World, 1948.

Miles, Siân, ed. *Simone Weil: An Anthology.* Trans. Emma Craufurd. New York: Weidenfeld & Nicolson, 1986.

Miller, J. Hillis. "Narrative." In *Critical Terms for Literary Study,* ed. Frank Lentricchia and Thomas McLaughlin. Chicago: University of Chicago Press, 1990.

Miller, James E. *The Passion of Michel Foucault.* New York: Simon & Schuster, 1993.

Miller, Nancy K. *Getting Personal.* New York: Routledge, 1991.

Modigliani, Jeanne. *Modigliani: Man and Myth.* New York: Orion, 1958.

Nevin, Thomas R. *Simone Weil: Portrait of a Self-Exiled Jew.* Chapel Hill: University of North Carolina Press, 1991.

Nietzsche, Friedrich. *The Antichrist.* In *The Portable Nietzsche.* Trans. and ed. Walter J. Kauffmann. New York: Viking, 1954.

Nietzsche, Friedrich. *Beyond Good and Evil.* Trans. Helen Zimmer. New York: Modern Library, 1917.

Nietzsche, Friedrich. *The Will to Power.* Trans. Walter J. Kaufmann and R. J. Hollingdale. New York: Random House, 1968.

O'Collins, Gerald, S.J., and Edward G. Farrugia, S.J. *A Concise Dictionary of Theology.* New York: Paulist Press, 1991.

Oxenhandler, Neal. *A Change of Gods.* New York: Harcourt, Brace, & World, 1962.

Oxenhandler, Neal. *Max Jacob and "Les Feux de Paris."* Berkeley: University of California Press, 1964.

Owens, Craig. "The Allegorical Impulse: Toward a Theory of Postmodernism," part 2. *October*, 13 (1980): 59–80.

Panichas, George A., ed. *The Simone Weil Reader*. New York: David McKay, 1977.

Parkes, Graham, ed. *Nietzsche and Asian Thought*. Chicago: University of Chicago Press, 1991.

Péguy, Charles. *The Modern World*. In *Men and Saints*, Trans. Anne and Julian Green. New York: Pantheon, 1944.

Pétrement, Simone. *La Vie de Simone Weil, I (1909–1934); II (1934–1943)*. Paris: Arthème Fayard, 1973.

Peyre, Henri. *French Novelists of Today*. New York: Oxford University Press, 1967.

Plantier, René. *L'Univers poétique de Max Jacob*. Paris: Klincksieck, 1976.

Preminger, Alex, ed. *Princeton Encyclopedia of Poetry & Poetics*. Princeton: Princeton University Press, 1974.

Radha, Swami Sivananda. *Kundalini Yoga for the West*. Boulder: Shambhala, 1981.

Rees, Richard, ed. *Selected Essays, 1934–1943, by Simone Weil*. London: Oxford University Press, 1962.

Rodden, John. *The Politics of Literary Reputation: The Making and Claiming of "St. George" Orwell*. New York: Oxford University Press, 1989.

Roskies, David G. *Against the Apocalypse: Responses to Catastrophe in Modern Jewish Culture*. Cambridge: Harvard University Press, 1984.

Sachs, Maurice. *Alias*. Paris: Gallimard, 1935.

Sacks, Oliver. *Migraine: Evolution of a Common Disorder*. Berkeley: University of California Press, 1970.

Schwarz-Bart, André. *The Last of the Just*. New York: Atheneum, 1960.

Showalter, Elaine. "On Hysterical Narrative," *Narrative*, I(1) (Jan. 1993): 24–35.

Spignesi, Angelyn. *Starving Women: A Psychology of Anorexia Nervosa*. Dallas: Spring Publications, 1983.

Suleiman, Susan Rubin. *Risking Who One Is: Encounters with Contemporary Art and Literature*. Cambridge: Harvard University Press, 1994.

Tarrow, Susan. *Exile from the Kingdom: A Political Rereading of Albert Camus*. Tuscaloosa: University of Alabama Press, 1985.

Weil, Simone. *La Connaissance surnaturelle*. Paris: Gallimard, 1950.

Weil, Simone. *Journal d'usine*. In *La Condition ouvrière*. Paris: Gallimard, 1951.

Weil, Simone. *Œuvres complètes: Ecrits historiques et politiques*, vol. II. Paris: Gallimard, 1989.

Weil, Simone. *Waiting for God*. Trans. Emma Craufurd. New York: Putnam, 1951.

Weil, Sylvie. *Les Reines du Luxembourg*. Paris: Flammarion, 1991.

Wiesel, Elie. *Night*. Trans. Stella Rodway. New York: Avon Books, 1960.

White, Alan. *Within Nietzsche's Labyrinth*. New York: Routledge, 1990.

Willeford, William. *Feeling, Imagination, and the Self: Transformations of the Mother–Infant Relationship*. Evanston, Ill.: Northwestern University Press, 1987.

University Press of New England publishes books under its own imprint and is the publisher for Brandeis University Press, Dartmouth College, Middlebury College Press, University of New Hampshire, University of Rhode Island, Tufts University, University of Vermont, Wesleyan University Press, and Salzburg Seminar.

Library of Congress Cataloging-in-Publication Data

Oxenhandler, Neal.
    Looking for heroes in postwar France : Albert Camus, Max Jacob, Simone Weil / Neal Oxenhandler.
      p.   cm.
    Includes bibliographical references.
    ISBN 0-87451-731-1 (alk. paper)
    1. French literature—20th century—History and criticism.
2. Camus, Albert, 1913-1960—Criticism and interpretation.
3. Jacob, Max, 1876-1944—Criticism and interpretation. 4. Weil, Simone, 1909-1943—Criticism and interpretation. I. Title.
PQ305.O94   1995
840.9'00914—dc20   95-11333